Raising Kids Who Will

DATE DUE		NOV 02
APR 2 5 2005		
GAYLORD		PRINTED IN U.S.A.

Raising Kids Who Will Make a Difference

Helping your family live
with integrity, value simplicity,
and care for others

SUSAN V. VOGT

LOYOLAPRESS.

CHICAGO

LOYOLAPRESS.

3441 N. ASHLAND AVENUE
CHICAGO, ILLINOIS 60657

The "Family Pledge of Nonviolence" that appears in chapter 7 is reprinted by permission of the Institute for Peace and Justice, 4144 Lindell Blvd. #408, St. Louis, MO 63108 ph: (314) 533-4445; e-mail: ipj@ipj-ppj.org; Web: www.ipj-ppj.org

The Scripture quotation contained herein is from the New Revised Standard Version Bible: Catholic Edition, copyright © 1993 and 1989 by the Division of Christian Education of the National Council of the Churches of Christ in the U.S.A. Used by permission.

Interior design by Eileen Wagner

Library of Congress Cataloging-in-Publication Data

Vogt, Susan.
Raising kids who will make a difference : helping your family live with integrity, value simplicity, and care for others / Susan Vogt.
p. cm.

Includes bibliographical references.
ISBN 0-8294-1792-3
1. Parenting--Religious aspects--Christianity. 2.
Family--Religious life. I. Title.
BV4529 .V64 2002
248.8'45--dc21

2002003575

Printed in the United States of America

02 03 04 05 M-V 10 9 8 7 6 5 4 3 2 1

To my husband, Jim; our children, Brian, Heidi, Dacian, and Aaron; and my own parents, Dr. Laurence and Charlotte Veihdeffer, who formed me and I them. We keep each other honest.

To Jim and Kathy McGinnis, who taught me that parenting and commitment to peace and justice were intertwined.

Contents

Preface ix

Hints for Reading This Book x

The Jones Family Christmas Letter xii

A Daughter's Response xix

1. IDENTITY
Nurturing Values of Honesty, Courage, Humility, and Integrity 1

2. TIME
Ideas for Taming the Calendar 25

3. MATERIALISM
The Simple Life Can Be Pretty Complex 57

4. ECOLOGY
What It's Worth to Care for the Earth 85

5. MEDIA
How to Use, Not Abuse, the Media 111

6. HEALTH
Life and Death Matters—Sex and Beyond 135

7. PEACEMAKING
How to Get On with Getting Along 157

8. SPIRITUALITY

Sharing Faith That Will Last after They Leave Home **179**

9. GLOBAL AWARENESS

From Being the Center of the Universe to Exploring the Universe **203**

10. DIVERSITY

What's the Difference—Black, White, and Everything In-between **219**

11. SERVICE

Life Beyond Myself, My Family, My Neighborhood.............................. **237**

12. MOTIVATION

How We Learn to Care about Caring **261**

Epilogue 1: Top That Flop **285**

Epilogue 2: Dear Mom **288**

Selected Bibliography **293**

Acknowledgments **295**

Preface

"Parenting is a hard job. It's often hard to know if you're doing the right thing."

–Susan and Jim Vogt

I had hoped to cowrite this book with my daughter, Heidi, since she has a reflective personality and loves to write. I thought it would be valuable for readers to see the art of parenting from both sides—not only through the eyes and memory of the parent, but also through the eyes of the child. Perhaps values and strategies that I thought were marvelous didn't feel so marvelous to our children—at least at the time. It would be interesting to see from a young adult's perspective what really made a difference to her and what backfired. Then my guinea pig, er, coauthor, joined the Peace Corps and ended up in Africa during the prime writing time. Communicating by snail mail and not having electricity, much less a computer, limited the way in which she could contribute. Thus Heidi's part takes the form of essays. Even though we were seldom able to communicate in person, Heidi kept giving me her perspective and thus influenced what I eventually wrote. Although her contributions are shorter and her name is not on the cover, I consider Heidi V. Vogt my coauthor.

Hints for Reading This Book

If you're like me, you don't necessarily read a book from front to back. I skim, pick out the parts that seem most important, and then perhaps go back and fill in the gaps. If this sounds like you, it might help to know the structure of this book and how different audiences might approach it.

Each chapter that deals with a parenting theme is divided into three parts:

1. Foundational principles that are gradually expanded on in both depth and difficulty. My daughter, Heidi, elaborates on each theme from the perspective of a young adult; our other children add comments where they feel inclined.

2. "Other Families' Stories," in which parents and young adults from many different family backgrounds share their insights on the chapter's theme.

3. Questions for reflection that can help parents apply the chapter's theme to their own lives.

If you are a relatively new parent:
Start at the beginning and read straight through or jump in anywhere you like. What freedom!

If you are the parent of a teen or young adult:
Read the epilogue first and reread it after every chapter. Many parents feel vulnerable and wonder if they've done a good job of parenting at this stage. I remember coming home from professional conferences feeling bad after hearing all the marvelous things my colleagues were doing. The cumulative effect of everyone's accomplishments made me feel inadequate.

It is important to remember that all the wonderful things other families have done did not happen in the same family or in one year.

If you are a parent with a particular interest or need:
Go to the chapter that deals with your concern.

If you enjoy gossip:
Go straight to Heidi's comments and those of the other Vogt children. You'll laugh and feel better.

If you have a voyeuristic streak:
Start by reading "Other Families' Stories." Some will inspire you; some will help you realize that your own situation could be worse.

If you are a teacher or very motivated parent:
Check out the exercises at the end of each chapter. They might give you grist for classroom or adult small-group discussion.

The Jones Family
Christmas Letter

Greetings to you all at Christmas. We'd like to fill you in on our family's comings and goings this past year.

Scott was just awarded a Fulbright Scholarship to study in England for a year. We're looking forward to taking the whole family over to visit him in May. Of course we'll need to take his brother and sisters out of school, but they're all very studious and conscientious, so I'm sure they'll make up the missed work quickly.

Mary led her soccer team to the state championship and was voted most valuable player. I don't know how she squeezes it all in between dating and being chosen homecoming queen.

Jenny won the city spelling bee for the second year in a row; but science is her real love, and she spent weeks working on her award-winning science project last year. We didn't mind the mess because we knew she would clean it all up when she was finished.

Jason's piano recital went so well that his teacher recommended him for the Governor's School for the Arts. He's not sure if he wants to go, however, since he has such a great group of friends at home who inspire him to do his best.

As for us, Bob just got a promotion at work, and we figure the extra money he'll make will pay for our trip to England. And here I am, busy writing Christmas letters and finishing my book.

How do you feel right now? If you're the writer of the above letter, you probably feel very proud of your children and pleased that you've done such a good job of parenting. If you're anyone else, you may be ready to vomit. It's not that you don't believe all the wonderful news about the Jones family. But you have to ask yourself, How realistic are the parents? Are they telling the whole truth? Are they blinded by pride? Was it really their excellent parenting that created such accomplished children? Maybe. Or maybe it was good genes, privilege, intense parental control, or blind luck.

What parent doesn't want his or her child to grow up to be successful in a career and in relationships? But is that really all we want for our child? Even if our child achieves great career heights, marries the prettiest or most handsome spouse, works hard and becomes wealthy, and so forth, will it bring abiding happiness?

The older I get, the more I realize that my hopes and dreams for my children need to be broadened and deepened. Success in the eyes of society is not enough. Happiness is fleeting, and in the end I think our greatest hope is that our children be people of integrity who know how to genuinely love. The prophet Micah said it poetically in the Old Testament: "What does the Lord require of you but to do justice, and to love kindness, and to walk humbly with your God" (Micah 6:8). This may not sound like a recipe for worldly success, but deeper happiness will be the unsought side effect.

BURNING QUESTIONS IN A PARENT'S MIND

If you cared enough to pick up this book, you likely have some of the same questions we did (and do). They are big questions with multiple answers.

How does one raise children who will become people of integrity?

As an energetic new parent, you might say, "Just give me the directions, and I'll follow them faithfully."

As an older, tired parent, you might say, "Hey, I'll settle for success in a career and in relationships. I'm barely hanging on and can't imagine doing one more thing. Our family life is already too complicated."

Often even the energetic, conscientious parent eventually becomes the older, tired parent who is tempted to settle for less.

The challenge is to focus on enduring values and character—the success that counts will fall into place. Less important concerns that crowd our lives will gradually disappear. Even if we're too busy, or if our children are not succeeding in the eyes of the world, by focusing on important values we will develop new eyes with which to see and understand our children. This is the grace that comes with aiming beyond superficial happiness.

This is not a book of answers but a book of ideas. I've selected key values that nurture a child's spirit and have tried to show ways that our own family, and others who have struggled with these same concerns, have tried to weave them into the fabric of everyday family life.

How do I know that if I do it, it will work?

Parenting theories come and go. One season it's permissiveness and the next it's tough love. Who knows what's right?

There are no guarantees in parenting. That's the frustration; that's why it takes maturity. You don't know if what you're doing is right until after your children are adults—and perhaps even later! They are the true test of whether anything "works." The unique gift of this book is the reflections of our own grown children on how the values we tried to share with them worked, or didn't, and what we all learned in the process.

I'd be a fool to set up our family as a model. If being a parent has taught me anything, it's to be humble. It drags all pride out of the honest parent to be called a hypocrite by one's kids, to have a child suspended from school, or to have them wear hairstyles and clothes that embarrass grandparents and pastors. But I can say that our children are honest and will give it to you straight. Make up your own mind about whether the various strategies we've used would be helpful with your own children.

Do remember, however, that sometimes the short-term resistance of a child may turn into appreciation later in life. We've all heard stories of how an adult looks back on a favorite teacher and says something like, "I hated that she gave us so much homework and was such a stickler for quality, but I'm the better person for it."

I can assure you that our children have made their share of mistakes and have had to live with the consequences, as have we. Our family crises have been embarrassing, even painful at times, but I'm confident that our children's hearts are in the right place. They are loving, young adults who want to make the world a better place. They want to make a difference.

In the end we can never control how our children will turn out. That is up to them. We are responsible for the process we use in parenting, not the outcome.

LOOKING BACK AND LOOKING AHEAD

Our friends were just a few years older than us, but their kids were a stage beyond ours; their oldest was in junior high while ours were still preschoolers. We shared the same values of wanting to raise thoughtful children with consciences, who would make this world a better place. They were exemplary parents in our eyes.

I was amazed, therefore, to hear them describe how disappointed they were that their oldest child seemed to resent some of the values they held so dear. For instance, the parents had a strong commitment to live a simple lifestyle, yet Caroline was complaining about never having what her schoolmates had and boldly stated that when she grew up she would make sure, above anything else, that she was rich. The parents were crestfallen, and we were surprised.

They seemed to have done everything right. They modeled what they believed by living frugally themselves. They took lots of time to play with their kids and have family outings. They cooked from scratch and made their own bread. They didn't even own a TV!

I watched and I learned: be careful of how you express your most dearly held values.

Because of the strength of these convictions, parents are tempted to impose them rigidly and in an extreme way on their children. During the early teen years, young people often choose to assert their independence in this area.

As a result of observing our friends, we decided to be cautious about how vigorously we enforced countercultural values. It doesn't mean that we gave up on the value, but rather we tried to listen hard to our children's deeper needs and make adjustments where appropriate.

But I learned another lesson beyond the obvious: It's worth paying attention to the experiences of older parents. Not everything in parenting is intuitive or can be learned in books. Talking with other parents who have been through it and watching what does and doesn't work contributes to wise decision making.

Years later, I would add a third insight: Not everything a child resists need be avoided. The challenge is to know when to compromise and when to hold fast. Most children don't like strange-looking vegetables, but they love desserts. Of course we don't feed them only desserts, no matter how much they plead. We know they'll thank us for it later as their bodies grow strong. Well, it may be *much* later when they are young adults or have children of their own.

One of the dilemmas of parenting, however, is that *later* is so long coming that we don't know if we're doing it right along the way. One of the goals of this book is to offer the reader the advantage of the reflections of both parents looking back on what worked and what didn't in raising responsible, caring, young adults; but also what the young adults themselves think about what made a difference in their lives for good or for ill.

What is the measure of a successful parent?

Is the measure of a successful parent a successful child? And how do we measure success? By income, awards, personality?

Parents want their children to grow up to be happy and healthy. But I believe that caring parents also want their children to care—and not just about themselves. We want them to make a positive difference in the world. Will the way we parent make a difference to them? Yes. Will they actually thank us for it later? That depends.

Although most of what I've written in this book is a result of my reflections on the journeys of our own children and others that I have observed or listened to, I am aware that my gleanings are vulnerable to parochialism. Perhaps my circles of friends and contacts do not accurately reflect the diversity of the contemporary culture that faces today's parents in the United States. I was delighted to come across research, therefore, by Parks, Daloz, Keen, and Keen (1996) that studied the lives of one hundred adults known for their commitment to the common good and whose lives had already made a significant difference. Although their categories are structured differently, their findings are consistent with my own. When asked "what single most crucial thing" a parent could do to raise a socially responsible child, they said:

> No single event can ensure that a person will or will not live a life of commitment to the common good. It is a mix of key ingredients that matters. Taken in isolation, many of the important experiences that we describe here—a loving home, for example—are desirable components of any healthy life. Clearly, there is no certainty that a child from a loving home will grow into a life of commitment, but add a parent who works actively for the public good and the possibility increases. Then add opportunities for service during adolescence, cross-cultural experiences, and a good mentoring experience in young adulthood, and the likelihood grows still stronger. In general, we have become persuaded that the greater the number and depth of certain key experiences one has, the greater the probability of living a committed life. . . ."

Read on and hear stories of our family and a variety of other families—of how some lessons stuck, some didn't, and what made the difference.

A Daughter's Response

My mother has been writing this book in her head since 1974—the year my older brother, Brian, was born. I, of course, wasn't there, but I can imagine her looking into her son's fresh blue eyes and asking my father, "Now how do we keep him from turning into a money-grabbing nuclear warhead manufacturer?" or something like that.

I have it on better authority that when I was born, two and a half years later, one of my parents' friends expressed relief, saying, "It's good that you have more than one child to save the first child from overzealous parenting." A few years later, with a third Vogt crawling around in diapers (the ecologically friendly cloth kind), my parents professionalized their dedication to their children by becoming family-life directors of a Catholic diocese in Kentucky.

My mother read Dr. Spock during pregnancy and kept reading and trying out new child-rearing techniques as we grew up. She and my father were passing on their successes in workshops while I was still in elementary school. My brothers and I served as guinea pigs for this new type of parenting that promised happy families and concerned kids. My childhood was the values of *Family Ties* crossed with the experimental method of *Cheaper by the Dozen*. I can personally attest that my mother's book has been well researched.

So if this is the book my mother's been waiting so long to write, what am I doing here, usurping part of her introduction? Well, she made one mistake. She waited just a little too long, until her guinea pigs were old enough to give their own opinions of the experiments.

And test subjects aren't known for being too complimentary of those who prod them. I wrote a good number of these reminiscences in my parents' basement, periodically interrupted by my mother coming downstairs holding my words in her hands, a worried expression on her face. "But Heidi," she said, "You make it sound like this rule didn't work? You'll ruin my credibility!" "Uh oh," I said, "that was one of my nicer ones."

As we traded drafts back and forth, we debated about things that happened fifteen years ago. "Heidi, you're exaggerating your dishonest streak," said my mother. "Mom, you have *no idea* how much we got away with," I replied. And this was just about TV.

To anyone who does not have a strong relationship with their parents, I strongly advise against attempting the endeavor my mother and I put before you.

But that, as I said in frustration to my mother as we poured over red-inked pages, is the point. I *am* close with my parents. Even more, I have great respect for them. I tell friends that they're two of the least hypocritical people I know. This isn't because their experiments worked, but because they never gave up on the test subjects.

And they must have been tempted. For every conversation my mother managed to wring out of me in the car when I was twelve and thirteen, there were countless drives of sullen silence and a few shouting matches. While I happily helped my father sort recyclables, I also cranked up the thermostat when he wasn't looking and insisted on driving rather than walking the four blocks to the corner store. Many of my parents' attempts to make us care about the world around us were lost on us—at least in a conscious sense.

And the impact those attempts did have wasn't always what my parents had planned. They often weren't prepared to deal with the impertinence that came with their emphasis on independent thought, the anger that came with their ever present community service, or the alienation that came as we decided that our parents "just didn't understand" the desire for designer clothes because they obviously had never wanted them.

But because they kept trying, one thing came across: they felt that certain ideals were important enough to accept short-term failures and aggravation. They took the good with the bad and gave in when they had to.

As a child, I saw their readiness to compromise as a weakness that I could exploit to get my way. As an adult, I have to admit that they slipped a little social responsibility under my skin when I wasn't looking.

Heidi

CHAPTER 1

Identity
Nurturing Values of Honesty, Courage, Humility, and Integrity

Here's an actual Christmas letter we received one year.

> MJ suspended her work at St. Al's to stimulate a process of mediation for a divisive conflict within our community. She's focusing more strongly on Peace Education, especially at the Peace Room of a new community service center in St. Al's neighborhood.
>
> Jerry's building the Peace Room, which we opened in September, then temp nursing at Montgomery County TB clinic.
>
> Both of us underwent a robbery at gunpoint before Christmas and are grateful for our new lease on life—thanks in part to the peaceful Spirit we could feel that calmed our assailant.
>
> Sarah's graduating from Oberlin, renting an apartment in DC, and starting her first job at Ayuda—helping immigrants with legal work to avoid deportation; she's also taking classes, jogging, and reexploring DC.
>
> Jonathan's moving from prison in Hagerstown, MD, to a closer

one in Baltimore, waiting to go to "Boot Camp" before release (mixed

feelings because of lack of preparation and structure to support his

freedom). We get to talk with him weekly and hope with him that he

is building his base for independent living. He may be released within

two years.

P.J.'s graduating from high school, doing a summer service project

in Brazil, and starting at Oberlin, playing soccer and enjoying his room-

mate from Japan, exploring psychology and spirituality.

Jimmy had an energetic spring outdoor adventure to Yosemite

and did summer camping in North Carolina. He's a sophomore at

Sidwell and playing soccer and basketball. He still enjoys art and

now history.

Timmy graduates from Ivymount into a new special education

school—Harbour School—in Annapolis (really a new light in his life,

and he is shining). He's coping with his Asperger's syndrome with a lot

of recreation therapy, structure, and help from his brothers. . . .

What I love about this Christmas letter is its honesty. The good stands side
by side with what some parents might consider embarrassing: a child in
prison and a special-needs child. The Park family's children are valued
simply because they are.

WHERE OUR VALUES COME FROM

So where did the Park family get their values? Where does anyone? The supermarket doesn't sell them. You can't buy them on the Internet. Our values come from somewhere, even if we can't always pinpoint the source.

For most of us, values start with parents, are taught by schools and churches, are reinforced or negated by friends and experience, and are stimulated by the culture and times. Not all these influences are positive ones, but they form us regardless. In time, we make personal choices. Do I focus primarily on my own comfort and getting ahead, or do I want to make this world a more fair and livable place for everyone including myself? What is the right thing to do?

As for me, the foundation was laid by my parents. They never said much directly about how I should live, but I never doubted their love for me and I knew that they expected me to do the right thing. Ours was a safe and loving home.

That's where it started, but that's never enough. Somewhere along the line, the notion that life is about more than my own achievements or comfort started knocking on my head. Because I was brought up Catholic, it started with traditional religious teachings about Jesus and how he taught his disciples to live. I accepted these teachings because they were all I knew and everyone around me believed the same things. It was easy: God was real, and life was good.

But I didn't know what I didn't know. I didn't know the whole story. I believed the Christian precepts about feeding the hungry, clothing the naked, and turning the other cheek, but I didn't know any really poor people, and seldom got into fights, much less was I tempted to kill someone.

Eventually my world got bigger and more complicated. I started seeing that there was selfishness and evil and pride in the world and in me. My understanding of religion had to grow to meet this new awareness or I would have to let it go. Whether it was grace, luck, or the prayers of my holy ancestors, I'll never know. I do know that I started to pray more genuinely and to understand that the scriptures were not just for good times or good people. The story of Christ's life was one of service, even self-sacrifice, and ultimately these values would bring me peace. Living for myself alone would leave my soul restless.

As my world widened even more, I started to see real poverty and real injustice in our world. I also saw that Christians were not the only ones who cared about addressing these needs but that people of other faith traditions said it in different words with different symbols. The instinct to serve humanity, even at one's own inconvenience, was common. Although the roots of my own values had been deeply planted, I saw that others shared a similar inspiration.

Fortunately, during my young adult years I found the company of soul mates in the form of a spouse, a vibrant faith community, challenging literature, and spiritual guides who honed and directed my understanding of what it meant to honestly live the Gospel. It would mean caring about others enough to make their lives a little better.

With the advent of our own children, however, making a difference in the world seemed too ambitious a task. I had diapers to change and kids' games to attend. The world would have to wait. Then the obvious dawned on me! I was making a difference. I was making a difference to our children. I was still making some contributions to the community, albeit not as grandiose as I had earlier imagined. I hoped to have time to make a more significant impact on society as the kids grew older, but I would also try to instill in them the desire to contribute to the common good—to make a difference—so that the transformation of the world might continue.

I imagine I could have come to similar values by a different route. I'm sure that others have come to very worthy values by taking different paths; but this is how it worked for me. I suspect that it will be harder for the next generation because there is not an easy consensus on what the best values are. But the odds are good that if they come from a searching heart and not just habit, the values will stick.

MOM ALWAYS LOVED YOU WORST

When we had only one child, I was convinced that I had been given an exceptionally hard-to-raise child as some kind of test or joke. When a friend introduced me to the term *high-maintenance child,* I knew it was the definition for Brian. By the time our second child, Heidi, came along, I started to realize that the first wasn't really so difficult (it was just parenting that was hard) but that certainly girls were harder on the nerves than boys (they whine a lot, especially during the preteen years). By the third child, Dacian, I realized I had a real challenge because he had a learning disability. After a few years with Aaron, number four, I realized that the "baby" years would always be the hardest since we were getting tired as parents and had begun to relax a lot of the rules that the older children took for granted. We barely had a TV with number one; with number four it was hard to keep track of TV time because someone else often had it on and the youngest would say, "Oh, I was just walking through the room, not really watching." Number one barely had a cookie before his second birthday as we guarded his teeth like dentists. Number four ate snacks with the older kids while he was teething and grew up much more quickly than we would have liked.

Eventually, I stopped making rash generalizations about our children. But it often seemed that other parents were having an easier time raising their children; their kids always seemed to be neatly dressed, polite, and brilliant—according to their parents. That's until I got to know the parents better and heard all the angst they were going through with one problem or another. They too wondered if they were doing it right.

Does adoption make parenting any easier? Other than not having your own genes to blame for any problems, probably not. The issue of identity— who am I and where did I come from?—looms even larger for adoptive children. In traditional closed adoptions, children may not even know the circumstances of their birth or whether they have biological siblings. Some of the parents I've known with the best parenting skills have been adoptive parents, and still many of their children tested their mettle, especially during the teenage years. Now that open adoptions are more common, the adopted child's identity is strengthened with knowledge about his or her biological history. We can hope that this will temper the crises that so many adopted children used to face.

Each child is worst and best in his or her own ways. This chapter is about helping children to know their true self, to maximize the best and minimize the worst. Growing up can be like walking through a labyrinth; when you get to the center you say, "Oh yes! Now I know who I am and where I stand. I'm centered." But we can't stay forever in the cocoon of the center. The rest of this book is about finding our way out.

STARTING THE SEARCH

To a great extent, raising children who will contribute to society in positive ways involves helping them to find themselves and to like what they find. The foundation of a healthy self-concept frees children to go beyond trying to constantly prove themselves worthy of love to extending care to others. Because they have experienced unconditional love, they feel secure in who they are and don't get hung up as easily on the question of who is worthy of their help. This doesn't guarantee that every child will turn out the way a parent wants. We are responsible for the process we use in parenting, not the outcome. Our children have free will and can choose their own paths, even destructive ones. We can guide, but we can't control.

So how do we raise children to become people of integrity with healthy identities? A lot of it involves standard parenting practices that are included in many books and classes. Most parents who have been nurtured well themselves know these practices almost by instinct. Lots of affirmation, good communication skills, sensitivity and care for the people in our neighborhoods, the cultivation of a generous and respectful spirit: these are all building blocks that support children's growing awareness that they can really make a positive difference in the world. When children grow up around these attitudes in their parents, they also receive the underlying message that working to improve our world is not going beyond the call of duty; it *is* our duty. We must give because we've been given to.

AFFIRMATION

Most parenting educators start with this concept of strengthening the self. We love our children and would sacrifice anything for them, but do *they* know it? In the course of ordinary events, parents communicate love to their children in two ways: they affirm how good the children are, and they impose restrictions for the children's protection. We do the former naturally through compliments, hugs, celebrations, and so forth. The latter sometimes involves tough love, and it doesn't feel as good to the parent or the child at the time. It involves saying "No, you can't go to the party since you've been sick at home all day" or, "You must return this candy to the store and explain to the clerk that you didn't pay for it" or, "No, I won't lend you money since you used up your allowance prematurely." It means looking like an ogre to your child.

Complimenting or praising our children seems like the easy part when compared with tough love, but it's also easy to let affirmation slide and to take one another for granted when we feel busy and overcommitted. And sometimes, in our determination to deal with negative behaviors, we forget about the day-to-day affirmations.

It's also easier to gush over our children when they are young: "How wonderful that you've learned to tie your shoes!" or "Mommy really appreciates your help with your baby brother." It may get harder to find things to genuinely praise as they grow older.

As we were just starting our own family, I looked up to the Foleys. They were a slightly older couple with six children. For us, they were mentors. Joan Foley told me that she looked for three things she could compliment each child for every day. One was a personality quality, one was an action, and one was a physical attribute. I thought this was admirable and decided to incorporate this into my own parenting repertoire. I quickly found out how frail was my human will and how forgetful my mind. I settled on just finding one thing a day for each child. Even this slipped through my fingers on many days, and I had only three children at that time.

Eventually, I used my morning-prayer time for thinking of things to praise in my children. I figured God would understand this as prayer because it was my attempt to look for the good in our mutual creation. Most of the time this worked. Although I tried to voice my compliment to each child sometime during the day, I found that even if I forgot, the discipline of looking for the good in someone who might not appear that lovable on a given day improved my attitude toward each child. I don't know if our children ever realized that I was consciously doing this.

To help our children appreciate their strengths, we invented something we called "Sweet Talk." We'd sometimes do this on Valentine's Day or a birthday. It involved focusing on one family member at a time and brainstorming all the positive qualities each of us recognized in that person. I suppose it would be better if this happened naturally, but some of us need a prompt to share what's in our hearts.

In regard to tough love, I still remember the guilt I felt the day I made one of my children walk to school because he had dawdled too long and missed the school bus. The school was not that far away, but it meant he would be late. This was not the first time he had missed the bus, and he had been warned of exactly what would happen, but I still wanted to get in the car and rescue him. It was quite a while before this child missed another bus. We went through subsequent variations on this with each child. You'd think they'd learn. I did; with each child it got easier for me to stick with the discipline.

Tough love is not about being vindictive but about showing children the natural or logical consequences of their actions. They learn that love doesn't mean always rescuing someone from mistakes and foolishness but letting that person learn the hard way sometimes. Tough love helps children face the realities of cause and effect.

In the long run, a combination of affirmation and tough love helps children understand that love involves much more than showering someone with gifts. Real love hurts sometimes, and it requires time and thought.

This kind of love experienced at home makes it easier for children to understand what it really means to help others. Sometimes the best way to help a panhandler may not be to give a handout but to give the resources to help him or her work to change the system that makes it hard to climb out of poverty. It's much easier (and it often feels better) to just hand out money, but lasting difference—and personal development—require effort.

HONESTY

No one likes to see their child lie or steal, but most kids at least try it when they are young. When my husband and I suspected lying we would tell the child that there would be a punishment for what they did wrong but that there would be a bigger punishment if he or she lied to cover it up. This usually took care of the run-of-the-mill lying associated with immaturity. If lying persists, it's often connected with a lack of self-esteem. Children think that they have to make themselves look better than they really are, so they lie about themselves or steal something that will give them status among their peers. In addition to dealing with why children don't feel good enough or important enough, it can help to talk about what is fair. Children are competitive and sensitive to not fitting in. They also pick up from the adult world that a person is what he or she owns. Parents can talk about how it isn't fair that some people have more than others, but that this isn't because of laziness or other personal flaws but due to circumstances that are often beyond a person's control. A person's worth is not dependent on looks or how much stuff he or she has.

The virtues that we try to nurture in our children sometimes get turned back on us. I remember when my husband, Jim, had just finished cowriting and publishing the Family Pledge of Nonviolence. We had already had several family meetings to discuss the pledge, and it seemed natural that our own family would take it. As parents we had been so concerned about the TV/media part of the pledge that we hadn't talked much about the final element: "To challenge violence in all its forms whenever I encounter it, whether at home, at school, at work, or in the community, and to stand with others who are treated unfairly." Just when we thought everyone in the family was committed to the pledge, Dacian (seventeen at the time) stated, "I can't sign this!"

He calmly explained that he didn't want to be in a position in which the pledge forced him to act in a way he considered ill-advised. "What if there is a fight brewing at school and I'm nearby? I don't know that I necessarily should try to break it up myself. I might, but I also might not think that's wise to do given the circumstances. I won't sign the pledge unless I can write 'as I see fit' after the 'Be Courageous' element." As an adult, I probably would have made this mental reservation automatically when signing something. As a teenager, though, he was really taking this seriously and wanted to be true to himself. His honesty helped us all look at the pledge more deeply and consider its consequences. It took courage to stand up for what he believed in, in the face of at least implicit parental pressure.

COURAGE

It takes courage to tell the truth and face the consequences. In *Parenting for Peace and Justice: Ten Years Later,* Kathleen and James McGinnis tell us that Gandhi used to require that five times a year each child in his schools do an individual thirty-minute performance of some kind.

> In this way, at least five times a year each child makes some public presentation at the daily assembly. Gandhi wanted to educate a nation of people able to stand up for what they believed, to stand up in public and not be embarrassed and speechless, to overcome the fears that keep people from acting courageously. We can imitate the spirit of this in many ways. Encouraging our children to act publicly—like reading during worship services, availing themselves of dramatic and musical opportunities, writing a letter to an editor, standing at a public vigil wearing a button on their shirt or coat—helps them develop confidence in themselves.

Sounds very noble coming from Gandhi, but I remember not being so fond of this "Speak truth to power" idea when our children first started to talk—and talk and talk. It seems we were raising a household debate team that would challenge every direction and every rule that we presented. Since we didn't want to stifle their spirits and hated to hear the words "Because I said so" come out of our mouths, we put up with it. But it started to wear us down. Must every decision be a debate? Consolation came much later when I realized that this same spirit that refused to accept my will just because I said so would also resist peer pressure to go along with the crowd and indeed would stand up for unpopular causes or the underdog. If I had it to do over again, however, I would have tried to discriminate between which decisions were up for debate and which were nonnegotiable or frivolous and not worth the arguing.

"But it's cold, I don't want to stand for an hour in silence protesting the cross that the KKK put up on Fountain Square!" There were several responses we usually had to these complaints.

- "You don't have to come, but here's why we think it's important to peacefully protest a hate group."

- When they were young: "Let's break it up with a half hour of standing and the rest of the time skating at the nearby ice rink."

- When they were older: "Your friend, Luke, will be coming too."

Sometimes courage takes a more subtle form. I learned only after we sold the car that Aaron, at age fifteen, felt embarrassed by the bumper stickers we had on it. One was in Spanish, and his friends all took French, so that wasn't a problem; but the one that read "Feminists for Life" hit a raw nerve. He wasn't opposed to the concept but was afraid that he would be seen as a wimp for being a feminist. He put up with it as long as I allowed his rock-band sticker.

Kids can turn the tables on their parents, however, and cause the parents to summon up their courage. In 1991, we had been talking at home about the Gulf War—its connection with our country's need for oil and what should be done. Brian and his friend Shane decided to write a letter protesting the war and send it to the editor of a local newspaper. This seemed like an appropriate civic response until Shane learned that the essay prize he had won in the "Voice of Democracy" contest was in jeopardy because of the opinions expressed in their letter.

Nonetheless, the two of them took it even further and decided to put up posters and a banner protesting the war at their high school. Although it was an unpopular stance at their school, it was a nonviolent act. Unfortunately, it was also prohibited since all posters were supposed to be approved. I started feeling nervous because they brainstormed even more dramatic symbolic actions, and I was aware that Brian had several college scholarships pending and needed good recommendations from the administration. Had we raised him to make too many waves, to make too much of a difference?

HUMILITY

Humility is the virtue of parenthood. It usually comes unbidden after the pride of being the perfect parent is punctured by our children's honesty and raw edges. There is little need to pass humility on directly because most people learn it soon enough just through the bumps of life. For those blessed with a smart or attractive or athletic child, the message that should permeate the air is that we rejoice in your life, but you aren't any more valuable or worthy than any other human being. For those blessed with a mediocre or awkward or less attractive child the message is the same. Each person is responsible for making the world a better place.

One of the hardest things I ever did had to do with jeans. I bought our teenager Aaron the jeans of his dreams and then later had to admit that I altered them so they wouldn't hang three inches below his shoes and be a walking hazard. They were expensive, and he loved them—but he wanted them long. Admitting I deceived him and taking them back to exchange them was hard. What was even harder was when my husband asked if I had told the clerk that I had altered the jeans. I sheepishly said I hadn't. I knew I had to call the store and offer to pay for the returned slacks. My son overheard the call.

Another time we were really short on money. I think this was during our unemployed/student/part-time-work phase of marriage. We had been offered a rather high speaking fee plus all expenses paid to talk at a conference. Since we weren't real familiar with the sponsoring organization, we checked into it and found that its values were at odds with ours. We decided to turn it down. Our kids overheard us discussing this decision. Maybe that's why none of them make a lot of money.

INTEGRITY

Integrity is about how our actions match our words. In fact, actions trump words.

Again and again, the parents I interviewed said that the biggest waste of time for them and the biggest turnoff for their children was lecturing and preaching. Actions were what counted. How do we teach that each person has worth regardless of status? By seeing the dignity in everyone, especially those who are unattractive to us, and meeting them with respect. By telling the truth about the flaws of a used car or appliance when trying to sell it. By publicly standing up for an oppressed person or unpopular cause at the risk of others making fun of me. By owning my limitations and mistakes as a parent or worker and then working hard to improve my work. By being a person of my word, following through on that promise to spend more time playing with my children. Accepting the consequence of less pay because I took time off work to do it. These are the times we teach, often without knowing it, and the lessons will stick.

The Vogt Kids Speak

I remember when Mom and Dad brought before us the finished version of the Family Pledge of Nonviolence. It seemed like just another one of the hokey things our family did, like the prayer chain during Advent, or the family meetings that always seemed to run around in circles before we finally came back to the starting point. However, I've never been one to go along with something simply to appease my parents, so I took the pledge seriously and noticed that I could not agree with the "to be courageous" statement. It seemed to me that in order to accomplish anything you need to pick your battles carefully and not go at it in a berserk state, attacking everything. If your friends are going to a movie that has violent content, standing up and denouncing them for their evil ways isn't going to get you anything. Likewise if you try to break up a fight between a couple of people you don't know, you'll probably end up with a black eye. To me being courageous also means being intelligent. When I was seventeen, I refused to sign the pledge unless I could put "as I see fit" next to my signature.

Dacian

One of the things that taught me honesty more than anything else was the fact that I knew that my parents were always 100 percent honest with me. Most parents don't intend to lie or mislead their children, but, often, difficult situations lead parents to commit white lies in order to maintain harmony or avoid an unpleasant issue. I knew of friends who didn't have this confidence in their parents. Leading by example in this arena, I feel, was very influential.

Brian

A Daughter's Response

"Of Barbie Dolls and Beauty Pageants"

The average American woman measures about 34-24-37. A life-size Barbie doll would measure about 38-18-24. She wouldn't be able to stand up, much less get chased around the pool by Ken. Her legs are too long, her breasts too big, and her waist too tiny. Barbie is everything that is antifeminist and bad body image. So of course, my mother never gave me a Barbie doll. True to the rules of childhood, I therefore prized Barbie dolls over any other toy. I saved up my allowance for months to buy one Barbie doll. I rushed straight to my friends' Barbie mansions and jealously looked over the seven or eight Barbies they might have lounging in different rooms or poolside. I tried to save money by using scraps of fabric or Kleenexes to create Barbie outfits, but they were never as good as the real thing. I could've spent hours in the Barbie aisle of Johnny's Toy Store just taking in all the Barbies, Barbie cars, Barbie clothes, and Barbie accessories. I was obsessed.

My mother wasn't pleased. She tried telling me I couldn't buy Barbies with my allowance money, only the clothes (hoping I would put them on other dolls). Luckily, my aunt occasionally overruled my mother by giving me a Barbie doll for Christmas or my birthday. Thanks to her, I owned Peaches 'n Cream Barbie, Day-to-Night Barbie, and Hawaiian Barbie. Peaches 'n Cream was my favorite. But Day-to-Night had smokier eyes.

My mother tried sitting me down and explaining why she was anti-Barbie. "Women are more than their looks," she said. I listened attentively and then begged her, couldn't I *please* have Astronaut Barbie?

At a certain point, she gave up and waited for me to grow out of it. Instead I grew into the idea of life-size Barbies. I became enamored with beauty pageants. I asked my mother about how to enter and when I would be old enough. She groaned. Miss America, Miss USA, Miss Teen USA, Miss World, Miss Universe: I wanted to watch them all. I wanted to live beauty vicariously through the women strutting down the runway. Unfortunately, these pageants were all two hours long and started after my bedtime.

Tentatively, I went up to my mother and asked her if I could stay up and watch extra TV in order to see the Miss America pageant. She said she'd think about it. I pouted. Eventually she agreed on two conditions: that she watch it with me, and that we discuss the show afterward. I jumped at the compromise. I planned to ignore her and enjoy the pageant. I was home free.

At 9:00 on the big night, my mother and I sat down to watch the Miss America broadcast live. We ate popcorn and drank Cokes and compared the evening gowns. We both agreed that the swimsuit competition was boring because they all wore the same bathing suit. My mom laughed, shocked at the idea of bathing suits and high heels (I was unfazed by this concept, having dressed my Barbies in very similar attire). She said she used to watch these pageants all the time at my age, and I realized she was enjoying this as much as I was. We tried to guess who would win. I didn't think our Miss Kentucky was beautiful at all. Then my mom explained that she had "poise," which the judges always liked. Miss Virginia had the best talent; she was a ventriloquist. My mother explained that singing and playing the piano were your safest bets. We forgot about body image and cheered them on. When Miss Kentucky was declared the winner, we smiled, proud that our state had produced the poise-filled beauty. Tired, we took the popcorn bowl and glasses to the kitchen and headed off to bed. My mother had completely forgotten to talk to me about the evils of pageants. I began to consider that my mother wasn't enemy #1 after all.

Heidi

Other Families' Stories

As a single parent I had that guilt, heaped on top of the normal uncertainty, that parents feel about whether they are doing the right thing. Then my son Keith told me a story. Keith had always been shy and found it difficult to speak in public. It seems that when he was taking a college class the professor made several references to "broken families" as a result of divorce. Keith summoned up all his courage and said, "My family is not broken! It was broken when my father was with us, but now it is whole."

M. N., soup kitchen director

It's hard to have your children question your decisions and put up a fight about discipline, but I figure if they're marshmallows for me now, they'll be marshmallows for peer pressure later.

Susan Brogden, mother of two teens, Harrison Ohio

Although my parents did a great job of parenting, the dumbest thing they did was to suggest, verbally and nonverbally, that they wanted at least one of us to be a minister or otherwise an important public figure. I think it got us all too obsessed with how we appear regardless of whether it's what we needed emotionally—the result has been too many martyr/Jesus complexes in our family over saving the world, and beating ourselves up over whether our lives fall short. I resented being shown off to others with the implication that my role was to reflect on my parents' value rather than do what I wanted to do. It took me about thirty years to learn how to listen to my own desires and emotions, rather than do what I thought others wanted me to do.

Anonymous lawyer, New York City

I would desperately like to see what Peter Maurin wanted: "A world where it is easier to be good." And I feel about God as Dorothy [Day] did when she said, "I don't have a conscience. A conscience has me." At times I'm sick of this conscience, but it's me and I see no way out.

John Stith, 26, Green Party organizer Montgomery, Alabama

Even though my parents acted like the "typical" Asian parents at times—overprotective and demanding—they gave my sister and me a lot of opportunities to pursue what *we* wanted to do. For instance, the fact that both my sister and I play both the violin and the piano—sure signs that the hand of an Asian parent is at work—the desire came from us, not from them. They encouraged us to travel in high school. They didn't pressure us to be in the honors classes at school, but somehow we always ended up in them. I think it was because early on they were so generous with their time and energy—always willing to help us with our homework every night. We also probably realized that our parents weren't exactly dummies (they both have doctoral degrees in engineering). That might have also been why we pushed ourselves to excel at school.

Jayme Linlin Yen, 23, graphic designer and rowing coach

I remember that my Dad always encouraged me to explore and discover. Once, as we were hiking, I started to climb a big rock and my Mom shouted something like, "Oh, Julia, honey, be careful, get down!" But my Dad replied, "Let her climb. She'll discover her own limits." Climbing up trees and rocks can be scary and intimidating, but only by doing it can a child learn to trust her instincts and come to know her capabilities and limitations. Because of subtle parenting skills like that I did learn to be confident and know myself. I'm not a parent, but I'm sure that this must be the most difficult aspect of the whole endeavor—allowing your children to take risks, knowing they may get hurt. Still, we often learn more from our bruises, scrapes, and scars than from our trophies, awards, and scholarships. My parents were also proactive, involved citizens, and thus I learned that the common person was capable of creating change. Somehow I got the message that I was in the good situation I was born into out of sheer luck, and that my good fortune carried with it certain social responsibilities. I was always told I should share my talents and use my opportunities to help others.

Julia Marie Graff, 23,
volunteer with Witness for Peace, Bogota, Colombia

My dad taught me a lot. When I was about eight, he took my sister and me to the Natural History Museum. With our curious, grubby hands we began touching the glass of the exhibits. My dad told us not to put our hands on the glass because "It's somebody's job to clean up around here." He refuses to buy products manufactured in countries he knows to have coercive population-control policies, no freedom of religion, and unfair labor practices. More than once this ethical consideration has caused him to continue wearing worn-out shoes and clothes for many months while he shopped for acceptable items. He plants trees that will never be tall enough in his lifetime to offer him shade. He once told me, "It takes a lot of work to be a principled person. Sometimes it's frustrating; other times you realize it's the only way to be." From my father I've learned the importance of striving to love and live truth even when it hurts, even when others won't understand, even in the face of ridicule, and even when the world will try to use you up and forget about you.

Kate Bergman, 24, graduate student and
Residential Counselor for Senate Pages, Washington, D.C.

Knowing Yourself, Knowing Your Child

HAVE YOU FIGURED OUT WHO YOU ARE YET?

What did your parents do while you were growing up that had a big influence on you becoming the person you are?

What was the smartest thing your parents did when you were growing up?

What was the dumbest?

Is there anything your parents insisted on when you were growing up that you disliked at the time but now thank them for?

What are the top five values that guide your life?

WHAT DO YOU WANT FOR YOUR CHILD?

If nothing else, you hope your child will be . . .

What did you like about your upbringing that you want to pass on to your own child?

What did you dislike about your upbringing that you want to avoid doing to your child?

What do you hope your child will thank you for later?

Number the following qualities or values that you might pass on to your child in order of their importance to you:

honest

generous

committed to a religious/faith
   system

loving

successful

sacrifices for others

physically attractive

hardworking

cares for the poor or powerless

has a spiritual core

has integrity

good communicator

physically healthy

intelligent

self-sufficient

loyal

committed

self-aware

compassionate

open

peacemaker

cares for creation

good friend

sexually chaste until marriage

creative

fair

other _____

If you feel frustrated doing this exercise, don't despair. As a parent you can work at all of the above. But knowing the values you hold *most* dear will help you choose your battles carefully and avoid trying to raise your child in your own image.

MONDAY	B—academic team, H—band, D—soccer practice Family Night
TUESDAY	S—nursery school car pool B—play practice H—band J—7:30 mtg S—7:30 mtg.
WEDNESDAY	B—academic team H—piano lesson, D—soccer practice D—Boy Scout mt S—aerobics class
THURSDAY	S—nursery school car pool J—Take car to shop, get ride to work, arrange for neighbors to pick up kids from band and play practice after school J—7:30 mtg.
FRIDAY	A—vaccination H—band A—birthday party J&S—date night
SATURDAY	B—play practice, D—soccer game (bring oranges)
SUNDAY	Church B—soup kitchen, H—Girl Scout banquet

CHAPTER 2

Time
Ideas for Taming
the Calendar

Does the schedule on page 24 look familiar? Your child may play baseball rather than soccer, or trumpet rather than piano. You may be taking care of elderly relatives instead of going to an evening meeting—or maybe you're doing all of the above. Why is it that with fast food, speed dial, e-mail, cell phones, and more cars than garage space, so many of us still feel as if we're not caught up?

I admit it: I am infected with busy sickness. I've been in recovery for about twenty years, but still I can never attend a meeting without my planner and the resolve to say "No." Of course this overflows to family life too. And it's not confined to dual-career marriages, either. People who have busy sickness deal with its symptoms no matter what their work and family situations. Worse still, those of us who have it are passing it on to our children.

We can start to deal with our busyness by evaluating the goals we have for our families. If raising children who care about the world around them is a priority for us, then spending time caring for those children makes a difference. That's the easy part. The hard part is figuring out how much direct parenting time is enough and how to weigh that against our responsibilities to make a living, nurture a marriage, and contribute to society ourselves—all while staying reasonably sane and happy. Here's how the balancing act typically plays out.

The more hours I work, the more money I earn. This is good. But the more hours I work, the less time I have to spend with my family and friends. This is unfortunate. But then again, if I work more, I can buy more time-saving conveniences, which means that I can spend more time focusing on the people in my life. This is good—and on and on.

But work can be a seductive mistress. It keeps asking for more. The goods I can buy with the extra money are very tangible, and the esteem of my colleagues can be addictive. It's tempting to give the best of myself to my job in the name of providing more for my family. This is not so good.

On the other hand, bills do have to be paid and it would be irresponsible for parents not to provide adequately for their children's material needs and sad for them not to provide for enrichment opportunities. To work is honorable and often brings satisfaction and contributes to the good of society. So, work is both necessary and good. But unless I am blessed with a very unusual job in which I get paid a lot for only a little of my time, finding the right balance becomes a constant struggle. Add to this the question of whether it is better for one of the parents to be at home with the children when they are young, and we are in the midst of the classic quality time versus quantity time debate.

QUALITY TIME OR QUANTITY TIME?

It takes a certain quantity of time to catch the quality times. The time it takes to listen to a child's worry may take less than a minute. Being there when the worry comes up may involve an entire day of just being around. Building a relationship of familiarity and comfort is difficult work, and a year or two may pass before your child is willing to show you that secret hideout in the woods. Catching a teenager in the right mood can take longer. Special events can be scheduled; crises and spontaneity can't.

One solution is to keep a parent at home most of the time. For many families, this is not possible. Does a parent have to stay at home while the child is young in order to get in enough quality time? Not necessarily, but it does make it easier.

Most successful dual-career parents that I have interviewed are super-organized and guard their family time with a vengeance. It doesn't hurt to have the income to pay for services that would otherwise take the time of a stay-at-home parent, such as quality child care, housecleaning, expensive convenience foods, camps, and so forth. Even with paid help, however, life will be stressful. Coordinating schedules to drop kids off at day care and get to at least some of their sporting events is challenging enough. Here are some survival techniques that help:

- Lower household cleanliness standards.

- Practice saying no to volunteer work.

- Guard weekends and evenings (or other off time) from commitments that don't involve the family.

- Choose recreation that everyone can do together.

- Buddy up with other parents who share your values and have kids close to the ages of your kids; they can be substitute parents when you're not available.

- Take time to organize daily life and chores so that time is not wasted looking for things or running to the store.

- Use cell phones to streamline transportation pickups and bring peace of mind. It connects spouses and children even when you are not physically in one another's presence.

- Consider how e-mail and other technologies may save time and keep you in communication with one another.

- Ideally, find a job with flexible hours and an understanding supervisor.

The suggestions listed above can also help the stay-at-home parent maximize quality time, but they are more crucial for the dual-career parent. Another alternative, of course, is to make more time for family by reducing the number of hours of paid employment. But this means spending time doing what I might otherwise pay others to do. It takes time to rely less on manufactured goods, to live in harmony with the environment, to save money by doing it myself (something discussed in chapter 3).

There are no easy answers, only tough choices. I can, however, share with you some wise one-liners that have helped me along the way. I constantly carry in my head an aphorism that originated with the family-life educator, Clayton Barbeau: "Where you put your time, you put your life." I figure out what is most important in my life and then spend my time on it. Most of the time (with the exception of sleep time), this has been a helpful guide. The other is a little poem that I have kept taped on my desk at work since our children were born. It pulls me back and gives me perspective.

> Cleaning and scrubbing can wait 'til tomorrow,
> For babies grow up, we've learned to our sorrow.
> So quiet down, cobwebs; dust, go to sleep,
> I'm nursing my baby, and babies don't keep.

Beyond sage sayings, however, taming time and putting it in the service of the family involves the hard work of prioritizing and ordering our lives. I have found it helpful to tackle this task by looking at three different dimensions of time: saving time, wasting time, and making time.

SAVING TIME

In the long run, saving time is probably not the most important of the three time dimensions, but it is the quickest and most fun, so we'll start with it. This is about being organized and efficient so that necessary tasks take less time. It's what many people think of when they hear the term *time management.* It is one of my loves, because my personality derives great joy and satisfaction from being able to do things quickly and minimize work.

Learn to multitask.

This is the default position of the high energy, achievement oriented, type A personality. For example, I seldom watch TV without folding laundry at the same time. When I had babies, I tried to always have a book nearby so I could read while I nursed. If a book wasn't handy, I used the time to pray. Other strategies that worked in our family include listening to work-related tapes while driving, listening to the news while cooking, holding family meetings during dinner, catching up on a child's life while driving him or her to school. The downside to multitasking is that our attention is divided. Reading the paper while my husband is talking to me, and later insisting that I heard every word, just doesn't cut it.

Get organized.

Most of the time I've wasted in my life has been looking for things that were lost—my own stuff and everybody else's. Some would call me over-responsible; my kids call me the "great finder." Perhaps this is because I put away more things than anyone else in our household. I have used a number of techniques to keep track of stuff: a message center where all phone calls and messages are noted; a pencil and paper by each phone; a tray for each child to keep mail and important papers in; shelves with containers for toys, art supplies, and sports equipment; and—my favorite—color coding (see chapter 4). My basic principle? Put like things together in a space close to where they are typically used.

Not everyone has the desire, or the knack, for the kind of organizing I do, and sometimes my kids feel that I go overboard. They still don't understand the pleasure I get from occasionally organizing all the Legos into categories of flat, one bump, two bumps, four bumps, double one bump, double two bumps, and so forth. Actually, I don't call this task "organizing"; for me it's recreation. In any case, it provides humor for the rest of the family.

Delegate wisely.

This is not the children's favorite timesaving strategy because they are usually the delegatees. In fact, it is not my favorite strategy either; any parent knows that it's often quicker to do it yourself. When I delegate, I have to accept a job that is not done the way I would have done it. Nevertheless, I keep reminding myself that parenting is a long-term project and that my goal is not just to get the house clean but to teach the children skills and responsibility. It may also eventually save me some work. It may not.

As with most families, our children had chores, such as setting or clearing the table, caring for pets, and cleaning. The process we used to delegate, however, may have been more important to the ultimate mindset of our children than the tasks themselves. Periodically, we would list all of the tasks that were needed to make the household run smoothly. This included everything from helping with dinner to feeding the hamster. We then posed the challenge to everyone to volunteer for the chores in a fair way. Age, skill, and time were factored in. If some tasks were not taken, we kept negotiating until everyone agreed on a fair distribution. The kids may not have liked their jobs, but they knew they were getting a fair shake. We hope that our delegation process instilled in our children a sense that everybody is responsible for contributing to the community and that sometimes we're going to have to do grunt work that we don't like. Did it save time? Yes—if you don't count time to inspect and nag. Did it teach our children an important value? I think so.

Lower your standards.

This may seem obvious, but one way to save time is simply to do less work. This is easier said than done in a family setting, though, because one person's necessity is another person's maybe. Jim and I have different cleaning standards; the children started with none. Contrary to the domestic stereotype, Jim has always been the more fastidious spouse in our house, and this has caused some marital strife. In time, and with the advent of more children, he graciously (and of necessity) lowered some of his housekeeping standards to meet mine—although he is still in charge of one bathroom.

This is a touchy subject because cleanliness is not only a health and aesthetic concern but it also can feel like a moral issue. "Cleanliness is next to godliness" didn't come from the Bible, but in many families it is treated like a holy rule. Some of us can easily slip into the attitude that we're superior because we clean more or because our homes are spotless—at least compared to other homes!

As far as I'm concerned, in the absence of physical health hazards, if you can't see it, it doesn't need to be cleaned. Since I'm short, I don't see all the cobwebs near the ceiling. This saves me time. It also has prepared our children to live in underdeveloped countries as adults.

If, however, you happen to be one of those families whose bathroom already looks like it belongs in a gas station, disregard the above.

Just say no.

Volunteering and being of service to the community are important values to instill in a child. These are the building blocks of a life committed to making the world a better place for everyone. A parent who volunteers not only provides a service, but he or she also models that this is a responsibility of caring adults.

But service can be overdone. Sometimes the responsible action is to say no—not forever; just for now. In a misguided desire to be the perfect parent, some feel that they have to bake cookies for every fundraiser, coach every team, and serve on every committee. This may be driven more by pride or guilt than by altruism. Choose very carefully what you say yes to. Not all good deeds have to be done during the active parenting years.

A friend told me about a traditional Hindu attitude toward service. Traditionally, the parents pull back from some things while their children are young. When the children are raised, they jump fully back into the service arena and give away many of the possessions that they needed when the kids were young. To everything there is a season.

This attitude teaches children that it is their responsibility to serve others, but it works best when service is thoughtfully chosen, not just an automatic reaction. Is it a request that I have a unique ability to respond to? Can someone else do it just as well? Is it something I can do with my spouse or my children? Will it interfere with dinner or other family time?

Once we really struggled with whether to allow one of our sons to join the wrestling team because their daily practice started at 5:30 P.M. This made it difficult to eat as a family either before or after practice. I talked with the coach to no avail. He had always done it this way. Eventually our son decided to drop wrestling for other reasons. I'm not sure what we would have done otherwise.

Even more disturbing was our parish's policy of scheduling religious education classes at 6:00 P.M., making a family dinner difficult. After much complaining and talk of respecting family time, I got nowhere. We could have done the religious education at home, as we sometimes have done. We could have changed parishes, but we didn't want to for other reasons. Since this was not a commitment we wanted to break, we resigned ourselves to juggling dinner one night a week.

Many parents fall into the trap of getting excessively involved in their children's sports. I love sports, have played organized sports myself, and support my children's involvement. Being on a team teaches a lot of life skills, builds relationships, and is fun. But there is a difference between being a support and being a slave. A parent doesn't have to be at *every* practice and game in order to be a good parent. My husband and I make it to most of our kids' games and often take turns with other parents driving to practices, but sometimes we have other commitments. Our children will not wither if we miss a few games.

WASTING TIME

Probably the most obvious example of wasting time is overuse of the TV and other screen-based media, such as videos and computer games. I don't mean the "I just finished my homework or an intensive day at the office and I want to relax for awhile" kind of TV, but the "I can't think of anything to do or am trying to avoid work" channel surfing. We'll talk about the media more in chapter 5; suffice it to say a lot of time can be saved by not wasting it on TV.

My personal struggle is with wasting time by worrying. This may come with the role of mother, but the challenge I face is discerning what is productive worry and what just drains me of energy and thus is a waste of time. Time spent worrying merges with our other daily activities, and this makes it hard to recognize. I may still cook, drive, and go to work, but my attention is divided because I'm worried about whether I made the right decision in disciplining a child. I start to be a nag or smother the child with interrogation. The rule of thumb I've developed is that if the worry can't change anything, it's time to let it go.

For a congenital worrier, however, this resolve is not enough. I have to buttress it with a substitute thought. What works for me is using the worry as a prompt to pray for the person or situation. Unloading on Jim usually helps too. Over the years I've learned to say, "I don't want a solution for this worry; I just want to ventilate." After listening, he often will defuse the worry with humor. All of the above also applies to wasting time by holding on to anger. Unless it moves toward a positive action, let it go.

Forgetfulness also wastes time; it means taking more trips to the store, retracing steps, and spending more idle time trying to remember what I've forgotten. Forgetfulness makes us feel out of control, which adds stress to our lives and robs us of energy. The time management gurus always recommend making "To Do" lists and using calendars. I think they're right. Helping an A.D.D. child to use these tools takes parental creativity and grace. Helping a parent with Alzheimer's to remember takes patience and forgiveness.

One final time waster is excessive travel. Choosing where to live in relation to a job is a decision most families make only a handful of times during their work lives, but the number of miles traveled to work multiplied by about five hundred times a year adds up to quite a few hours in the car. If it's time to move, choose your location carefully, with an eye to travel time. Beyond commuting to work, think of all the other places the family drives to regularly: school, the shopping center, and friends' houses. Living in an urban environment often makes these trips shorter. Better yet, if the destination is within walking distance, the child doesn't need to waste a parent's driving time. Less driving also saves wear and tear on the car, the environment, and the nerves.

WASTING THE RIGHT TIME

Ordinarily I do not relish chauffeuring our children around. Not only is it not the best use of my time, but it also uses gas and therefore money, the pollution hurts the environment, and car trips rob the kids of exercise. Currently, I drive one child to school every day. He could take the bus, and it's not out of the question to walk. So much for being socially conscious.

Why do I betray my values? Because I'm aiming at a higher goal: conversation. Over the years I have noticed that something strange happens to boys around the time they reach age fifteen. They lose the power of speech around parents. When our first child entered this stage, I became so frustrated that I made son #2 (who was still in the "I want to please" stage) sign a contract promising that when he turned fifteen he would not "be a cranky, uncommunicative, whiny, critical, ungrateful, grunting ogre." I resigned myself to having failed with the first child, but maybe I could salvage the others. By the time son #3 hit puberty, he had learned from the older ones and refused to sign anything. They later told me that a contract signed under duress is invalid anyway. I knew this, but I thought it might at least be a conversation starter.

So driving in the car has sometimes afforded natural conversation opportunities. Our rule is no radio during these drives. Some mornings we say nothing. But given enough days, some interesting snippets slip out. After all, he can't hide behind TV or homework when he's in the car, and since my eyes are on the road I won't see his eyes if he rolls them. If I'm brief, I can tackle a sensitive subject without the embarrassment of the child and me having to look each other in the eye. There's no escape. This technique is even more effective when chauffeuring a group of teens. The only rule here is that the parent doesn't say anything. I just listen. I learn a lot.

Keep Sabbath time.

I put Sabbath time under "wasting time" only because, in today's world, enjoying a true Sabbath makes no sense; you're not making money or getting any work done. Yet for people of faith (and many others besides) the Sabbath is not a waste but is helpful for a balanced life.

For Jewish people the Sabbath is Saturday; for Christians, Sunday; and for Muslims, Friday. The particular day of the week is not important; the concept is what matters. The Sabbath is a time when we can step back, get some perspective on what makes us so busy throughout the rest of the week, and make sure our priorities are in line. Traditionally it has also been a family time. Unfortunately, today it is often primarily a shopping day. We can catch up on work and buy things that we didn't have time to get earlier; our own family sometimes does these things, but at what cost? Whether or not you consider yourself religious is not the point. Stopping to rest and take stock of my life's direction helps the spirit revive and focus. People who are motivated to change the world need periodic times of rest. This is not just physical rest but rest for the spirit. Neglecting this custom creates some driven and compulsive social activists. Eventually, burnout and resentment take their toll.

So how does a family take full advantage of this special day when soccer starts at 8:00 and Mass is at 10:00? Not without soul-searching. Technically, we could just about make Mass at 10:00, but it was hardly a restful beginning to the day. After the obligatory but ineffectual complaining to the soccer league, we decided to focus on the time after worship. We would make an effort to have a special family breakfast, with lingering.

Even though our daughter decided to quit the team after one season, it prompted our family to think of other ways to celebrate Sunday as our day of rest. Chores were planned for Saturday. We accepted some work-related activities that fulfilled a need for renewal and a change of pace. Thus we could consider gardening and some shopping recreational. Playing sports in the afternoon was OK, even better if they were informal and not organized sports. We planned some outings to places of interest, which forced us to do the cleaning and shopping on other days. In the name of lessening stress, we allowed last-minute trips to the store to get supplies for the school project that was due the next day—but we didn't like it.

Ironically, for those of us in church ministry, Sunday is often a day of intense work. We'd substitute another day of rest when this happened. Taking time to rest is not a waste.

Take vacations without guilt.

Taking a vacation is another way to "waste" time that has been especially meaningful for our family. We've always loved to travel but haven't always had the means to fly. When our children were young, we'd take a camping trip somewhere in the United States almost every year. This took a lot of planning and work, but the bonding, memories, and lessons learned were worth it.

Besides learning numerous car games, we also learned that bucket seats make better siblings, fast food preferences are negotiable, bribery has its uses, and the car never stops when babies are sleeping no matter how much the driver needs to go to the bathroom or how low the gas gauge registers. Today, car travel is made easier by videos and air conditioning, but look at the learning opportunities that have been lost.

Our family also absorbed some more serious lessons on vacations, such as an appreciation for the fragility of nature through camping, how helpful strangers can be to strangers, and how to make our own fun. We also learned what a variety exists when it comes to people's homes, lands, and customs—yet how basically human we all are. Sometimes the only resources we had were the woods around us and one another's company. Besides spending time together and bonding, we also exposed the children to the needs of the wider world. They learned that not everyone lives the way we do. They also learned how to solve conflicts when cooped up with people they can't get away from.

MAKING TIME

In my opinion, this is the most difficult task, but one of the most important parts of taming time. It's difficult because it demands discipline, hard choices, and initiative. Without it, however, it doesn't matter how much time we save because we might not be doing the important things that will make a difference in our children's lives and influence them to make a difference in others' lives.

Eat together.

Let's start with dinner. I remember one episode clearly because it shocked me at the time. Brian, at age eight, said, "Why do I have to come in for dinner now? None of my friends eat dinner as a family!" I quickly retorted with, "That's an exaggeration! Sure, some neighborhood children may not eat dinner as a family but what about Jonathan and . . . and . . . uh . . ." Oh dear, I wasn't really sure that I could name anyone beyond the one family that was part of our small faith community who shared the value of eating dinner as a family. Upon closer examination, I realized that to a great extent Brian was right.

What's so sacred about dinner? It happens every day. We face one another. We eat. We talk. It doesn't matter that some of the talk is trivial or full of complaints. We're sharing our day, warts and all. It doesn't matter if the food is plain or even unappetizing. We have food. It doesn't even matter if we come to the table angry with one another or if we get angry as a result of being together. We have to face and deal with people who push our buttons—and then push beyond it. We might even find the grace to forgive. Actually, it doesn't matter that dinner together happens every day as long as it happens most days. Need it be dinner? No, although for most families that is the most convenient time. I know one family that couldn't eat dinner together because of work schedules. They substituted breakfast as their check-in time. The "almost every day" of it does matter since it is a way of staying connected with the people who are important to us and serving one another in the simple and necessary tasks of survival.

Ideally, everyone contributes to the meal according to his or her ability. Someone cooks, someone sets the table, someone leads a prayer, someone cleans up, someone brings a story or problem, someone brings humor or a solution to a problem. We hope that someone gives thanks. Not every meal is this idyllic, but that's why it's important to do it often. We can afford to have some miserable meals because there will be others that aren't, when the principle works. Not all the ingredients of perfection will be present in each meal, but if you do it enough, you'll catch most of them.

The other value of working together to make meals happen is that it models service according to one's ability. Obviously, babies aren't able to contribute in any significant way other than by making more work or being a distraction. Sometimes the family members who are older, more experienced, have more time or more training have to carry the load of the weaker ones. It doesn't mean they are superior people but that they have been blessed with capabilities and are responsible for sharing these with those who can't yet do it for themselves.

Schedule family nights.

Most families have pretty complex schedules during the active parenting years. Most parents can barely imagine adding one more activity to the weekly schedule. It is precisely because we are going in so many different directions, however, that saving one night a week to be home together is important. There are several different styles of family nights that families might choose.

For some families it might simply mean reserving one night that no one has any outside meetings. (Parents, that includes long phone calls and doing business at home.) For families with several children, finding a common night might be a feat. Maybe nothing is organized, but everyone agrees to be home and to let happen whatever happens. This is good in itself.

Others may take a more proactive stance and plan some recreational activity for the family night. Possibilities include watching a TV show together, playing a board game, doing a puzzle, taking a bike ride or a walk, or going out for ice cream. These are all great.

When our children were young, Jim and I took this a step further by creating a family night that included a moral. For us, family night was once a week, and it did take a lot of work because we designed a lesson, activity, prayer, and treat around a different theme each week. Right now I feel tired just thinking about the energy we put into it—but it was worth it. We used this time in part to do family-centered religious education. To spread the load, Jim and I would alternate, with one of us planning how to convey the theme and the other making a special dessert. It has provided all of us not only with fond memories but also with lots to laugh about.

Although this kind of family night worked for us, it did take a lot of work. Don't let the perfect be the enemy of the good. Find what works for you. It's better to do something than nothing.

Establish a date night.

After a while Jim and I realized that we were pouring so much energy into our kids that there was little special time for our marriage. Our years of dealing with other couples in marriage ministry had taught us that focusing on our children at the expense of our marriage would do them no favor. But we had no time and less money. We did it anyway: we agreed to have a date once a week. Our custom was to alternate who planned it so that neither of us would feel burdened and each of us would get a chance to do something we really liked. Sometimes the planner would keep the activity a surprise, which added to the mystique. It didn't have to involve going out or spending money, but it had to be intentional, not just sitting around and saying, "What do you feel like doing?"

Our children were young when we started this, and we were both generally tired most of the time, so one of the tricks we learned was to give each other time for a nap early in the evening. With the energy to stay up later, our "date" would start after we put the children to bed. Some of our best dates were playing Scrabble by candlelight (and by my rules!) or walking along the riverfront and spreading out a tablecloth for wine. Our policy was, and still is, to not talk about the kids or problems, just about our dreams and ourselves.

Take your kids on dates.

Even though we had family night once a week, as our children got older we realized that they had different needs and that in trying to span a thirteen-year age difference we would lose the older ones. Our own date night was going so well that we decided to extend it to the kids. Four kids fit neatly into a once-a-month rotation. Each child got to choose what he or she would do with a parent during our one-on-one time, once a month. In order to avoid breaking the bank, they needed to alternate choosing an activity that cost money with one that cost less than five dollars.

This date night with each child made sense in theory, and it worked well for several years. But the logistics of scheduling everything started to get too complicated. It faded out of use as the children moved into high school and didn't ask for it anymore. Not all good things are forever.

HOW MUCH IS TOO MUCH?

Active, giving people are usually busy people. We want to encourage our children to develop skills and to mix with a lot of different people in our community rather than just doing passive activities at home. Every family needs to find its own balance, however, lest we be always racing from one meeting or game to another. Because Jim and I only worked at one job outside the home when the children were young, one of us was generally home with them during the day. We did, however, have a lot of evening meetings, many of them involving both of us. (That's what you get for being in marriage ministry.) We could have gone out every night of the week had we been willing. We weren't. Our rule of thumb was that we would not get baby-sitters more than two weeknights in a row. Dual-career parents probably want to limit nights out even more.

In regard to our children's activities, we agreed with them that they would play no more than one sport per season. Other clubs and lessons were negotiable, depending on whether they required transportation from us. Thus, after-school activities such as Scouts and academic clubs put little stress on the family schedule; the kids could walk home or take the bus.

Lessons that required parental chauffeuring were more of a pain and more limited (although we sometimes gave in because we valued the enrichment, as in the case of music and drama activities).

TO WORK, OR NOT TO WORK (OUTSIDE THE HOME)?

I keep coming back to this issue because work life is the greatest factor in how much time we have for our kids. Unfortunately, single parents seldom have the freedom to stay at home, and in some families, financial and health-insurance needs force both parents to work full-time. In yet other families, both parents feel truly called to work that is outside the home and more or less full-time.

We have to think creatively when it comes to work life and not be pressured by what is considered normal, or even right, by others' standards. It doesn't always have to be the wife who stays home. If it's the wife who initially stays home, it doesn't mean the husband might not later be the one, or vice versa. You don't have to be at home full time, and most important, it doesn't have to be forever. You should put it on the table for a thoughtful decision, however, so it's not just something you fall into.

Jim and I have done a little of everything. I stayed home; he stayed home. We split one full-time job. We both worked full-time, and we both were unemployed for a while. We also did the student/job/homemaker combination for a time. When we job-shared, we alternated days at the office and at home. Although this was a unique situation, not transferable to most families, I gained some insights that may be instructive to those who don't have the advantage of living in both worlds. When I was at the office, I thought the better life would be the flexibility and fun of being with our young children. The days I was home, however, I found myself yearning for the feeling of accomplishment and appreciation that goes with paid employment. The grass is always greener on the other side. Both Jim and I agree that if we had to say which job is harder, it would be staying home with preschoolers.

If you are a single parent working outside the home, hopefully the other parent of your children also is actively involved in the parenting. Regardless, you need a strong support network of family and friends. Take on only what you can. This is no time for guilt or false pride. Ask for what you need, and sometimes you'll get it.

So must we resign ourselves to the role of victim, stressed-out and behind in this modern, fast-paced culture? Even as I write these lines I find the concept amusing. How is it that we who have so many time- and labor-saving conveniences seem to be rushing more than previous generations? Are we happier because of it?

After spending a month with our daughter in Africa, I was struck by the different pace of life there. I seldom saw people rushing. Her village had no clocks, so being late wasn't obvious. They had no electricity, no running water. By Western standards it would be judged a harsh and primitive life. But they seemed happy and generally content. Who has the saner, better life? It depends on how you look at it. We all have the same twenty-four hours to work with.

The Vogt Kids Speak

I remember enjoying family vacations as a child. We would get together and go camping somewhere. It was always camping, and hasty alliances would be forged en route. Basically, whoever annoyed you least during the car ride was your best friend. This worked out well, because there was always something to do with my older siblings. However, as time went on, my two older siblings continued to get older, and soon there was no one to do anything with during these forays. As a result, our family vacations lost a lot of the appeal they had for me in the past, since there was no longer anyone to run around and play with.

Dacian

Now, I would have to say that calling the coach is something that I certainly would not recommend. There are times when parents need to take matters into their own hands, but I don't think that going so far as to plot to reschedule a team's practice so that one family can eat dinner together is appropriate.

The truth here is that the value my mom places on sports is certainly minimal. The degree of commitment that a sport might entail is not something that would be supported by my mother if it superceded other activities that she felt were more valuable. With that said, I must admit that I appreciate the fact that my parents did not come out to all of my sporting events. Frequent shows of support were sufficient for me, and I was actually glad that I was not one of those kids who had their parents watching every single game or match I had. It made me feel independent.

Some of my fondest childhood memories are of the extensive camping vacations that my family took. Sometimes I felt jealous of friends who would fly to beach resorts for a vacation, while I spent a great amount of time in the car just getting to where we were going. But now when I look back on this, I feel that the ability to see the country this way was a true gift. These trips were even better the few times we traveled together with another family or friends. We would go off for three weeks at a time and see parts of the country that most of my friends in Kentucky had never seen. I feel extremely lucky now to have seen nearly forty of the U.S. states. This is certainly something that I will encourage when I have a family.

Actually, I don't remember a whole lot about the family nights, although I did look forward to the dessert at the end, which was often the enticement to participate. I imagine that there were probably very good discussions during these activities. My parents stopped insisting that I participate in these family nights by the time I was thirteen or so, otherwise I probably would have resented it. At some point, you just have to understand that older children will not want to do the same kind of stuff as younger ones.

I thought that the "kid's date" was a good idea, although I generally preferred the date that we could spend money on. I remember thinking that I could use this date to my advantage by suggesting that we go to the toy store as the "date" and then use the money to buy a toy. I guess this probably wasn't very much in the spirit of the activity. My parents tolerated this date about once and then said that the date could not be used merely to buy something.

Brian

A Daughter's Response

The Dinner Table

"Dad, we need to buy a new car."

"We bought new cars before we had children."

"Aaron, what did you do at school today?"

"Mom, I'm trying to eat!"

"But, Dad, the Celica is more rust than car!"

"Dacian, why did you pour me milk? You know I drink ice water!"

"So?"

"Then tell me about school between mouthfuls."

"Dacian, it was your mistake. Go pour the milk back."

"Pour it back yourself."

Welcome to dinner at the Vogt household. At approximately 6:00 every evening we had a mandatory gathering of sulky children, tired parents, and individualized salads. It was ritualized chaos.

The six of us sat in the same seats every night, a tactical arrangement that I had devised at the age of nine to reduce dinnertime blowups. It went like this.

Mom and Dad sat at the heads of the table. This was my nod to tradition. Aaron, the youngest, was to Mom's left because at that time he was still in a high chair and needed her assistance. Dacian, next in age, was to Mom's right because he was then in a period of mother-worship and didn't realize that she would be watching every extra blueberry muffin and uneaten Brussels sprout. For this very reason, my older brother, Brian, and I were at Dad's left and right, respectively. We had to give our opinions on various social injustices a little more regularly at Dad's end of the table, but he rarely noticed what we ate.

This arrangement also took into account that Dacian and Aaron couldn't sit next to each other (they would fight), and that Dacian and I couldn't sit directly across from each other (we would kick each other under the table). Brian had already matured from physical combat to verbal abuse. What's miraculous is that we managed to sit down to the anachronistic family dinner at all. Yet we did, every evening, despite the fact that dinner itself was more often the scene of family blowups than Cleaver-style harmony. While the time, place, and seats were set, the conversation was no-holds-barred.

There was the time Brian filled his plate up with the last of the noodles without asking if anyone else wanted any. I complained, so Brian promptly bent his head down and licked all over the pile of noodles in front of him. "Want them now, Heidi?" Yelling ensued.

There was the time my father pulled out yet another op-ed piece about poverty or war or somebody getting treated badly somewhere, and the rest of us just talked over him. He kept trying to read, and my brothers and I kept arguing over who needed to pass the butter. In the middle of our debate, my father set his lips, pushed his chair back, and left the table. We all got very quiet and looked to my mother. "*Somebody* ought to go apologize," she said. The four of us just sat there, no one willing to be somebody.

There were the countless times that one of us sat sulkily, giving everyone the silent treatment or saying, "This food sucks, why can't we go to Kentucky Fried Chicken?" or asking, "Why don't you two make more money?" or demanding that allowances get raised, that chores alter, and that purchases of Cap'n Crunch increase.

And often, when I recall these dinners, I also recall one of the four children running away from the table crying or being sent away from the table and stomping out of the room. Or I recall my Mom losing control and yelling at us to please be more civilized.

I loved it when soccer games or band practices or school plays made me, to my mother's horror, miss dinner. The last thing I wanted to do as a teenager was communicate with my parents. And dinner was my parents' attempt to force their way into my life, but I'm sort of glad they did. Because I also remember getting let into my parents' lives as they discussed people at work or extended family. I also remember shining moments like when I came to dinner fresh from a fifth-grade current-events class, asking if they knew that black people were treated like servants in Africa. Brian said, "Duh! Everybody knows that!" but my mother said, "Yes, it's terrible, and it's called apartheid, but it's not all of Africa."

"Yes, that's the word!" I said, impressed that I had parents who knew about these things and who were just as upset. And I also remember that at dinner my parents presented a united front. Any other time it was divide and conquer. But I never remember my parents fighting with each other over dinner. It might have been just because they had to work so hard to contain their "free-spirited" children, but they were a team. Together they made us sit down to dinner, and together they put up with our insolence. And together they created a space where the family was forced to be a unit. For other families it might be car pools or shopping. For us, it was dinner.

These days, when a holiday finds all six of us back in our assigned seats, it feels natural. We're a little more polite to each other now (except, well, Aaron *is* fifteen) and there are a lot fewer shouting matches. But the dinner table is just as noisy with political disagreements, work problems, and, every so often, the four children banding together to tell our parents how they could have raised us better.

"You're right, we really messed up," says my father. "Will you pass the corn?"

Heidi

A Daughter's Response

Dating My Dad

First of all, I thought it was *weird* that my parents went on dates. Granted, lots of things that Mom and Dad did were weird: my mom always looked like she had stepped out of 1973, and my dad was always saying hello to people on the street who he didn't even *know*. But this was weird in a completely different way. My mom would get all giggly and put makeup on. My dad would start humming. They would leave in a flurry of fancy clothes and excitement, while my brothers and I were left with a baby-sitter. This was a "weird" that I felt left out of.

So when my parents said they were going to start having dates with us, I didn't know whether to be scared or excited. I was a little of both.

Then they said that we would get to choose what we did for these dates, and I knew there had to be a catch. What if I want to go to Hardee's? Sure, they said. I was reticent, but soon I was putt-putting with Dad and going out to lunch with Mom. My younger brother went to a movie with her. My older brother got to drive go-carts around the track with Dad.

The Vogt family is competitive. Brian, Dacian, and I were used to fighting with one another during outings, either for sibling dominance or for attention from our parents. "Discussions" were often won by out-shouting your opponent. More than any of the ways my parents tried to get the family to spend time together, the best was the one that separated us from one another, made shouting unnecessary, and made just one of us the star for the evening.

Heidi

Other Families' Stories

Having met in college, each committed to pursuing excellence in our chosen fields, it never dawned on us that one of us would someday have to give up—at least for awhile—a professional career. But five years after the birth of our first child, we finally came to the realization that the extra income simply was not worth it. In a very real sense, we used my salary to purchase a hugely improved standard of living. Having done that four years ago, you couldn't pay us to return to that lifestyle.

Heidi Clark, 36, mother of one biological child, one adopted child, two foster children, Houston, Texas

For our family the most important thing was having a time for supper that we were expected to observe. We did not allow anything that consistently interfered with eating dinner together, but what made it so important were the discussions. That was where all the issues came up. We had to explain that we were not having much beef in our meat sauce to protest cutting down the rain forests in Brazil for cattle grazing. We were part of the Campbells Soup boycott when Campbells was using migrant children in the fields (and all my children's friends were collecting can labels to bring to school which translated into Campbells donating tape recorders and gifts to the school, once enough were collected). We did the "Rice Bowl Project" to collect funds for hungry families. We talked about political issues, and my husband was always dragging out a globe or an atlas or an encyclopedia to help everyone check things out. By the time the kids were in middle school, they were running to get a book to defend their position in a fight. Our dining-room table is filled with the notes and marks of those conversations. None of the three kids will let us refinish it. We got to share our views and learned to listen to theirs, but I know we would not have done it without the meal.

Kathleen Chesto, mother of three young adults, author and teacher, Southbury, Connecticut

I have worked full-time ever since our daughter was born, and even though my husband has been a willing and active parent with jobs that allowed him to be home many days, I still had to call home at 8:00 P.M. every night when Lynea was two to sing her a lullaby. What's ironic is that Steve is a much better singer than I am.

Laura and Steve Domienik, parents of a fourteen year old, Kennedy Heights, Ohio

My parents spent lots of time with us, both as a family and individually. We did lots of family activities together, including long trips around the country; but each of my brothers and I also had our individual "nights out" alone with my parents, when we got to pick both the dinner and the activity. I think it's a brilliant way to raise kids, to emphasize family but also make each child feel important.

Robert Honeywell, 36, lawyer, actor, playwright, New York, New York

When our children were little, we tried to continue to do too many organized social-justice-type activities that didn't accommodate our children's temperaments. Even though I cut down the hours I worked, I continued too many of my church and social-justice commitments. Children take a lot of time, and if you don't put the time in with the child, all of your words and meetings are meaningless. Some children are more high-strung than others, and rushing this type of child is not going to make him or her a kinder, gentler person! We left our children with too many teenage baby-sitters so that we could play music at church. We should have prioritized our home activities. We were rushing too much and didn't take enough time to structure our home environment. Also, I don't think that I realized early enough that parenting takes a lot of time. If you are too busy with too many other life goals, your kids can become an obstacle to those goals. That is a terrible thing to do to kids. It's better to just enjoy the time with them and realize that raising wonderful kids is a great contribution to society. It is okay not to do everything! I understand why there is the section in the Bible about the poor being with us always. It is meant for people who think that they can solve all of society's ills by being workaholics for social justice.

**Cathy Bookser-Feister, mother of two teenagers and one preteen,
Cincinnati, Ohio**

Since I work a lot of evenings and Saturdays, we instituted something my wife calls "Mornings and Mondays." It means when I worked an evening I would take the next morning off. When I worked a whole Saturday I would take the next Monday off. Before the children were in school, this gave me some special time with them and gave Rene a break. After they were in school, it gave Rene and I more time together.

**Leif Kehrwald, father of one teen and one young adult,
Portland, Oregon**

I've worked part-time throughout my marriage. My husband supported me in taking time to go to the park with the kids when I got home instead of cleaning the house. I had a tough time juggling time, but most of it was of my own making—trying to be supermom. For me, parenting was such a difficult and draining occupation that I worked for my sanity. I looked at oncology as a break.

**Jo Ann Schwartz, mother of two young adults, oncology nurse,
Ft. Thomas, Kentucky**

At times we have both worked full-time outside the home. I have worked part-time, and I have stayed at home full-time. Several times I chose a less prestigious position that allowed a great amount of flexibility of work hours and that also had bosses and coworkers who supported my desire for being very involved in my children's well-being. My husband and I both worked full-time from the time our first child, Paul, was eight weeks to two and a half years old. As I look back, nine years later, I believe this worked for us because a) it was a temporary situation; b) Paul was taken care of by a loving and nurturing woman in her home; and c) we said "no" a lot to other commitments and outside responsibilities. Still, I missed out on a lot of my son's early childhood. But the career experience that I gained "bought" me the flexibility that I now enjoy. Maybe situations can work and be OK, but certainly we have a better balance now with me working only part-time.

**Christi Kern, 38, mother of three (ages eighteen months, six,
and nine), postdoctoral research assistant, Mt. Pleasant, South Carolina**

Taking My Time Temperature

Although you may feel tempted to choose all of the following, pick up to three of your top needs.

I wish I had more time for

- myself (private, quiet time; educational or health pursuits; recreation)

- my marriage (time to talk, have fun together, work together on projects)

- spirituality (time for prayer, reflection, worship)

- my job (time to do a better job, get more done)

- my children (time to play with, work with, listen and talk with)

- service to others (time for civic or church involvements; responding to people in need locally or globally; ecology)

- other

I spend too much time . . .

If my wish for more time were granted, I would . . .

If I had to reduce, or cut out, an activity that I'm already doing to make room for a higher priority, I would . . .

CHAPTER 3

Materialism
The Simple Life Can Be Pretty Complex

- What's wrong with making a lot of money and having nice things?

- As long as I work hard and honestly for my wealth, why should I feel guilty?

- Does it do anybody any good if I give everything away and become poor myself?

- I should be able to enjoy the fruits of my labor as long as I don't hurt anyone.

- What if we're generous with our possessions and regularly donate money to charity?

- Yes, I make a high salary, but my professional work makes a valuable contribution to society—and besides, I invested a lot in my education.

- Material goods, paying for help, and technology all make my life easier, more pleasant, and I can get more done.

Some fine people have made the above comments over the years. These statements hold important truths and make a lot of sense, but there's another side to the issue that starts to raise a dilemma.

IT'S NOT JUST ABOUT MONEY

Simplifying one's life is about getting rid of clutter in order to pay attention to what's really important. If I say that my relationships (with spouse, children, friends, and those in need) are my ultimate values, then I need to make room for them. "Stuff" crowds not only our physical space but also our time. This happens directly through crowded schedules and distracted minds but also indirectly when Mom takes an extra job or Dad lengthens his hours at work in order to pay for more stuff. Is the stuff worth the time stolen from relationships or solitude?

Crowded time is not good for the spirit.

Consider the frenetic life many of us lead. We may thrive on it for a while, but eventually it takes a toll not only on our health but also on our family time and on our spirit. Often the frenzy is driven by both parents working outside the home, although it is certainly possible to have a stay-at-home-parent so overcommitted to other causes that time given to them equals a paid job.

A balance of manual and intellectual labor is good for the body and soul.

Doing some of the household manual labor (cooking, cleaning, child-care, repairing, gardening) not only teaches important life and survival skills, it keeps our bodies active, our spirits humble, and our relationships in balance. Sure, you can pay someone to clean the house or you can go out to eat rather than cook. Sometimes the family's needs require this, but too much of a good thing can be bad. Time taken in seemingly tedious chores can give our minds a break and remind us that not everyone in our world has access to the conveniences and luxuries that are available to us. Sometimes the labor is pure drudgery, but sometimes it can be renewing and inspiring. We don't always know which it will be, so a certain amount of grunt work just has to be done to let the inspiration slip in.

Too many possessions can make more work or make us lazy.

This may seem like a contradiction because much of modern technology is meant to free us of repetitive or menial tasks so that we can be more productive. Surely automatic washers and dryers free up a day that might be devoted to interaction with children. Computers speed up communication and maximize the number of people we can be in touch with. But do you find yourself washing clothes more often (even if they're not really dirty) or getting more junk e-mail and spending more time on the Internet just because it's so easy? Besides, do we really need more things to dust, repair, and protect from theft?

On the other hand, who is going to voluntarily offer to walk to the store if a car is available, or wash dishes by hand if a dishwasher is right there? If children have all kinds of stimulating electronic games and gadgets to occupy their free time, will they think to take a hike or create a neighborhood play?

Waiting, longing, and working for something increases appreciation.

Even if we can afford many toys or lavish vacations, we do our children a disservice if we provide too much. It may make us feel better for not spending time with them, but it takes away their need to stretch, to delay gratification, to savor what they have and long for something else. A toy or experience that has been "longed for" is much more appreciated. Ungrateful children usually have too much stuff.

Attachment to possessions can stunt children's ability to share and compromise.

If we're trying to lay the foundation for our children to care about others and make a difference in the world, they need to learn to be generous with their possessions, time, and ideas. It's easy to share if I have a hundred cookies and only a couple of friends. But our planet has more than one hundred eighty countries. What if most of the cookies are in my own country? We all need to learn what our fair share is and how to distribute the cookies so that no one goes hungry.

Consuming less is good for our planet.

Even if we could provide for everyone on earth to enjoy a typical North American lifestyle, would that be desirable? Besides being unattainable, it couldn't last. Everyone would be equal, but if every family in the world owned two cars, had an air conditioned home with typical appliances and computers, used disposable products to the extent that we do, and matched our present level of energy consumption, the resulting pollution would strangle the earth. Realistically, most of us are not going to make drastic changes in our lifestyle, but reducing unnecessary consumption can at least clear our minds and reduce the strain on air, land, and water resources.

Consuming less is a small step toward a more just world.

It just doesn't seem right that some people on our earth have much more than they need while others lack the basic necessities. Can one person living more simply make a difference? Not much. Can a family influence a society to reduce consumption so that others can have a little more? In time, step by step, yes. That is what this book is about—making our world a better place to live for all, through the actions of those who care, starting at home. The increasing gap between the rich and the poor just is not fair.

Keeping greed in check is not a choice.

It seems universal to all mainline religions that care for the poor is essential and that the rich are urged to share their wealth. It seems fair to say that even if we are not called to sell all that we have (Luke 18:22), we probably are called to not *buy* everything that it is possible to buy. This is not because the goods of the world are bad but because too much "stuff" can distract us from our deepest goals in life. How much is too much? It would be presumptuous of me to judge precisely what is a luxury and exactly what income level or lifestyle is "more than enough." I haven't figured that out for myself yet. Be that as it may, all people of faith must confront this issue honestly.

The goods of this world are not inherently bad. The goal is balance. How do we find the right balance between enough and too much? I don't have a perfect answer, but I think it probably has to do with keeping the needs of others in sight. Whenever I walk through a poor neighborhood or spend time with a person whose income or advantages are less than my own, my conscience prompts me to look more honestly at my real needs versus my wants masquerading as needs.

LIVING SIMPLY CAN TAKE A LOT OF TIME AND WORK

It takes a different kind of effort to live more simply, but deeper satisfaction and a better quality of life are the rewards. Children who are not overindulged have a natural compassion for the have-nots of our society. Children who are encouraged to meet their needs for play through creative means rather than too many store-bought toys develop a resourcefulness that will help them make a difference in whatever they undertake. Ultimately, our children benefit from our "presence" more than our "presents."

Spending time foolishly with meaningless work is time wasted. Spending time reading to our children or taking a hike with them is an investment in the future. Sure, some things are going to take more time. It takes longer to cook a meal at home than to resort to fast food. It's more work to repair a toy than to just go out and buy a new one. But what is the real cost if you factor in the building of family relationships and the development of a human being who might contribute innumerable graces to society? Or, conversely, what is the cost to society of a generation of kids who know how to run a computer program but not their lives? A life focused on what I own will always be a poor substitute for one focused on knowing who I am.

More time or more money?

Some of us have more time than money; some more money than time. Many of us feel we have neither. What's complex about this is that money has a direct relationship to time. As one goes up, the other often goes down. Earning more money often means working longer hours, which takes time away from spouse and children. Maximizing time with the family often means decreasing or delaying needs or wants. There are choices to make, and they're not always easy.

Lest we drift into a lifestyle that is driven more by advertising and our neighbor's admiration than our own beliefs and values, it is important to be intentional about decisions of how to spend our time and money. It takes time to save money by preparing home-cooked meals, buying cloth diapers, hanging laundry out to dry, tending a vegetable garden, or cleaning the house. It takes time to focus on people rather than on things by helping with homework, being around the house during a teen's noisy party, or cleaning out a closet to give clothes to Goodwill. It takes time to be kind to the earth by recycling, walking or taking the bus, or composting. It also sometimes costs money to save money. We have to buy garden tools and seeds, cleaning supplies, a washing machine, and so forth. It's not just a matter of buying less and giving all our surplus to the poor. Living more simply can be pretty complicated.

Which leads us to a simpler life—saving time by paying someone to do tedious chores so we can spend more quality time with our families, or saving money by doing those chores ourselves and thereby reducing the need for paid employment that takes us away from our families?

Both can be legitimate choices, but both are also vulnerable to self-deception and rationalization. Time considerations have been discussed earlier, but let's look at some intangible traps we might find in either approach.

Yes, money can buy you quality time, but the significant moments or questions in a child's life can't always be scheduled. The toddler's first step; being home when children return from school to hear the day's joys and trials while still fresh in their minds; witnessing a child's squabble rather than hearing complaints later—all take a fair amount of just "hanging out" to catch the quality moment.

Yes, taking time to do it yourself and be with your children can build character and bonds, but sometimes we can get so wrapped up in being the perfect parent that we get strangled by smugness. The challenge to the "Martha Stewart parent" is a spiritual one. We must take care to not over-control our children or become too proud of how little we own and consume. Our children and friends will resent our self-righteousness. And our souls will suffer from arrogance.

Can cheap be expensive?

The other complexity of simplicity is that sometimes it is cheaper (or better for the planet) to pay more. When our children were young, we bought a cheap plastic swimming pool. It barely lasted one summer. Eventually, we invested in a more durable one that lasted many years. Buying a few quality toys that will last till there are grandchildren is worth the extra expense.

For clothes that the children will soon outgrow, cheap is fine. For health care or education that will affect them over a lifetime, go for quality.

DOING IT YOURSELF WHEN YOU'RE NOT THERE TO DO IT

Many parents struggle to find the time their families need and want from them. This is especially true for single parents or for families in which both parents hold full-time jobs away from home.

Indeed, there are legitimate economic circumstances in which both parents need to work outside the home. Both incomes may be modest, one income may be unreliable or erratic, or both parents' careers may not lend themselves to part-time schedules or interruptions during the childbearing years. The prudent couple has very little choice in these cases unless they are exceptionally creative or willing to make dramatic changes in their life such as a career change or living a very austere lifestyle. This situation requires a lot of self-discipline, frequent checking of how relationships and emotional health are going, organization, and flexibility. Ideally, it's not a permanent situation.

Then there are situations in which both parents work outside the home for personal fulfillment, to contribute an important service to society, or to live out a life calling. These are hard calls. But it's important to make a thoughtful decision about working outside the home rather than assume that "I don't have a choice about this because you can't really raise a family on one income these days." There are nearly always more options than are apparent at first.

For the good of the family, some parents of young children will choose to continue to both work outside the home and use the extra income to pay for services that will maximize the time the parents can be present to their children. I have seen many conscientious (and highly organized) parents make this work. But it's not as easy as it sounds. Sometimes the marriage suffers, sometimes it's just a matter of feeling frenzied and tired. It may be a sacrifice you're willing to make. But I challenge you not to make that decision too quickly and to always leave the door open for reconsideration. Often we can temporarily find alternative ways to fulfill ourselves or keep up with a professional career while the children are young and at home most of the time.

Make work outside the home work.

Having picked the brains of successful dual-career parents and drawn on our own occasional experience, following are some tips for making it work:

- When home, spend time on priorities that you can't meet with money, i.e., playing with a child, talking with your spouse, laughing and relaxing together.

- If your income is sufficient, pay for services you might otherwise do yourself, i.e., housecleaning, eating out, yard work, personalized childcare.

- Lower housekeeping standards. This might be necessary even if you pay for housecleaning; you certainly don't want to spend time recleaning something just because the way it was cleaned doesn't suit your style. Assuming your house meets basic health standards, decide what's essential and let go of the *House Beautiful* image. Some parents said that keeping the entryway and a "public/relaxing room" rather tidy was enough for their mental health until there was time to do serious cleaning and organizing.

- Free yourself of gender stereotypes regarding chores. It's a waste of time and emotional collateral to assign some jobs only to females and others to males. If only the women cook and only the men mow the lawn, there's dead time when the right person is not around to do the work. In our family we use three criteria to assign chores: interest, skill, and time. We usually take turns doing the jobs that neither of us have an interest in, like taking out the garbage (it requires no particular skill).

■ Cultivate efficiency. Organize clutter, multitask when possible, minimize time wasters like TV; see chapter 2 on time.

■ Control your calendar. Say "no" to nonessential requests. Just because there's a party doesn't mean you have to go. Just because there's a bake sale doesn't mean you have to bake.

■ Sleep less. This may sound inhuman or obvious for parents of babies, but some parents find that they can get by on less sleep if they take a "power nap" during the day or early evening. Not everyone's constitution or work environment will allow this practice, but my husband swears by it.

■ Be vigilant about saving time for your relationship. It may seem selfish to take time and money for a date but think of it as an investment in your children's future. In the long run, crabby parents seldom make their children's lives happier.

■ Cultivate flexibility and let go of perfectionism. Sure, you're going to be late for some appointments and not caught up on some work, but you don't need to spend energy fretting over limitations or things that can't be changed.

Mix it up.

Even though dual-career parenting is a viable option and a necessity for many, remain open to other options. We can often find alternative ways to fulfill ourselves or keep up with a professional career while the children are young and at home most of the time. Many parents find that one and a half jobs sufficiently meet their economic and professional needs and allow the flexibility to attend school functions and run errands. Our family doctor is in a group practice and works two and a half days a week. If one of us has a medical emergency on a day she's not in, we just see one of the other doctors. Others use their professional skills in a volunteer capacity, which allows them to take on only as many jobs as they want and at a time that's convenient for them. A talented TV professional in my community agreed to produce a video for my office free of charge. She had the expertise, the contacts, and the commitment to do the job. We gladly provided an opportunity for her to keep her skills current and were willing to fit it in to her personal schedule. Some jobs allow parents to make their own work schedules, thus minimizing the need for outside child care. Of course they then need to be protective of the little couple time left over. A single-parent scientist friend of ours took a job editing a scientific journal while her children were young. Much of her work was done at midnight. With a computer and the Internet we can rethink the form and location of many jobs.

Know that single parents are not alone.

Yet single parents do have special challenges. Not only are there fewer hands to do the work, there's the emotional burden of making daily decisions without a partner to consult. Of course, unless you are widowed, no one is totally a single parent. Theoretically, divorced, noncustodial, or unmarried spouses should still both be actively involved in the care and upbringing of their children. This may be complicated, but it's not impossible. In the real world, however, not all parents meet their responsibilities. Doing it yourself can be a formidable task, especially when you have little time *and* little money. Though not an impossible mission, you deserve all the help you can get.

Ask for that help. Put energy into developing a strong support system. After you are through the initial trauma of a divorce, family and friends may not know what kind of ongoing help you need. Perhaps a regular dinner with relatives or an outing with the kids will give you a break. Some single parents find it helpful to trade child care with one another. This way they know their child is getting personalized, quality care while the parent has a little time to him- or herself. Often churches or communities offer support groups. Some are designed to help people cope and heal after a divorce; others are more for socializing with people who are in similar circumstances. If your child is not the same gender as you, Big Brothers/Sisters can help support preteens and teens who lack relatives or close friends who can fulfill that role.

For those single parents who still need to work outside the home, use all the shortcuts you can and don't feel guilty about it. Use convenience foods even if they do cost more. Take advantage of school or neighborhood events as a way to entertain your children and get some adult companionship. Teach your kids homemaking skills. Everyone should have them, and you'll be surprised at how much your kids can help. "Buddy up" when there's a party that needs a gift or food contribution. Pool your money or time and take turns with other parents meeting the request. Let the others do the volunteer work. Your plate is full. You are "doing it yourself" and making a difference simply by raising your child. Let go of all the rest.

DEALING WITH FEELING OVERWHELMED OR GUILTY

About now you may be thinking, *Maybe we really should sell the house and move to the inner city. Is that the only way to do justice to our kids?*

Maybe—and maybe not. A radical downsizing is not impossible, but, for most of us, fighting materialism entails curbing consumption and growing in generosity. The goal is not to become destitute but to nurture solidarity with those who are poor so that we might be sensitive and responsive to their needs.

One of the land mines of covering the topic of simple lifestyle and consumerism is that everyone has a different idea of what is necessary and how much is enough. I'm sure that there are families that live more simply than we do, and I would be embarrassed to have them visit my home and see all the creature comforts we've bought. I also know that I can be an efficiency freak and often pack way too much into a day at the expense of being a serene parent. My fear is that you, gentle reader, will hear the examples in this book and dismiss them as unrealistic or too much work for your own family. The way I generally deal with this demon is by breaking it down into smaller pieces. I don't need to sell the house and move to the inner city, but whatever I have, it probably is a little more than I need. Can I take one more step to let go?

The other temptation is to feel historical guilt. "Whoops! Using cloth diapers sounds like a good idea, but my kids are past that stage now. I guess I've blown it." I face this each time I second-guess a purchase. I recently bought shelving for our basement and found out afterward that I could have saved about one hundred dollars at a different store. It's times like this that I have to force myself to let go emotionally. That's poverty of spirit—not being attached to always being right. Prayer can help here.

If all else fails, lighten up. Humor heals and puts things in perspective. Trust that you made the best decision you knew how to make at the time.

SAYING NO (OR YES) TO OUR CHILDREN'S WHIMS (OR NEEDS)

When our oldest son, Brian, turned thirteen, he also turned into a conspicuous consumer—or at least it seemed that way to us. We had worked hard to impress upon our children the value of people over material possessions and the value of creative recreational pursuits—like hiking, homemade plays and circuses, camping, bicycling, and board games. We watched with admiration as our children made hideouts by gathering up all the blankets in the house and laying them over the furniture.

But then Nintendo was invented! Oh, it had probably been around for a few years, but suddenly everybody at school (meaning probably three friends) had this new video game system. Brian not only felt deprived, he was bitter at us for responding to his requests with "We really don't want to spend the money on that." To him that translated into "We're poor." He begged, he pleaded, he mobilized the younger children, persuading them to add their voices to the appeal: "Can't we please get Nintendo?" We weren't thrilled with the idea because we had heard about the violence connected with many of the games, and besides, we were short on income at the time.

Brian was so persistent that eventually we compromised. We would pay half, and the children old enough to get an allowance would contribute money according to their income. We agreed that they wouldn't buy games that were unduly violent. (Later we discovered the value of writing these agreements down and defining the terms; for example, "What qualifies as violent?" and "Does 'buying' include renting or watching at a friend's house?") We had checked with a few friends, and it seemed that this indeed was a growing fad and was probably going to be around a while. Besides, Brian was pretty sensitive about not fitting in at this stage, and we wanted to show that we cared about his feelings.

This was also around the time that Brian became very conscious of what brand labels were on the outside of his clothes. He was embarrassed to wear clothing with a generic label and refused to wear anything that came from the nearby discount store, no matter what the brand name. (It no longer worked to take off the tags so he couldn't tell where the clothing came from.) Our daughter, Heidi, although several years younger, was starting to express similar feelings about her clothes. It was starting to become a constant struggle to go shopping and listen to their complaints. We didn't always glide smoothly through these conflicts, but we tried a couple of things that seemed to work more often than not.

Try a clothing allowance.

I'm not sure if it was inspiration or desperation, but one of our best parental policies came out of the clothing quandary. We instituted a clothing allowance. We agreed on a dollar amount that each child would get for clothing for a full year. It would not include coats, and we would pay half of the cost of shoes. The amount sounded like a windfall to them because they were not experienced in calculating costs over a full year. And they could always ask for clothes for birthdays and Christmas. Perhaps we took advantage of their naiveté, but they both readily agreed.

Sometimes they faced the hard reality of the money being almost gone long before the year was out ("But it's only July!"). It didn't take long, however, before they were singing the praises of Value City, and eventually they decided that it was rather cool to get bargains at Goodwill. As a parent, the part I appreciated most about this arrangement was that it took the arguing out of clothes buying. It was up to them to decide whether they wanted to pace themselves and pay modest prices or blow most of their allowance on a pair of popular athletic shoes.

Get Christmas under control.

Everybody complains about how Christmas has lost its meaning and gift giving has gotten out of hand. I know a family that was going through hard times one year when the father lost his job; they decided to have a "moneyless" Christmas: no presents that cost any money, only homemade ones or gifts of service. Their kids were older, and it was only for one year, but I admire their values and their decision. I'm not sure our family would buy it.

Many extended families pick names to control the number of gifts, or they set a dollar amount on what can be spent. This helps. The problem is that traditions die hard, and everyone is afraid of hurt feelings or seeming cheap. Sometimes the magnitude of a gift is seen as a measure of love. It became apparent once we had children that we could not gracefully control grandparents' gift giving. We suggested fewer gifts but ones of high quality, or gifts of time spent doing a favorite activity. Eventually we got very specific about recommendations so there wasn't a lot of waste or overlap.

Some families take well to simplifying gift giving; others don't. Regardless, we have better control over what happens in the nuclear family. Our own custom has been to give each child three gifts: one heart's desire, one piece of clothing, and one "gift to grow on" (usually a book). As they got older, the heart's desire might merge with the piece of clothing. Later on, all three items merged into a computer for college.

Sounds simple now. It didn't come without pain, however. There was the Christmas that we moved six-year-old Brian into a bedroom that didn't have a closet. I worked industriously for a month making a clothes tree with enameled hooks of various colors. I nailed it, stained it, polyurethaned it, and was very proud of it—a true labor of love. We got him a couple of other presents, but the major one, the clothes tree, flopped miserably. My convictions got in the way of my heart that time, and thus the "heart's desire" category was born.

WHEN TO BE THRIFTY AND WHEN TO SPLURGE

Our children might tell you that we were heavy on the thrift and light on the splurge or that our idea of a splurge was camping in a park that had flush toilets. They might be right. Given our economic situation when they were young, however, it was part voluntary simplicity, part necessity.

I had very little patience for products that were popular just because of a brand name or advertising. Clothes needed to be attractive and well made, but if you couldn't see the defect or repair, I went for discount or generic. I told our children that not eating fast food was for the sake of nutrition, although it was probably just as much to save money.

Religious beliefs helped in that we could remind the children that Christmas is first about Jesus' birth and that gift giving flows from our joy over this. Likewise, wearing hand-me-downs and passing them on to others is an expression of stewardship to which our faith calls us.

When our children were younger, they usually accepted our lifestyle and thinking because we were the parents and it was all they knew. As they got older, it got harder. We heard complaints and disgruntlement as they noticed we were different from the world around them and from what they saw on TV. This didn't come as a surprise, but it was still disconcerting. We had raised them to be independent thinkers and to stand on their own two feet, and they were doing just that.

In response, we parents needed to become more clever and creative. If a particular clothes brand was a symbol of being cool, and cool counted more than reason, we'd let it be a birthday gift. We looked for ways to treat the kids that might surprise them, like going to the circus or a water park.

Where we splurged most, however, was on trips. Partly this was because trips could always be justified as having an educational component, and besides, both Jim and I like to travel. We could counter "Why can't I have…" with "Because we're saving to take a cross-country road trip or go to Russia, France, or Jamaica."

We also splurged on lessons or growth experiences. We bought flutes and trombones, paid for piano and swimming lessons, basketball and drama clinics, and we vigorously searched out remedial and enrichment resources when our children needed them, regardless of cost. Yes, we also did braces and medications that probably didn't feel like enjoyable splurges at the time. We hope they thank us for it later.

The bottom line: if it was an artificial need created by advertising, we discouraged it, but if it encouraged growth, we supported it. We made exceptions freely, however, based on the emotional needs of the child.

The Vogt Kids Speak

Heck, I spend so little money, and have throughout my life, that I never noticed we were being frugal.

Dacian

Yes, my parents were cheap. However, in retrospect, it was a very selective cheapness. They were very unlikely to spend much money on the latest toy or fad. But when it came to things like educational experiences or long-lasting goods, such as bicycles, they were much more generous. One of my most influential memories comes from when I was thirteen and trying to get money together to participate in an exchange program to France. The cost of the program was about twelve hundred dollars, which was a lot of money for my family. Although I contributed what I could, I couldn't put much of a dent in that large a sum. My parents didn't have that kind of cash on hand either. Therefore, my dad took on a temporary job delivering phone books to help cover the cost of this trip and also to help pay the cost of my sister's summer camp. Now, delivering phone books is probably not the most enjoyable job to do on a hot summer day, but I will always look on that experience as a symbol of the type of commitment that my parents had to providing for things that they truly felt were important.

Overall, I liked the clothing-allowance concept. It allowed me the choice to spend money on clothing that I wanted but also placed realistic constraints on my purchases. One year I was limited by the finite amount of money in my clothing allowance. I remember frequently seeing tension between my friends and their parents because of disputes over buying clothes. The clothing-allowance approach avoids these conflicts, while still allowing freedom of choice.

I can't say that I really have an opinion on cloth versus disposable diapers. Although I certainly did appreciate the option of having disposable diapers available when I was taking care of my youngest brother, Aaron!

Well, OK, we did go to the water park. However, I think my mom took the money-saving attitude to an extreme here. We usually went to Sunlight pool along with another family that had a son who looked somewhat like me. Well, the son wasn't going along on this trip, and he just happened to have a season's pass to the park. My mom quickly saw this as an opportunity to save money, and so I entered the water park using Matt's ID card. We might have been short on money, but this was going a little too far.

Brian

A Daughter's Response

The Dress

The dress was navy blue rayon with short sleeves and a turned-over collar, like a woman's business suit. Two rows of gold-edged, white filigree buttons ran down from the just-deep-enough V neck. The satiny rayon glistened in the fluorescent store lights as I admired myself in the mirror. Best of all, that glimmery rayon only fell to midthigh. Thigh to knee was a thin gauzy material that swept around my legs like silky air. The dress was sophisticated, feminine, and even slightly sexy—but not too much for a thirteen year old. It was The Perfect Dress.

My mother agreed. Then she looked at the price tag: $70. "Eighth graders don't buy seventy-dollar dresses," she firmly pointed out. I persisted. We had been scouring the mall for a full morning, and this was the first dress we had agreed on, but she held her ground. "No, Heidi." I whined. She remained unaffected. Eventually we stopped tormenting the saleslady with our indecision, put the dress on hold, and drove home for further discussion with "your father."

I wasn't overly worried. I knew the procedure. Every six months or so there was an "event"—a wedding, an awards ceremony, or a holiday for which I discovered I needed a new dress. I had an annual clothing allowance of $120, and these big-ticket items often threatened to overrun it in one purchase. The clothing allowance successfully kept my parents and I from wrangling over every new t-shirt, but I refused to surrender the battle of the "event dress" to mere budgetary limitations. Once I found the Perfect Dress, the bargaining began. On a good day, my parents would agree to pay for most of the dress, only taking a fraction out of my clothing allowance. On a bad day I'd agree to do some yard work to earn my dress.

I was adept at wiggling out of these promises, but doing so meant a lot of heated conversations about why I hadn't painted the garage or cleaned out the basement as I'd agreed to do.

I needed this particular perfect dress to usher me into the annual marching-band banquet. Yes, it was more expensive than other purchases I had wheedled out of my parents, but the process would be the same. I expected to have that dress in my closet in two days' time.

Then my parents sat me down and introduced a roadblock I wasn't prepared for. "We think you should find a less expensive dress," said my mother.

"I understand it's a lot of money, but it's really the only one I want."

"No, we don't think an eighth grader needs a seventy-dollar dress," said my father.

"Well, that's why I was thinking I could work off half of it," I said, deciding it was time to compromise.

"Even if you paid for the entire dress up front by yourself, we wouldn't let you buy it," he said. "It's the principle of it."

The principle?

At thirteen, I saw no place for the principle of anything in this discussion. Who buys clothes on principle? It's a simple exchange. One person has money. Another has a dress. They trade. Supply and demand. I had learned about this in school. Principle? Principle was for writing letters to the editor and opposing the death penalty, not for my beautiful new band-banquet dress.

I yelled. I pleaded. I cried. Eventually, I got the dress. I probably promised to paint the entire house. I *know* that I swore to wear that dress to every formal event until graduation. While their principles were strong, my adolescent will was just a little bit stronger. But every time I put on that dress, I remembered two things: (1) my parents had some pretty high standards for living in this world, and (2) they cared enough about me to make an exception every once in awhile.

Heidi

Other Families' Stories

When I was thirteen, I desperately wanted a sixty-five dollar purse made by Polo. My mom thought it cost too much and wouldn't buy it for me. I saved up all my baby-sitting money and finally was able to buy it. One year later I regretted buying that Polo bag—not just because it cost a lot, but also because I realized I only did it to be part of the crowd. If I could take it back now I would. What changed? I don't know. Just getting older I suppose. I graduated from grade school and started high school with a different crowd.

Kate Hunter, 14, New York, New York

We use technology in our family to maximize our time with the kids, but it also complicates our lives. We have a cell phone. We have two computers in our house, one that is connected to the Internet. In fact, I'm talking to my computer with a special headset and software application that transcribes in real-time what I'm saying. These items aid me in efficiently completing my work and, theoretically, should allow me more time for the family. Not always the case. We recently purchased a DVD player and still have a VCR, both of which enable us to watch the programs that we want to watch when we want to watch them. We tape educational programs for replay at a later time. For entertainment purposes, the children have a GameBoy and a Nintendo console. We also have a baby monitor that allows us to closely check on the baby, Maribeth, while she is sleeping and we are doing things around the house. This facilitates greater freedom to do what needs to be done, or what we want to do, while also giving us great comfort that she is OK. It's a lot of stuff, but it's all geared to helping our family run more smoothly.

Michael Kern, father of three children, assistant professor and research scientist, Mt. Pleasant, South Carolina

Probably most important, my parents did work they believed in. Mom works as a family-life educator, and my Dad made a midcareer switch to similar work, even though it was less lucrative. Their example was the strongest influence on my belief that you have to do work you believe in regardless of whether it's high-status, high-paying, or conventional.

Robert Honeywell, lawyer, actor, playwright, New York, New York

My parents insisted that we live a very simple lifestyle. We never bought brand new cars or fancy things, and I remember hating this when I was growing up! I knew my parents had the money to buy all the stuff my friends had, but their priorities were very different. Now I realize that their priorities were to send us to any college we chose, to take our whole family to the Soviet Union to visit our exchange students, to take family trips across the country. . . . They saved because they thought that our education and our experiences were more important than having a new car or a bigger house. I love the fact that they raised us that way. When I get something I've wanted I really value it, and stuff is becoming less and less important to me. Also my parents were such savers, I have a very easy time with money now. Most of my friends are in debt because they just buy tons of stuff. Even when I'm only working part time, I have enough to pay my bills and not worry.

Jeannie Stith, voice-over artist, Philadelphia, Pennsylvania

One practice that my parents really instilled in me was almost obsessive frugality with money. I also learned the connection between faith and one's personal responsibility for addressing the challenges of the world. And now my dad feels I've taken my personal responsibilities too far with my radical ideas, but I take some comfort in the suspicion that his parents probably thought the same of him.

John Stith, Green Party organizer, Montgomery, Alabama

Although it was more for health reasons than to combat consumerism, after Halloween we used to buy back a lot of the candy our kids collected. They got some money, and we got to throw away junk food.

Leif and Rene Kehrwald, parents of one teen and one young adult,
Portland, Oregon

Taking Stock

Following are some reflections that I have found useful in evaluating my own lifestyle. Reflect on these, choose what fits, and add your own.

- What is my most prized possession? (Don't count people or virtues. Think of something tangible.) Could I give it up if it was getting in the way of a relationship? Principle: People are more important than things.

- Do I consider myself rich, poor, or in the middle? (Most people in the United States think of themselves as middle class.) What would it take for me to have exposure to those who have less money than I do? Principle: Solidarity with the poor can keep one honest about what is a need and what is a want. Solidarity with the poor can keep me honest about what I actually need.

- Remember the home and car my family had during my early childhood. How does the home and car I have now differ? Has the difference made our family happier than I was as a child? Principle: Rein in "creature-comfort creep," which can fool us into gradually escalating our possessions. Usually as one's income rises so do one's "needs."

- What do I currently spend money on that may be a splurge but is really worth it? (Consider education, travel, quality toys, charities, hobbies, recreation.) Principle: Don't be tight; be balanced.

- Am I self-righteous or compulsive about attaining a simple lifestyle? Do I feel proud that I don't have as much as others or waste less than others? Principle: Practice acceptance and generosity of time, treasure, and talent.

- What's one thing I could do that would put less stress on the environment while still not stressing me unduly? (Consider transportation, packaging, doing it yourself, eating less meat.) Principle: Make the earth an ally.

- What's the single biggest thing that's complicating my life right now? (not enough time, money, quiet; health; stressed relationships; too much stuff) What one step could I take to make it better without hurting myself (or anyone else)? Principle: Take one more step to let go.

CHAPTER 4

Ecology
What It's Worth to Care for the Earth

I love fruit. We had already planted blackberries, raspberries, and blueberries, so when the seed catalog came I was ready to go for something bigger: apples. I could envision the kids picking all those nutritious apples that would keep the doctor away, climbing the strong branches that would give them free recreation and a love for nature, and me reading and relaxing under the tree in the summer while the shade cooled our house, allowing us to use the air conditioning less often. What a deal for ten dollars per tree! I ordered two trees, one of each of my favorite varieties of apple. We sang about Johnny Appleseed before meals, and I prepared to write a letter to the local medical school that they could just close up shop.

The trees—or should I say saplings—finally arrived. In my head I knew they would be small, but the sticks we got were a little dispiriting. We planted, we watered, we waited. I knew that it would be several years before we actually got any fruit, but it was hard to wait. Being the eternal optimist, however, I figured if the catalog said three years, certainly we would have apples by year two because we would love these trees so much. Eventually we mostly forgot about them.

But then a spring came; blossoms came; bees came. Small fruit began to set; I counted all five of them. By late summer, however, the magical disappearing act occurred. I don't know if it was birds, squirrels, neighborhood kids, or simply the course of nature, but by harvesting time there were no apples. I decided to get serious.

I read, I consulted, I had serious talks with the kids about how eating green apples would make them sick. These were not Granny Smiths! Eventually I came to the sad conclusion that I would have to resort to— sigh!—chemicals. Jim, the purist, said, "No, way!" I said, "I'll only do the minimum since I don't care about beautiful looking apples, just edible ones." I researched what would be least toxic to the environment and decided to do one application of dormant oil spray in the spring. Then I read the label. When I sprayed I looked as if I had just stepped out of a spaceship, with goggles, gloves, and every inch of skin covered. Disposing of unused spray responsibly strained my conscience, so I just kept spraying till it was gone. Eventually this job became a punishment for the kids. So much for the love of nature.

Did I succeed? Sort of. We did get apples, albeit small and discolored ones. The brown spots dissuaded the kids from eating them despite my insistence that they could eat around the spots and that the apples tasted fine. I made applesauce a few times, but it took a while to cut out all those brown mushy spots. Our maple trees were better for climbing. Apparently the kind of apple trees I chose had low branches, which meant that they were difficult to sit under and provided little shade for our house. I'm sure I could have done this better, but at least we're providing food for some neighborhood critters.

Perhaps you've had a similar experience. It would have been easier, less expensive, quicker, and perhaps better for our health if we had bought the apples at the store. Any kind of gardening raises these same dilemmas. Caring for the earth and being concerned with ecology is inevitably inter-twined with living simply and carries the same pitfalls. It often takes more time and money to do it right.

Yet I still plant flowers, vegetables, and trees—and hope. Maybe it's the wholesome feeling I get from being outdoors with my hands in the dirt; maybe it's the thrill of actually seeing green sprouts and watching them grow; maybe it's the feeling of self sufficiency I get from being able to eat something I've grown; maybe I'm just a sucker for Earth Day sentimentality. But I won't give it up. Each seed turned into a plant is my statement of hope for the future—of our earth and its people.

We can get involved with a lot of social issues that can improve life on earth, but ecology has the advantage of being down-to-earth and tangible. The difference one person can make is often visible. Unlike aiming for world peace or eliminating poverty, the difference a group can make can be measured in our lifetime. The Cuyahoga River no longer burns, Lake Erie is alive again, and bald eagles and buffalo are no longer on the endangered species list. Caring for the earth, air, water, animals, and plants is not the only cause worth working on, but it carries an even greater weight when we realize that respecting the environment mirrors our respect for human life.

The cardinal rules that cover most ecology issues are: reduce, reuse, recycle, and repair. And since I like alliteration, I will use them here.

REDUCE

How you reduce your impact on the environment will depend a lot on where you live. City people and country dwellers have their unique challenges and solutions. For instance, you can't use a public transportation system that doesn't exist. But transportation and consumerism represent major areas in which all of us can be more thoughtful and intentional as we make both large and small choices.

Drive less.

The challenges of responsible transportation illustrate just how complex environmental problems and solutions can be. I once suggested that, as an experiment, our family try to live on a welfare family's income for one month. Not everyone in the family was enthused with this idea, but it was Lent and there were no better proposals, so we proceeded. I figured out how much the grant would be for a family of six, and we kept track of all expenditures, trying to limit ourselves to necessities.

We found that we could squeak by till it came to transportation. Our experiment allowed that we already had a car and even that it was paid for and that there were no repairs during the month. Gas alone was the budget breaker—and Jim works at home! Clearly, if our goal was to live on less money and reduce pollution, getting rid of a car would be at the top of the list.

Of course it's not that simple. My husband constantly urges me to depend less on the car. We, like most Americans, have two of these conveniences. Our cars, however, give us ample opportunity to experiment as a car-free family because one or the other auto visits the repair shop frequently. During these times our lives become very complex. We try to minimize trips or miles by creating intricate schedules for who will pick up whom; we consider which friend, neighbor, or coworker to bum a ride from this time; one of us takes the bus or rides a bike.

Coordinating schedules is complex and stressful, and it adds extra miles and hours to our day. Asking others for rides is fine occasionally but leaves us feeling indebted. Riding a bike is all right during pleasant weather if I am healthy, don't need to dress professionally, don't have too far to go or too much to carry. I actually end up feeling quite virtuous and fit during these outings. Getting all these criteria to mesh, however, doesn't happen often. That leaves me with public transportation, which is usually a bus. I do this, but I don't like it. Even though we live on a bus line and don't live that far from my job, it takes a transfer and an hour longer to get there by bus. If the simple life is about having more time and less stress and clutter, this doesn't qualify. Living more simply can be pretty complex.

So cars were another issue of dispute in our family. Jim and I looked on cars as a functional device to get us where we needed to go. We were also concerned about minimizing our impact on the environment through auto pollution. To many young people, including our children, cars were a visible status symbol. Our urgings to walk or take the bus were resisted and only tolerated as a last resort. Were we damaging our children's self-esteem by making them different from some of their friends, whose parents gave them the latest tech toy for good grades or a car for graduation?

Buy less.

Despite manufacturers' and politicians' encouragement to buy more to keep the economy strong and growing, it makes sense that the less we buy, the less energy needs to be used to manufacture goods. The downside of this is that the economy might lag, jeopardizing investments; unemployment could rise, thus hurting many families; and of course we might not have something we want or need. It is a complex balance, and since I am not an economist it would be irresponsible of me to suggest a simplistic solution.

Our own family's approach, therefore, has been to focus on making thoughtful decisions on what we buy. This involves evaluating whether it is a need or a want, whether there is a more environmentally friendly way to meet this need, and—if it is a want—whether it supports one of our values (such as family harmony or renewing our spirit) or is a frivolous fad that will be clutter or yard-sale fodder in a year or so.

On a societal level, my hunch is that the problem is not unsolvable, but it takes political will to redirect manufacturing to goods that are worth having and to build incentives to support environmentally friendly energy policies. Currently, it is not cost-effective to build much that is powered by solar, wind, or alternative energy sources. But what if our nation looked to conversions such as this as a solution to the energy crisis? People would need to be employed, new companies would emerge to invest in, and mass production would reduce cost. I know it's more complicated than this, but that's why we need more than social workers to make a difference in the world. It starts with people imbued with both the commitment to honor our environment and the will and skill to make a difference. Scientists, economists, technicians, and entrepreneurs with a social conscience are needed.

Maybe you do care about the environment and want to help, but there are lots of causes out there, and you can't do everything. In fact, you may not have the science, business, or political knowledge necessary to make a significant dent in this area. So what can you do while waiting for the right people to come forward? What can you do to nurture children who might be the ones?

What you can do is take a step or two. It doesn't matter where one starts because one step leads to another. I started this section with transportation because the Union of Concerned Scientists recently studied the subject of what ecological steps really made the biggest impact on the environment and energy consumption. Reducing our dependence upon automobiles was the single biggest change most Americans could make. But downsizing to one or no car, moving closer to work, and taking public transportation are major life changes for most of us. All the more reason to bring up our kids with this awareness. It may be too late or too disruptive for some of us to make a major move or downsize the number of cars we depend on. But it's not too late to raise children who can more intentionally consider energy factors when they decide where they will live and work.

Here are some other minor steps we tried to reduce our negative impact on the environment.

Since I do the laundry in our family, I decided that on nice days I would hang the sheets out to dry. The authentic earth woman would not buy an electric dryer and would dry *everything* on a line. That would be good, but it would take more time. And I have to admit that I like the softness of underwear that's been dried in a machine. My compromise? It hardly takes any time to hang out sheets because they're large, and it saves me one load a week. (Don't tell my mother, but I also learned that we would not all die of dirt disease if I don't change the sheets every week. I learned this from our kids in college.) When our old dryer died, we replaced it with a gas dryer that was more energy efficient.

My other reduction tip that has not yet been embraced by the rest of the family is reduced packaging. I keep at least one cloth bag in each car, and whenever I go into a store I take the bag with me. At the checkout line I repeat the mantra, "I don't need a bag" and use my own. It's a symbolic gesture. It's simple. It's small. It may be insignificant. But it is a step, and it raises my own consciousness. The hardest part was remembering to take the bag into the store with me. Now it's a habit. Not everyone in our family does this, so there are always plenty of plastic bags around if I need one.

REUSE

Once upon a time milk was delivered in glass bottles that were picked up when empty and then refilled. That may never happen again on a wide scale, but we should be encouraged by remembering all the ways we reused things before all the plastic and paper took over our space.

Avoid disposables.

I once heard about a person who separated two-ply toilet paper to make it stretch further. At least they weren't reusing it. I don't know if that is an urban myth, but even *I* don't go that far. Many of us already avoid using too many disposable products such as plates, cups, utensils, and other paper products. Some would argue that the electricity and water used by a dishwasher wipe out any energy or money saved by using real tableware. It's also quicker to use disposable.

My own experience is that it's barely quicker once you get into the habit of washing. Doing the dishes can be a good time to talk with your kids; it can even teach them teamwork. Sometimes it's a battle, and I guess that teaches conflict resolution or forgiveness. I have to admit, however, that when the kids were young, I often looked forward to having no help with the dishes. It was the only peace I got all day. Bottom line? It's less expensive to reuse. Do I ever use disposable products? Of course.

One of our more successful ways to cut back on paper products was the reduction of paper towel use. The methodology was simple. We still bought paper towels but put them in an inconvenient place, such as under the sink. The quaint, wooden paper towel rack became the holder for a couple of cloth hand towels. A bucket of rags was under the sink next to the paper towels. It was so easy to use the reusables that the paper towels were used only for cleaning up grease and nonwashables.

Color-code to save resources and keep the peace.

On good days our teens tolerated it as whimsy or "Mom being Mom"; other days they called it compulsive or neurotic. I call color-coding a convenience and a way to minimize waste and hassle. I do believe that when they were younger, however, each of our children became quite fond of his or her color. It all started with the fervor of being a new mom and an old tightwad. I soon noticed how many plastic glasses of milk and juice we went through each day. Being both lazy and ecologically opposed to doing more dishes than necessary, I suggested to my husband that each family member have a uniquely colored plastic glass to use for the whole day. Since our toddler had red hair, his color became red. When each additional child was born, I looked at him or her, gave a name, and assigned a color.

As our children multiplied so did my ideas of things to color code. It started out innocently enough with toothbrushes, towels, and napkins. I was especially proud of the napkin variation. I wanted to use cloth napkins instead of disposable paper ones. This would meet my dual goals of saving money by not making unnecessary purchases and saving the earth by not creating more garbage. To avoid mounds of laundry, however, I needed to find a way for each family member to keep the same napkin for a week. I diligently looked for similar napkins in different colors. Eventually I even sewed a set myself. Boy, was I energetic in those days! It worked—sort of. One of the adult members of our family just couldn't seem to remember his color. Luckily he wasn't usually the one setting the table.

Eventually, everything I saw became an opportunity to color code. To distinguish Christmas presents, each child knew to look for his or her color ribbon; the same with Easter baskets. The family calendar had each person's activities written in the appropriate color. Any time I bought multiples of something to give the children, I tried to find each one's color. Generally, this helped us all keep track of what belonged to whom and avoid some arguments. Fortunately, I stopped short of dressing each child only in her or his designated color.

Consider cloth diapers.

Color-coding is one way to reduce the need for consumption by reusing items. Another, perhaps more controversial, way is the use of cloth rather than disposable diapers. For most modern parents it's not even an issue, but my husband and I started raising our children when disposable diapers were not that common. Purists say that cloth prevents diaper rash and is softer and healthier for babies. Other purists say that disposables prevent diaper rash and are healthier for the baby since they wick the urine away from the skin. Both say that in the long run, their way is more cost-effective and better for the environment. Both have research to support their views. Here's how the decision to use cloth diapers unfolded in our lives.

My husband, Jim, relates that "before our first child was born, the thought of changing any diaper, cloth or disposable, seemed repulsive. It only took a few weeks of frequent changings, however, for my awkwardness to change to ho-hum. This is no big deal." So it also was when we used cloth diapers. At first we did it because someone had given us one month's diaper service as a baby gift. We got into the habit of using cloth and found that neither disposables nor cloth were foolproof—both occasionally leaked. The clincher was that using cloth was so much less expensive.

Initially, we would revert to disposables for trips and camping but eventually decided that it wasn't significantly easier since we had a routine and a plastic bag that sealed. It meant one extra load of wash a week with one extra rinse cycle since we used bleach. Because the same diapers spanned several kids and doubled as spit-up cloths, we figure that we saved thousands of dollars even after factoring in laundry detergent, extra water, and electricity. The washer and dryer we had anyway. The effect of disposables on the environment is still debatable, but from the standpoint of consumerism we saved a lot of money without much hassle. The one exception we made was to keep a supply of disposables available for relatives and baby-sitters. Keeping these people happy was a higher priority.

Using cloth diapers is not a matter of morality, but it's not as hard as most people presume. If saving money in order to allow a parent to be at home more is important to you, don't dismiss it as an option. The kind of diaper a child wears is not going to make a difference in the kind of person he or she becomes, but the time parents spend with the child and the attitude of conserving and reusing that permeates the home will.

Hand it down or share.

Many families have the time-honored tradition of handing clothes down from one sibling to the next and eventually to nieces and nephews and so forth. Yard sales are just a money-making variation of this. I've heard kids on the bottom end of the hand-me-down cycle complain that they never get anything new, but that's easily remedied by periodically supplementing the tradition with new clothes.

Clothes aren't the only things that can be reused. Books and toys are naturals. Sometimes it's more a matter of sharing than giving up ownership. Once our lawn mower broke, and we were about to shop for a new one when my husband had the idea of having a neighborhood lawn-mower pool. He expanded the idea to include any major tools that we use infrequently. He wondered why we couldn't just set up a system of sharing. The idea would take a bit of organization, and I imagine there would be some abuse, loss, and damage, but the amount of money saved by each family not buying duplicate items would easily make up for this.

The plan never materialized because the first few people we approached said they would be happy to lend us their mower for a while but really wanted to retain ownership. Understandable, especially in this mobile society. But wouldn't it be nice if our neighborhoods could become more of a community than a grouping of independent entities. It's hard to let go of owning something new or having something that's mine alone.

We do have a sharing agreement with some close friends. It involves car use, and so far it has worked. Each family has two cars, but with a combined mileage of 540,000 one or the other is often in the repair shop. We also have teenagers. This means that sometimes a car is completely totaled, and it takes a while to find another good used car. Since we live close to each other we figured that all we really needed was three cars between the two families. When a car goes out of commission, we drive each other to work, and whoever needs the third car uses it. It's like a swing car. This works because we can walk to each other's house, we go to a lot of the same activities, we have the same values, and we trust each other.

RECYCLE

I recently received a strange letter. Although the sender had addressed it by hand, his name was not one I recognized. And it was from a country I'd never heard of. It was bulky and a mystery. Probably a request for a donation. Surprise! It contained one AA battery and a note. Apparently Mike Roman, a Peace Corps volunteer on the remote island of Tamana, Kiribati in the central Pacific Ocean, got my name from his parents and wanted to offer some ideas for this book. The battery? It was explained by the postscript "Could you throw this battery away for me? Thank you!" I later learned from his parents that he almost always includes a battery in his letters to them too. On a small island, trash is a big deal. If you can't burn it, there's no safe way to get rid of it and no room for a landfill. Because the island doesn't have electricity, batteries are a common source of energy. My conscience was pricked that day as I called our city to find out what was the responsible way to dispose of a battery. They chuckled when they found out it wasn't a car battery and said small batteries for home use could be put in the regular trash or I could take it to the hazardous waste collection site next October. I think I'll keep it as a reminder.

Take it to the curb.

We've come a long way from the days of unlimited landfills, when recycling meant trekking all over town to drop paper at one place, cans at another, bottles at still another—and nobody took plastic! Few people recycled because it took too much work. Now curbside recycling is common, and lots of people do it because it's easy. After a number of years of good intentions and not much follow-through, I believe that the secret to most recycling efforts is awareness and a usable system. The awareness takes no extra time or money. The system depends primarily on convenience. That's why curbside recycling has been so successful. The goal in the family, then, is to make getting it to the curb convenient.

In our house we put all newspapers in a crate and have a plastic container that has separate sections in which we put bottles, cans, aluminum foil, and plastic bags. That's nice, but it's not the most important thing. The secret ingredient is keeping it next to the kitchen garbage can. It takes no more effort to toss something into recycling than to toss it into the garbage. Well, almost none. We usually flatten our cans and plastics, but it's not required; it just saves space. Will this make a big difference in saving our earth's resources? Some, if many people do it. How big a difference is hard to evaluate, but it does make a difference in our children's attitude about how they use and dispose of items. I do remember being proud of Brian when he was eighteen and on a camping trip with friends. He insisted they pack their empty pop cans out of the woods until they found a receptacle. Maybe water or juice would have been a more nutritious beverage, but at least the recycling had taken hold.

Compost it.

Recycling usually makes us feel clean. And then there's composting. Most people resist composting because it's dirty, there's no good place to do it, and it takes too much work. I admire people who compost scientifically and get great yields. For those who care, but not that much, here's the Vogt simplified version. We have a plastic container with a lid that sits on the kitchen counter. (The lid is important.) We have a spot behind the garage where we dump the container whenever it's full—about once a week depending on the season. We pile on yard waste and leaves in the fall. Come spring gardening time, Jim digs to the bottom of the compost pile and finds enough good dirt to spread in the garden before planting. If we had a big garden we'd probably have to get more serious. It's not the most effective way, but it fits our needs. No building a compost bin, no turning it every month, no adding worms or checking soil balance. (It did help, however, when we had a rabbit.)

Pass it on.

Recycling need not be limited to returning elements to the land or their source. In the reusing category we talked about handing down clothes in families. Not all families are big or in need. Taking used clothes to Goodwill, St. Vincent de Paul, or similar used-clothing centers is a good way to recycle good but tired clothes. I've been on both sides of this experience. Once when shopping at Goodwill, I found a dress I had donated. I knew it was mine because it was hand sewn. At least I had the presence of mind not to buy it. It's a hassle to transport the clothes, but that's what a teen with a new driver's license is for.

Get something new, get rid of something old.

Everybody likes new clothes (with the exception perhaps of many preteen boys). The "one in, one out" system has helped keep our family honest about our needs and encouraged us to make those trips to Goodwill. When I get the desire to buy a new piece of clothing, I consider whether there's room for it in my closet and what I might give away to keep it a zero-sum operation. In other words, we resist the urge to build bigger closets in which to store more clothes. When the space gets too stuffed, it's time to prune or to refrain from buying anything new.

REPAIR

Perhaps the hardest part of being environmentally responsible is repairing items rather than throwing them away. Repairing things takes time; it also requires knowledge and skill. It takes twice as many trips to the hardware store than you had expected. For some it can be a hobby or an occasion for bonding with a child. For others it's pure drudgery. It's great for the environment but it does involve a judgment call in terms of time. One approach is to buy quality items that will not break or wear out quickly—but this is not fail-safe. Eventually, we all ask the question, To repair or not to repair?

Some criteria that could help with this decision might be:

- Is it a high ticket item, such as a car or washing machine, for which the cost of repair is a relatively small percentage of the cost of a new one—and for which disposal would be ecologically problematic?

- Is it a repair I know how to do myself?

- Do I have the tools and the time to do the job?

- Is the the item even worth saving?

- Would I enjoy doing this project, or would it simply become a chore and make me grumpy?

Repair Christmas.

One of my favorite fix-it episodes happened several years ago around Christmas. I decided to make one of the three presents we got each child a gift of repair. Some of the repairs were easy, such as mending a favorite dress; some were more difficult and required taking an electronic item to a repair shop. I did what I could myself but figured that part of the gift was the phone calls and and running around I would have to do to get the item fixed. In some cases, the kids could have done it themselves, but I was saving them time and trouble. I was proud of my ingenuity. I *think* they appreciated the gifts. I don't imagine it would have worked real well when they were young or if that had been their only gift. I suggested we make this a family custom. So far no one's taken me up on it.

How long can it go?

My parents always bought new cars. When Jim and I first got married, we did the same. Then somewhere between car one and car two, prices more than doubled. We have been happy reusers ever since. The first time we had a car reach 100,000 miles, I walked home to get a camera so I could take a picture of the odometer. (OK, so I was only a block away.) After a while, 100,000 was no big deal, but *200,000,* now that was something to be proud of. Jim came up with the idea of a family contest: Guess That Date.

About two months before our once-totaled and often-repaired Toyota hit round numbers, we sent out the word. Whoever came up with the closest date to the car hitting 200,000 won a whopping twenty-five dollars. Those away from home e-mailed their bids, more for the fame than the cash. With a little coaching, Aaron, the youngest, realized that he had the advantage of watching the day-to-day progress of the car and knew what trips were coming up. He also could pick a date just before or just after one of the older kids' guesses. Since twenty-five dollars would be more meaningful to him than the others, we didn't call a foul on him for his strategy. Jim and I made pretty unrealistic bids. Aaron won. Just goes to show you that sometimes repairs can pay off. With his head for strategy we're training him for *Survivor.*

COMMUNING WITH NATURE

Some folks have a natural fondness for nature, while for others, "roughing it" means spending the night in a Holiday Inn without cable. For our family, I don't know if it was genetic or simply an acquired taste. The goal was to have fun and see the country. The vehicle was camping. The result was an appreciation of creation and the natural world. Camping doesn't fit every family, but for us it fit the desire to travel with the need to do it inexpensively. We learned to like it. One of the reasons it probably worked for us was that we started young, while the kids still thought it was cool to go to the bathroom in a pit toilet and we could convince them that running through tall grass was just like being on an African safari. We played up the adventurous and challenging aspects of camping. For some, it became an ongoing love; others graduated to indoor video games during the teen years. But all of them hiked, got dirty, and learned to live without electricity for a few weeks. They saw the interdependence of humans, animals, land, water, and air. They survived. The nice thing about nature is that it teaches without preaching.

For those not inclined or able to camp, connecting with nature and protecting the environment can be fostered through walking, biking, picking up litter, planting a flower, or generally conserving natural resources. If our planet doesn't survive, neither do we.

The Vogt Kids Speak

I hated taking the bus, and usually weaseled my way out of it. I can see reasons now, but try explaining that to a kid and see how far you get.

I save water and electricity and avoid unnecessary pollution by not doing my laundry that often.

Dacian

Although I often argued with my parents about my mode of transportation to different activities, one thing that I did appreciate was the freedom to go basically anywhere I wanted, as long as I came up with the means of getting there. If I wanted to ride my bike or take the bus, my parents were willing to let me go. This taught me independence and showed me how to get around on my own. Although I remember trying to convince my parents to spend more money on our two cars so that I wouldn't be embarrassed to ride in them, I now find myself, at the age of 27, still not having owned a car. I generally get around by bicycle, walking, or subway. It's good for my health and wallet and it puts less stress on the environment. I also appreciate the fact that my parents chose to live in the city, which gave me the option at a relatively young age to go places on my own. I felt sorry for friends who lived in the suburbs and relied on their parents to drive them wherever they needed to go.

Brian

My mom can be embarrassing at times. She's always saying to store clerks, "I don't need a bag," and then she whips out her cloth bag. I don't mind her doing this as long as she doesn't expect me to do the same thing.

We recycle a lot of stuff (cans, paper, plastic), as I suppose many people do these days. When I was younger, I liked stomping on the pop cans to flatten them before we put them into the recycling bin. Now, it's just a pain, so my friends and I just line them up in the kitchen and magically the next day someone has put them in recycling. I do get mad, though, if I see someone throwing a can or bottle out of a car window. It's not that hard to recycle.

Aaron

A Daughter's Response

Two-Wheel Drive

My father biked to work, to meetings, to the grocery store. For the most part, we ignored him. As kids, our bikes were for coasting down Myrtle Hill, for sticking baseball cards in the spokes, and for racing to the corner store. They had to look cool, carry two, and be ridden yelling "No hands!" into the wind. At the end of the day our bikes were put in the garage and stored until playtime returned. Kids' bikes weren't for getting places.

Until the summer Dad introduced the downtown ride. He proposed it one hot June afternoon over dinner. "How about taking a bike ride to downtown Cincinnati?" he asked. I didn't think he was serious. Downtown was three miles away from our house, a six-mile round trip. And it was the kind of place you went in a *car.* "We could have breakfast at the downtown McDonald's," he added. I was daunted, but I was in; so were my brothers and my noncycling mother.

Biking downtown meant getting up *early.* A little after dawn my brothers and I pulled our bikes out of the garage and filled up water bottles while Dad checked the air in the tires. Downtown didn't seem any closer to me in the early morning, but the others looked so confident, I kept my apprehension to myself as we set off on our adventure.

There were so few cars early on a Sunday morning that we were able to ride in the middle of the lane and coast through red lights, just because there wasn't anyone coming. We waved at the people we passed. We asked my father about the neighborhoods we biked through. We took in cracks in the road, flowers edging sidewalks, and the smell of exhaust. As we biked across the suspension bridge that spanned the Ohio River, I wondered why I hadn't noticed how amazingly big the river was from the back seat of the car.

When we arrived in the awakening bustle of downtown Cincinnati, I had a secret. I was sure the people on the street saw me on my bike and assumed that I lived around there, that I was just any neighborhood kid practicing riding with no hands. How could they guess that I had come from a whole three miles away? They *certainly* had no idea how good that McDonald's breakfast tasted.

The summer downtown ride became a semiannual event, incorporating different neighbors and different Vogts at different times, fading out as we all got past being intimidated by a six-mile bike tour. But my father kept biking to places when I would have driven, and sometimes a few of us joined him.

It was a quiet message, but one that lasted. A car isn't the only way to get somewhere. We just have to embrace the alternatives, which can be closer than we think. I've kept biking, partly for the joy of it, partly because it's a lot cheaper than a car, and partly because I need to keep reminding myself what my father showed me: that the quickest way from point A to point B isn't always the best.

Heidi

Other Families' Stories

One of our more effective stewardship strategies was when we decided to encourage our children to turn the lights out whenever they left a room and to live with lower thermostat settings in the winter and less air-conditioning in the summer. The money we saved went to creating an energy savings that we would later divide between a family fun event and Energy Care (a fund for those who can't pay their utility bills). Whenever we would get our monthly gas and electric bills, we would compare these amounts with the amounts of energy we used during that same month the previous year (we had saved our receipts and showed the children how to read the bills). We would multiply the units of energy we saved that month by the current year's rate, to calculate our financial savings. Half the savings went to Energy Care; half to us, usually to finance a family bowling night. The children did the math calculations—good practice—and became much more willing to save energy. We think the fifty-fifty split was the key.

**Jim and Kathy McGinnis, parents of three young adults, founders of
the Parenting for Peace and Justice Network, St. Louis, Missouri**

Lynea has picked up a lot of causes from us, but one thing she didn't want to pick up was the trash at 8:30 on a Saturday morning. Cleaning the earth wasn't the problem; it was a teenager and 8:30 A.M.

**Laura and Steve Domienik, parents of a fourteen year old,
Kennedy Heights, Ohio**

We recycled, reused, and composted way before it was popular to do so. I tried to limit laundry by explaining to the kids that they didn't need a fresh towel every time they took a shower and that if they bought a new piece of clothing, something else should go. We insisted that our kids learn how to take public transportation. But raising worms in the basement seemed like going too far to our kids—at least in the beginning. Knowing my commitment to composting, my sister had given me worms as a birthday gift. I kept them in two bins in the basement. The kids' job was to take leftover vegetables to the worm bin in the basement. They hated that job, not so much because of the worms but the fruitflies it attracted. Eventually they accepted that conservation was important and that composting was nature's way of renewing the earth. We've taken over this animal's space outside, and this is one way to give back. Eventually the worms became our family's claim to fame, as my daughter wrote an essay about them for the newspaper.

Jo Ann Schwartz, mother of two young adults, nurse,
Ft. Thomas, Kentucky

I have been strongly influenced by Native American philosophy . . . and want to get closer to survival. I recently went backpacking for a week with some of my friends. The simple acts of setting up camp, fetching and purifying water, protecting ourselves from rain, and trying to start fires for heat made each moment meaningful. At the same time, our sense of community and friendship deepened because we had to work together, and we depended on one another for survival.

Nicolo Kehrwald, 20, Portland, Oregon

My two kids think I'm pretty weird at times because I have very strong beliefs about recycling, nutrition, TV, and so forth that differ from the beliefs of many of their friends. When they were young, I had more control over their environment, but now there's a lot of compromising on both our parts. We always used reusable plastic containers and insulated bags for our lunches when we were out. When Ben started going to school at age thirteen, he wanted to fit in, so I agreed to buy plastic and paper bags as long as he would bring them home to be reused. He said kids made fun of him for bringing organic foods, apparently because of an organic spritzer (pop) I sent. I reminded him of my compromises in packaging and buying ham instead of soy cheese for his lunches. In turn, he needed to understand that how I shop and what I feed him reflect my concern for the environment and our health. He felt proud one day that he sold someone his spritzer and bought a Coke for a fraction of the price until we discussed why I pay extra for good foods. We talk about my values, and he has some understanding, but it's hard to know what will stick. His main concern right now is how to fit in with his peers. I think being too dogmatic will only push him away from my values.

**Kim Thompson, divorced mother of two children,
self-employed day-care provider, graduate student, Cincinnati, Ohio**

What's It Worth to Save the Earth?

Caring for the earth is often an extension of our great respect for human life. Sometimes it works the other way around; the awesome beauty and power of natural creation lead us to see how humans and the whole universe are connected in a web of life.

Beyond the fundamental respect for human life, what environmental causes do you care most about?

- air pollution
- water pollution
- land pollution
- energy conservation
- nuclear contamination
- garbage and landfills
- litter and visual clutter
- preservation of trees, ecosystems
- preservation of animals (land, water, air)
- recycling
- gardening
- eating low on the food chain
- political activism
- organic gardening

What does our family already do to respect and protect the environment?

What's one more step we could take?

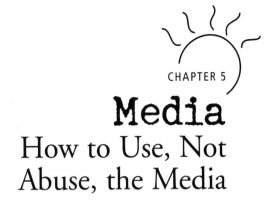

CHAPTER 5

Media
How to Use, Not Abuse, the Media

"No, it doesn't!"

"Yes, it does!"

"No, it doesn't!"

"Yes, it does!"

"Look, just because I watch violence on TV or play a violent video game doesn't mean I'm going to go out and hurt somebody. I know it's just pretend, just a game."

"Yes, but what about the shootings at Columbine and other schools? What about the gang fights in our own city? Heck, what about you and your brother wrangling here at home?"

"Hey, we're just playing. Even when we're really mad, nobody's gotten seriously hurt. We get over it."

"Maybe you do, but what about the other kids who don't? We don't live on an island, separated from kids who might be a little more on the emotional edge, and you just might be in the wrong place at the wrong time."

"Look, Mom, it's not going to hurt me. I can take care of myself. Don't worry about it."

The above scenario has been repeated in various forms in my own family more often than I'd like to admit. Sometimes I wonder if it's a battle worth fighting. Does exposure to a lot of violent play really harm a child? Does it really make any difference? If parents limit or censor their children's exposure to violence (or promiscuous sex) in the media, will it make any difference in how these children treat other people and what they contribute to society? These are controversial questions. Good parents have different answers, depending on their child's age, gender, or how tired the parent is at the moment.

As you might expect from a family-life educator and middle-aged mother whose kids like to characterize her as being terrorized by cartoons, I have serious concerns about the media. Let's start with the issue of violence. I'll try to be fair.

DOES VIOLENCE IN MEDIA HURT?

Seeing one bad movie, watching an occasional violent TV program, or trying out a violent video game is not generally going to scar a person for life. A steady diet of the above, however, desensitizes our society, our families, and ourselves to violence—and the ante has been rising. What used to pass for violence in the fifties is tame compared to today's standards. Yes, I am guilty as charged of being a wimp when it comes to violence on the screen. This is partly because I haven't been hardened by years of watching escalating violence. It is probably due partly to my temperament. Perhaps the biggest disagreements that I've had with my own children have been over use of video entertainment, including TV, video games, computers, and movies.

Media violence desensitizes us.

Even though watching one violent movie or program may indeed have no harmful effect, what I am concerned about is the cumulative effect of hours and years of graphic scenes of the torture and killing of human beings. At first it's mild violence aimed at young children, maybe punching and kicking. As children build up a tolerance for that, they need more and stronger violence to achieve the same level of excitement. The intensity and frequency of the violence has to increase in order to keep the audience interested. It's almost like an addiction. Newer and more intense stimulants are needed to reach the same thrill level. This is one situation in which tolerance may be a vice.

I've heard this argument in various forms at various times: "But I grew up watching Westerns, and I didn't turn out to be an ax murderer. My kids play violent video games, and they're doing fine. In fact they say it releases tension and keeps them from doing the real thing."

Congratulations, you've beat the odds. But not everybody has. According to a joint statement made in July 2000 to the U.S. Congress by the American Medical Association, the American Psychological Association, the American Academy of Pediatrics, and the American Academy of Child and Adolescent Psychiatry, "Well over 1,000 studies point overwhelmingly to a causal connection between media violence and aggressive behavior in some children." In addition, Thomas Robinson, M.D., M.P.H., and a researcher at Stanford University, has found that if we take media violence out of a child's life, violent behavior will go down. You can read his report, "The Effects of Reducing Television, Videotape, and Video Game Use on Children's Health and Behavior" at the following Web site: www.med.stanford.edu/school/scrdp/research/studies/youth_video_reduction.html

Lieutenant Colonel Dave Grossman, a psychologist who travels the world training medical, law enforcement, and U.S. military personnel about the realities of warfare, confirms Robinson's findings: "Today the data linking violence in the media to violence in society are superior to those linking cancer and tobacco."

Video games create conditioned responses.

Grossman explains the use of operant conditioning in the military to train soldiers to respond to orders quickly and reflexively.

The military and law enforcement community have made killing a conditioned response. . . . Soldiers learn to fire at realistic, man-shaped silhouettes that pop into their field of view. That is the stimulus. The trainees have only a split second to engage the target. The conditioned response is to shoot the target, and then it drops. Stimulus-response, stimulus-response, stimulus-response—soldiers or police officers experience hundreds of repetitions. Later, when soldiers are on the battlefield or a police officer is walking a beat and somebody pops up with a gun, they will shoot reflexively and shoot to kill. . . . Every time a child plays an interactive video game, he is learning the exact same conditioned reflex skills as a soldier or police officer in training.

For further information see www.killology.com

It's not enough to monitor only your own children's use of media.

Of course, to be fair, media violence does not affect all young people equally. Those with a healthy, loving family life usually have internal ego strength and enough personality development to help keep impulses in check. But we don't live in isolation. Even if parents could have absolute control over the televisions, video games, and computers in their own homes, we don't have perfect control over what happens in our neighbor's home or the homes of our children's classmates. Other kids, who might not be so emotionally mature or whose parents don't monitor their media use, are interacting with our kids, if not in the neighborhood, maybe in a restaurant or on the road. Just keeping our own kids safe is impossible. We can't cover it all.

FIGHTING VIOLENCE WITH ACTION

So what can we do? Should we just give up and hope that we're lucky? One of the best antidotes to hopelessness and despair is action. Just because censoring the worst of violent media may not prevent all violence doesn't mean we shouldn't do it. Most responsible parents have rules about which shows, games, or chat rooms, if any, a child can use. Some finesse the problem because their children are heavily involved in sports or some other activity that takes up a lot of discretionary time. Some parents go cold turkey and just get rid of the TV or only have a video player.

Becoming politically active around this issue can really make a difference, although it takes some effort. Families Against Violence Advocacy Network (FAVAN) is a national coalition of organizations working to influence the government and society on a variety of violence-prevention initiatives including violence in the media. (Individuals, families, and organizations who are interested in learning more about FAVAN can do so by calling (314) 533-4445, or sending an e-mail to ipj@ipj-ppj.org, or visiting their Web site at http://www.ipj-ppj.org.)

In hindsight, when our children were young the actions we took were fairly easy. Basically, we limited what programs or games they could watch or play. We had family meetings about it and did some compromising, but ultimately we had veto power. The kids believed us when we said something wasn't good for them. They complained sometimes, but we had relative control over their lives.

It became harder, however, when they became teens. One action Jim and I wanted to take when we had two teenage boys still living at home was to take the Family Pledge of Nonviolence. We were optimistic, but we weren't fools. We were well aware that one of the principles of the pledge was "to select entertainment and toys that support our family's values and to avoid entertainment that makes violence look exciting, funny, or acceptable." We knew we would have to approach this very delicately. Our kids certainly weren't warmongers, but they were typical teenage boys who played video games and were really into role-playing games such as

Dungeons and Dragons. We had already agreed that they would not play video games that showed graphic killing of humans. But the pledge of nonviolence took this to a higher level.

After reading the pledge and agreeing that TV and video games were a sticking point, we decided to list all the kinds of game violence that we thought should be acceptable as well as those that would not be in the spirit of the pledge. After a couple of weeks we had a decent list. We eventually negotiated that historical, futuristic, or symbolic violence would be acceptable but that graphic violence aimed at human beings would not. This allowed bows and arrows and other medieval weapons. It allowed movies like *Star Wars* and the crashing of vehicles in video games. Some parents, especially those of younger children, might still find this objectionable. In a perfect world I would have liked a more comprehensive definition of violence, but I could live with this agreement, and it allowed us to go forward. Perhaps more important than the specific compromise we came up with was the discussion it took to get there. By the time we had done all the talking and listing, we all better understood the reasons behind our positions.

OTHER REASONS TO BE VIGILANT ABOUT MEDIA

Violence is not the only, or even the most important, issue surrounding the use of media. It's not only a matter of what screen-based media promote, but what they prevent.

We lose creative play.

Much has already been written about the passivity of sitting in front of a TV for hours. Interactive games and computer work are more participatory, but they are still sedentary. Sometimes we need relaxation, and it's enjoyable to just sit back and be entertained. This is not bad, but it becomes a problem when the time we spend doing it becomes excessive.

What's excessive? That's a good question for a family meeting. For us, it changed over the years with the advent of more children, the arrival of new technology, and our fatigue quotient. We got our first TV when our first child was three. Half an hour a day of public TV was fine for him. He didn't know any better for about a year. When our fourth child was three, he was used to seeing the older kids watching TV, and it wasn't all public television. We had long since increased the time to an hour per day, with exceptions for news, special movies, holidays, being sick, programs Mom and Dad really wanted them to watch, and a few others. Eventually we expanded this to an hour and a half per day, with all the previous exceptions in addition to educational games, homework on the computer, fifteen minutes online during the day (because we have only one phone line), and unlimited online time after 10:00 P.M. until bedtime.

Keeping track of the time and exceptions is wearying, and I'm not sure this is the best approach. Some days I just want to throw the TV out, but I have a bad back. In desperation, I have been known to announce that the TV is dead and to put ribbons around both of them as a reminder. Sometimes I get Jim to carry it to the basement for storage. The kids think I'm overreacting, and they might be right, but sometimes I just want them to go play with Legos, draw a picture, build a fort, play some basketball, even go out in the snow and walk to the store for bread as I did when I was a child. Call it nostalgia or call it a mother's instinct; I still feel that this part of our life is out of balance.

Having children spaced over a twelve-year span has given me the perspective of watching how our children played before and since video games and computers were common. My observations don't rise to the level of scientific research, but I have noticed that the younger ones don't initiate as much open-ended, free play as the older ones did. I wonder if it's because video and computer games take less creative energy? It's easier to play passively. When we call a moratorium on "screens" as a discipline or for a season such as Lent, the younger children initially gripe, but when that wears off they rediscover toys and pursuits they wouldn't have if the TV were readily available. Camping allows some of the same dynamics to take place. With no electricity, we're forced to make our own fun. A certain amount of boredom is a necessary prerequisite for creativity.

The media lowers sexual standards.

Chapter 6 deals more extensively with sexuality, but in terms of the media, the standards have been gradually changing. I used to scoff at people who wanted to censor television and movies, thinking they were just prudes. We've gone way beyond prudishness today. People with multiple sexual partners and no permanent commitment to their relationships are shown as typical. Is it any wonder that couples are finding it more difficult to make and keep marriage vows when promiscuity is portrayed as normative on the sitcoms?

How can any of this change? Talking with our own children is a start, but they are influenced by more than just what happens in the home. Their peers and the pervading culture need higher standards; they need transformation. It takes public pressure, boycotts, organizing, and lobbying to make a societal shift. Advocates can make a difference. It also takes people of courage who are willing to speak out for their values at the risk of being ridiculed and labeled old-fashioned or prudish.

Is there anything beyond sex (and violence, and wasting our time) that we can lay at the feet of the media? At the risk of overkill, I'd like to suggest that TV can also promote excessive consumerism and materialism. Commercials sell us things we don't need and create the desire for more; but a subtler influence is simply the lifestyle portrayed on most sitcoms and many dramas. Few TV families live modest or simple lifestyles. It's easy to be fooled into thinking that the majority of people in the U.S. live an upper-middle-class lifestyle and that we are entitled to the same. We feel poor by comparison even if all our daily needs are met. We might feel unhappy and not recognize why. We just know we don't have enough.

STRATEGIES THAT HELP

You can make decisions that are healthy and reasonable for your family when it comes to media exposure. Here are some ideas that have worked for us and for other families.

Monitor the monitor.

All the families and young people I interviewed had some kind of guidelines for what they could watch—time limit, time of day, nature of program, or contingent on finished homework and other responsibilities. There is no one formula that works for all, but monitoring screen use is a given. Even shows that slip by the monitoring stage can be the occasion for discussing values and options. It's helpful to watch controversial programs with your children.

Limit the number of screens and their locations. Avoid individual sets in children's bedrooms. Computers are best in common rooms where an adult might walk by at any time. (For a long time we had a really ugly den that was also pretty cold in the winter. It was uncomfortable enough to sit in that we figured it qualified as a good room for the TV.)

Watch it live.

Much of what we see on screens is even better in real life. Why settle for a sitcom when you've got community theater right in the neighborhood? (The acting may not be as professional, but the bloopers don't get edited out either.) Why vegetate in front of reruns when you can hear live music not far from where you live? City dwellers have more access to live entertainment than do folks further out, but there is often something going on in the community that is not only entertaining but also won't break the bank. This encourages kids to get out from in front of the screen; it also provides them with opportunities to be involved in live forms of entertainment

Use rating systems.

Movies, games, music, and programs have ratings. These may not meet your standards because they are often determined by the people who are trying to sell you something. But you can use them as a minimum criteria. Ultimately, these judgments are the parents' responsibility. An excellent resource is the Web site of the National Institute on Media and the Family, which evaluates video and computer games, videos, and television shows from a family-friendly perspective.

Make the computer your servant, not your master.

Some families don't answer the phone during mealtime or after a certain hour of the day. Even before telemarketers disturbed us several times a day, we had to learn that the telephone was a convenience, not a device that controlled our schedules. We have to look at the computer in the same way. If your home is hooked up to the Internet, there will always be a message from someone, a new headline being posted, or a new chat room discussion beginning. Set limits, not just for the kids, but for everybody.

Use parental controls and a filtering program on your computer. Even with the computer in a conspicuous place in the home, children run the risk of chasing the wrong phrase through an online search and ending up in an unsavory location. One woman was simply searching for vacation information concerning a certain international city and logged onto a pornographic site. There are a number of filtering systems available. Learn what they are and how to use them.

WHAT'S GOOD ABOUT THE MEDIA

In the beginning, I said I would be fair, and most of what I've written so far sounds pretty biased against the media. So here's the fair part: There are many commendable uses of the media. For example, television

- Expands our vision beyond our home

- Brings us the Olympics, sports, news, and some truly great shows

- Entertains us when we're bored or sick

- Makes us laugh and cry

- Provides opportunities for family interaction and discussion

In addition to the positive elements mentioned about TV, cable

- Makes TV available in remote areas that don't have good network reception

- Lets discriminating viewers select certain channels with quality programming and limited commercials

- Provides coverage of community meetings and events

With video and computer games

- There are no commercials

- Children become familiar with computers

- Children can be kept quiet and focused for long periods of time

- Some are educational (see the Games Project Web site at: http://www.gamesproject.org)

The benefits of videos are that

- When wisely chosen, parents control the content

- There are no commercials (well, usually not beyond advertisements for other movies and movie products)

- They are less expensive than going to a movie

- They provide opportunities for family interaction and discussion

Computers have several benefits, including:

- They are good tools and resources for homework and general information gathering

- They help us communicate with friends and family via e-mail

- They can save time by allowing us to shop online, find reading resources without going to the library, access articles without searching through old magazines, and so forth

- When they work well, they bring helpful information to us quickly; when they don't work well, they teach us patience

- They allow us to say to our children, "I remember what it was like B.C. (before computers)."

Ultimately, the media can provide us with three "eyes":

1. Inspiration: shows can lift our spirits and prompt us to do great things.

2. Influence: the media can turn public attention and opinion to many good causes.

3. Information: the media educate and inform us.

In all of these ways, media can help us become well-informed, well-rounded people who pay attention to the world and try to make a positive impact on it.

The Vogt Kids Speak

I found myself agreeing with my mother on many points, yet I still believe that there were some things she overlooked in her section on the media. While it is true that violence and mature themes have been growing in the media, it is pointless to try to stop it. It is a force not unlike evolution where it grows and changes to fit its surroundings. By trying to limit exposure to these things, it only makes the urge to witness them more compelling. If my mother had not tried to stop me from viewing this, I believe I would have accepted it as a fact of life (which it is) and realized that it is a fictional representation of life created to appeal to the viewing audience. This may not be a good thing, but it cannot be stopped, unless we were to convert to a communist government where the government decides what we are exposed to. But we're a democracy, and all the freedoms we have given the media cannot be taken away, and they can display what they want in their own way.

Aaron

I do agree that you should limit your children when they are young, because I have seen many young kids who make me say, "Geez! I wish someone had paid more attention to what this kid was doing." However, in order to keep your kids following your beliefs, at some point you need to cut back on all the restrictions; otherwise your kids will simply rebel. I believe that after a certain point, if you have raised your children correctly, they will be able to think for themselves and won't let the media sway their beliefs.

Dacian

When I was younger, few of my friends had any limits on their use of screen entertainment, outside of some of the "countercultural" friends of my parents. This made life very difficult for me. It wasn't until I went to college that I actually met other kids, outside of my parents' group of friends, who actually had similar restrictions. It was at that point that I supported these restrictions.

Brian

A Daughter's Response

Stolen Pleasures

I was eight and I detested *Captain Kangaroo*. Why was I supposed to be enthralled by a woman talking to her hand because she'd had the forethought to stick a sock on it first? And the guy in the red jacket needed a good haircut. He was always chuckling to himself over jokes he must have been old enough to know weren't funny. Listening to their patter was worse than my mom's dinnertime, "How was your day at school today?"

Yet I watched it. *Captain Kangaroo* was the only show on at 6:00 on Saturday morning.

My younger brother and I had a ritual that developed out of my parents' TV restrictions. Every normal day of the week we were limited to an hour of television, not including news or public television. (*Entertainment Tonight* or *20/20* did not qualify as news.) But on Saturday mornings we were allowed to watch as much TV as we wanted, and the two of us weren't going to miss a minute of it.

So early every Saturday morning, when it was still dark out, my little brother and I would creep downstairs to the den and turn on the television. We didn't need alarm clocks. We woke up from pure anticipation, just like on Christmas morning.

Around 5:30 A.M. I would settle down on my stomach on the yellow shag carpet, cup my chin in my hands, prop myself up on my elbows, and stare at the color bars. I would turn the sound off so I didn't have to hear that screeching tone that accompanied them. And then I would watch and wait. The color bars weren't on the same channel that showed *Captain Kangaroo*. That was channel 64, a local Cincinnati channel that only played boring fuzz until 6:00. Only the major networks had color bars.

As the clock approached 6:00 the debate started:

"Heidi, let's turn to 64 for *Captain Kangaroo,*" says the recently arrived brother.

"No, let's wait till 6:30."

"C'mon, this is *boring.*"

"So is *Captain Kangaroo.*"

It was at 7:00 that Saturday morning really started to kick into high gear. *Snorks, Smurfs, GoBots, Garfield and Friends, G.I. Joe, Transformers, Rainbow Brite, Strawberry Shortcake, Pac-Man, Richie Rich, Inspector Gadget, Archie*—we watched them all. Dacian and I fought over conflicting shows and struck deals ("Okay, you can watch *G.I. Joe* if I get the second half-hour of *Smurfs*") or solved our disputes by turning the TV knob to the channel of our choice and then taking off the knob and hiding it from the other party. In this case, sibling number two would go running for the pliers, which I eventually learned to hide when I first came downstairs in the morning.

But whatever the injustice, however heated the dispute, we tried our best to keep it from waking up our primary enemies: Mom and Dad. We both knew that at any time they could walk in and say, "OK, it's time to clean your rooms" (our Saturday chore). They often did this just as the *really* good shows were coming on at eleven. And we had been waiting *so long* for those shows!

Television was the stolen pleasure of my childhood, always snatched from behind my parents' backs and enjoyed with a guilty pleasure. Saturday morning marathons were supplemented by similar TV binges at relatives' houses on the holidays. We watched TV all day (and they had cable!) while the adults sipped strange drinks and commented on the football game or which parish priest was dying. I reinterpreted the television restrictions for baby-sitters with a courtroom lawyer's finesse. I went across the street to "play" by watching Nickelodeon all afternoon. If my mother walked into the den to see me reclining on the couch an hour and a half into a movie, I had always "just turned it on." And of course, I didn't know the name of the movie, so she couldn't decide whether or not it was age inappropriate.

My methods got more sophisticated as I got older. I volunteered to wash the dinner dishes, taking two hours to do it between commercials. If found in the den, I had "just stepped in for a second," and couldn't they see that I was in the middle of washing the dishes?

My brothers and I watched one another's backs (unless we couldn't agree on which show to watch). When my older brother started baby-sitting the rest of us, all pretense of television restrictions was dropped as soon as our parents stepped out the door. We were in this war together and we were going to win it.

Yes, we all knew what our parents were after. At ten, I could spout soliloquies about the brain-eroding effects of television, about the dangers of violence in children's shows, about the benefits of "creative play." I had heard it all plenty of times from my mother. I had heard it often enough that I knew how to prove that *G.I. Joe* wasn't violent, that *Days of Our Lives* wasn't a soap opera, and that Saturday morning didn't end until 2 P.M.

So, should they have just left me alone with Dolby surround sound and a cable box and considered their job done? Would I have then gotten bored and gone outside to play capture the flag?

I don't see it happening. I think they were fighting a losing battle. My attention span is just too long and my desire for canned laughter too deep for them to ever succeed. But at least they never surrendered. They had a principle, they stuck to it, and I admire them for that.

And some battle strategies paid off. My parents made a strong statement to me by never putting money into my television addiction. Our

TVs were always castoffs from upgrading relatives. We never got cable, however much the children schemed, and we were the last on our block to get a VCR. But the rule that impacted me most was the allowance of public television. Because I needed my TV fix and I was allowed to watch as much public television as I wanted, I became a fan of *Newton's Apple, 321 Contact, Ghostwriter,* and even *Nova* at a young age. While I would have rather been watching *Saved by the Bell,* I gradually discovered more and more to like on public television in the afternoon. And what I didn't like actually *was* boring enough to force me toward capture the flag every once in awhile.

Heidi

Other Families' Stories

I watched a lot of TV when I was growing up in the sixties, but watching Andy Griffith was way milder than even today's cartoons. We order cable only during college basketball season and then cancel it.

Dave Brogden, father of two teens, Harrison, Ohio

In the summer we require that the children get themselves ready for the day (breakfast, make their beds, brush their teeth, and pick up their rooms) before they were allowed to use any "electronics." We defined electronics as TV, computer, GameBoy, and Nintendo. They were limited to a total of 2.5 hours per day after their "work" was finished. Normally during school days they were limited to an hour. This was, and remains, a source of difficulty in learning about consequences within our family. As we became stretched, worn out, and submerged in grant deadlines, we frequently extended the kids' time with electronics. If they played educational computer games or watched educational shows on TV, we also extended their time, so that this did not affect their quota. In general it has worked well, but what is required is close parental monitoring.

Michael Kern, father of three, assistant professor, and research scientist, Mt. Pleasant, South Carolina

We had limitations on violent content on TV. This worked for a while, but as they got older, our boys started watching all of their TV at other people's houses. Then I had no control at all over what they watched. Also, my one son became fascinated with what we would not allow. He ended up getting in big trouble in school for making a joke about violence. He made up a game on his calculator that had students dueling/killing teachers. He thought it was funny; his eighth-grade friends thought it was funny. The teachers did not think it was funny and wanted to expel him and press criminal-menacing charges against him. It was awful for him and for us. When I look at this situation, I believe that he had turned us off completely about TV/video violence. He was watching stuff at other people's houses and not telling us about it so that he could be with his peers. Consequently, we lost an area of communication with him. He figured we were way out of touch with society, and he turned us off. Unfortunately, he turned off everything we said in this area, and he underestimated adult responses at school. The interesting thing was that he responded fairly responsibly to getting in trouble. He was honest with the administrators and tried to apologize and make restitution. Somehow, he listened to us in the area of dealing decently with people. I think he turned the preaching off but followed the example.

Anonymous, mother of three teens, Cincinnati, Ohio

I work in telecommunications security and have seen enough investigations that the main Internet rule I have for my remaining teen at home is, "No chatrooms."

**Joe Niehaus, parent of four, grandparent of eight,
Crestview Hills, Kentucky**

I was annoyed that my media access was limited compared to a lot of my peers. I think I felt left out for a time when everyone my age had cultural references that I didn't have. But even as early as high school I think I felt I'd gotten a gift. I'd read so much more and traveled more and had a better, broader imagination than most people I knew. I've only been happy about it since, and I've seen some of the shows and movies I thought I was deprived of, and I think the world might be a better place if no one had seen a lot of them.

M.B., 28, social worker, Brooklyn, New York

When I lived at home, I was allowed one hour of video games after homework. Although I love video games, when I have children I will limit their use of "fighter" games like Mortal Combat and first-person shooter games.

Jim Rice, 21, college student, Woodbury, Connecticut

When I was growing up, there was nothing on TV that contradicted what I believe, but it's different now. We have an adopted daughter, and her birth mother's parents said that in retrospect they underestimated the power of the media to influence their daughter, who became pregnant. It challenged their values about sexual morality, and the media won.

Karen Elfers, adoptive parent of two children, Edgewood, Kentucky

Taming the Beast

Reflecting on the issues of stereotypes, violence, and consumerism, ask yourself the following questions:

What are the best TV shows/movies/games?

What are the worst TV shows/movies/games?

How do the media enrich your life?

How do the media negatively influence your life?

What rules does your family have for using media? Do they work?

If you couldn't use a screen for entertainment for a week, how would you spend your time differently?

CHAPTER 6

Health
Life and Death Matters—Sex and Beyond

"Mom, I need to talk with you. Kevin and I have been getting pretty serious about each other and even though we're still in high school, we think we're ready to have sex. We've been talking about this for several months and haven't come to this decision lightly. We really care for each other. I know you'd like me to wait till marriage, but I've always been able to talk with you about stuff like this, and I know you think it's important to be responsible about sexual decisions and not bring a baby into this world before we're ready, so I was hoping that you would go with me to our family doctor to get birth control pills."

This is how parents earn their stripes and gray hair. We know that preaching doesn't work, and it's too late at this point anyway. If you are the parent of younger children, you may dismiss this as something that will never happen to you. Perhaps you are right, but indeed it does happen even to conscientious parents who have tried their best to help their children understand the serious risks of premarital sex. It is in the nature of teenagers to become infatuated and to call it love. What can the wise parent do? Granted, this is a personal crisis for the above family, but does the teen's decision and mother's response make any difference to the health of humanity? Let me deal with the second question first.

Sexuality (and other life-and-death issues such as substance abuse, nutrition, and mental health) are ultimately about respecting yourself, your body, and others. On one level, health in these areas makes a difference because obviously a person who is not alive, healthy, and functioning well can't be of much help to others. On a deeper level, the same emotional maturity and self-discipline that it takes to have a healthy body are the traits necessary to make and keep commitments and to put oneself at the service of others.

What are some of those traits?

Self-confidence

We all know that this is not about being self-centered, but about knowing oneself—strengths and weaknesses—and accepting oneself with humble honesty. Self-confidence is related to the identity issues covered in chapter 1. The more self-aware and self-confident I am, the more I don't look to other people, activities, or things to make me whole. It doesn't mean I am the perfect specimen of human mind and body but that I know who I am and am at peace with it.

Self-confidence cleans up the motivational landscape because I'm not performing in order to impress someone, gain their love, or fix myself. I'm doing it because it is right and good to do. Of course no one has reached this level of self-actualization, but I believe it's what we must aim for, in our own lives and in the lives of our children.

Delayed gratification

This is not most people's favorite virtue, especially for children and teens. But one of the hallmarks of maturity is learning to wait for something good: to wait until after the meal for dessert, to wait patiently for my birthday or Christmas, to wait to lose pounds till a healthy diet and exercise take effect, to wait to have sex until a permanent commitment is desired and practical.

If our goal is to make the world a better place, a lot of our projects are going to take a heck of a long time, and we'd better be prepared to keep going while we wait for the right time or for the results to show.

Sacrifice for the good of another

Sometimes the mature person needs to look beyond even their legitimate wants and needs and say, "I will voluntarily discipline myself or accept hardship because of my love for another." A person who decides not to drink alcohol in order to provide a safe ride for others does this. A mother of an unborn baby who makes an adoption plan or decides to raise her baby rather than have an abortion makes a wrenching sacrifice. The parent who dedicates him- or herself to the care of a handicapped child sacrifices a lot of daily ease. Children who watch the adults in their lives put the good of another before their own comfort receive the seeds of sacrifice.

Giving up something good (like sleep, food, money, or sex) for a time is hard, but it may not feel as difficult as giving up a bad habit even if it is for my own good. It might be the desire to quit smoking or to stop abusing alcohol or drugs. It might mean not giving in to the peer pressure to begin with. Usually, abandoning these addictions is not merely a matter of willpower; it may also involve giving up one's pride and seeking professional help. Giving up something or standing up to others are not easy or popular things to do. Both require courage and self-discipline—the same traits required to stand up to injustice.

A clear vision of the goal

Often the reason young people (and even the rest of us) get into trouble is that our goal is too vague or too short term. A person contemplating suicide can't see past his or her immediate despair to a livable future. An anorexic person sees a distorted goal of physical beauty and misses the bigger goal of being a lovable person. Young people experimenting with sex see the immediate goal of physical pleasure or feeling loved and don't realize that there's a bigger goal out there—the joy and trust that comes with an enduring committed love. If we focus on the small goals, we may miss our heart's real desire.

SEX AND THE WISE PARENT

Of course the wise parent starts to talk about human sexuality way before a child becomes a teenager. It starts when they are toddlers, and we calmly name their body parts while giving them a bath or take opportunities to comment on sexual messages we see in the media. But even parents who have tried to do everything right might still find themselves faced with a child who makes an unwise choice. We don't have absolute control over what our children think and do unless we lock them up in a tower until they're twenty-one, and then there would be other problems.

I know the mother in the opening scenario and consider her a wise parent. What did she do? She knew her daughter was painfully aware of the potential consequences of her actions because an older sister had become pregnant in her teens. She struggled between wanting to protect her daughter from a possible pregnancy yet also wanting to stand firm in her belief that sex belongs in an adult, married relationship. She had had many frank talks with her daughter about sexuality and the sacredness of life. She hoped that all this history would kick in, and she decided to trust her daughter to do the right thing. She did not agree to take her to get birth control pills because that would give the erroneous impression that she condoned her daughter's decision. As I know her to be a faith-filled person, I'm sure she prayed too.

Some may disagree with this response. A case can be made that the daughter may become sexually active anyway and that the mother should help her protect herself from an unwanted pregnancy, a sexually transmitted disease, or even AIDS. I give this mother credit, however, for standing by her convictions and treating her daughter with respect and love. They both will have to live with the consequences of their decisions.

But respecting our sexuality starts before the point of making a decision about becoming sexually active or bringing new life into the world. Often it's a matter of respecting the human life in front of us or beside us. In our own home we tried to show respect for both genders by not stereotyping jobs as being only for males or only for females. We looked at each individual's talent and time when deciding chores. Although Jim never did get the hang of sewing, he did discover that he enjoyed cooking and became quite good at it.

We discussed pornography with our teens. Few people would defend pornography, but an argument could be made that at least it's a private vice and only hurts the viewer. We countered that by saying pornography degrades women and that for some men it leads to acts of violence against women. Because it has the potential to threaten the safety of women, it becomes a public and justice concern, not just a private act. It's natural for teens to be curious about sex and pornography and perhaps to experiment, but it's easy to be tempted to go beyond curiosity to addiction, especially with easy access to the Internet. Some questions to pose to young people might be:

- How would you feel if it was your mother shown in a pornographic magazine?

■ If there's nothing wrong with pornography, would you be fine with your grandmother watching it with you?

■ Even if sexually explicit material doesn't affect *you,* how would you feel if your girlfriend or friend was the victim of a rape because of someone else's distorted view of women?

Although usually I am supportive of our constitutional right to free speech, this is one area in which I support limits on the media's freedom to say and show anything they want. The protection of our children and the good of society require governmental legislation. Even with rules and filters, it's impossible for even the most vigilant parent to monitor every lurid screen, script, or lyric.

Decisions about sexual actions don't appear out of thin air but follow years of exposure to the values of one's family, peers, and society, many of them subtle and subliminal. The faithfulness of spouses to each other teaches the value of sexual intimacy in marriage. Conversely, if someone has no qualms about being promiscuous before marriage, what confidence can a young person have that he or she won't be promiscuous within a marriage? Pam Stenzel, sexuality educator, explains it like this, "Your first experience of sexual intimacy is a time of special bonding. It's like putting duct tape on your arm. It sticks pretty tight and hurts to pull it off. Put that same duct tape on later and it will not stick as well. Each time you use it and pull it off, it loses some of its ability to bond. Intimate relationships are like this too. Each time you break up with someone you've been sexually intimate with, it's harder to make the next one stick. Save the tape for the real and final commitment."

Frank discussions with preteens about the physical and emotional dangers of sexual intimacy outside of marriage are important for any parent-child relationship. Single parents may want to enlist the assistance of a respected adult of the opposite gender to reinforce their values. Factual and value-based sex education classes in school are important supports as long as they include parental involvement and reflect the parents' values. Of course, both married and single parents' lives must be congruent with this message.

Regardless of whether the issue is premarital sex, abortion, sexually transmitted diseases, AIDS, or working to assist people in a third-world country, the principles are the same. Respect and love the person, give accurate, factual information, and live what you believe. The message that should undergird all lessons and conversations is that no mistake, no matter how horrible it may seem to them, is unforgivable.

SUBSTANCE ABUSE

Abuse of tobacco, alcohol, and other drugs are all manifestations of insecurity. I'm not good enough, cool enough, attractive, funny, or loved enough just the way I am. I want to change the way my body naturally functions because I'm not happy or satisfied with it. Some argue that these are private vices and don't hurt anyone else. I should be allowed to do what I want with my own body, even if it hurts me. But we now realize that secondhand smoke is not only uncomfortable for those around us but raises their risk of cancer. Alcoholism can destroy a family, and drunk drivers kill. Drug abuse often leads to other crimes against society.

Much has been written about how to prevent substance abuse, and government and educational programs abound to treat it. Generally, the approach is to strengthen self-esteem and decrease the allure of unhealthy practices through counteradvertising. Both these tactics make sense and should be supported. I decided to take a different approach and asked a number of young adults what influenced them to say "no" to drugs now or when they were teens. Their answers clustered around the following themes:

- Model your belief. "My parents didn't smoke or abuse alcohol."

- Lead a full life. "I had plenty of other interesting things to do."

- Pick good friends. "None of my friends were doing it."

- Take a stand. "Teachers took a clear stand against substance abuse and explained why it was bad."

- Have a purpose in life. "I had a bigger goal in life that kept me focused."

For parents this translates into: Don't flirt with abuse yourself—and tell your children why they shouldn't. Encourage them in a full and meaningful life. There's not a whole lot you can do about peer influence if your child is easily led. The goal is to help your children build a strong enough ego and self-respect that they won't feel tempted. It's not foolproof, but it's a plan.

HEALTHY BODIES AND MINDS

Some kids need to be urged to eat; some need to be urged to stop. In the United States, nutrition issues do not so much revolve around hunger but rather a balanced diet or emotional balance.

When our kids were young, they turned up their noses at the healthy, vegetarian casseroles my husband would make. They called tofu "toad food." We had more food rules and battles than needed, but since there was a variety of healthy foods around and snacks were limited to after dinner, they survived. Because we generally served balanced meals, our kids got an intuitive sense that they should have different colors on their plate, that ketchup doesn't count as a vegetable, and that the darker the green vegetable, the better. We scaled back on eating meat, but I don't know whether they realized it was because we were trying to eat lower on the food chain or surmised it was just for health. Having a diabetic child raised our awareness about the delicate relationship between food and life. I don't know that all of them can fill in the food pyramid, but they may have learned something more important. Just because I want that piece of pie right now doesn't mean I can't wait until after dinner: delayed gratification. Just because I have a whole bag of chips doesn't mean I should eat them all: self-discipline. Just because I bought the gum doesn't mean I should hoard it: sharing. These are the same skills needed to be a success in any area of life. But we often learn them first in relation to our personal, physical selves.

On a more somber level, there are children who are driven to eating disorders due to unmet emotional needs. Certainly our culture's projection of overly thin body images plays a role, prompting some young people to doubt their self-worth and even move toward self-loathing. But for many young people it's not so much about weight as control—not self-control but control of their lives. The fast pace and crowded schedules of some socially active parents just might tip the scale in the direction of an eating disorder for a child who is susceptible. Eating disorders can be related to the perfectionist personality type in that both try to achieve control over their environment by stretching a good to the extreme.

Signs that might indicate that your child (most often a daughter) is at risk for an eating disorder are:

- The child is consumed with losing weight, talks a lot about food, and diets a lot (much of this is normal, so don't overreact, but notice whether such behavior is combined with other triggers).

- Around the age of puberty, the child seems to be unduly afraid of growing up.

- The child is sensitive to change, such as changing schools or moving, and seems to go through extreme distress.

- Because of her involvement in certain activities, such as ballet or gymnastics, she is hypersensitive about her weight—or he is hypersensitive about bulking up.

Ways to prevent problems in this area include not making food too big a deal, not using food as a primary reward or punishment, and being attentive to giving children a way to influence decisions about their lives, their schedules, and their time so that they don't feel that their lives are beyond their control. Eating may be the only area over which a child still has any personal control.

And what does America's search for the perfect body have to say to people with a physical disability, whether it be congenital or from accident or disease? Fortunately, there are many services available to help disabled people cope both physically and emotionally with their handicaps. The breakthrough for able-bodied people often comes when they recognize their own strengths and weaknesses. Some disabilities are just more visible and obvious than others. Accepting our limitations is a step toward seeing that our worth (and a neighbor's worth) is not dependent on the strength or shape of the body.

Some people are born healthy; some are not—at least not in the physical sense. Here we are, genes and all, regardless of our own will or merit. A lot of it is luck. The challenge is to take the cards that are dealt us and make the most of them.

An unhealthy mind may be harder to deal with than a physical problem because it's more invisible. In families whose members have high ideals and want to be of service to others, mental distress may come in the form of perfectionism or burnout. Depression is the sister of these maladies because it says "I'm not good enough." Parents can model a balanced life of work, play, rest, and spirituality. Self-forgiveness teaches that mistakes are not the end of the world.

Just as we are born with differing physical attributes, each of us—and each of our children—comes into this world with differing mental abilities and emotional fragility. Wise parenting can encourage and enhance one's natural ability, but in the end the child is his or her own person. Parents cannot make them smart, or sensible, or control their sexual orientation. We can only love them and stand by them, just the way they are. Most religions of the world support this idea of unconditional love. As a Catholic, I am reminded of Mary's relationship with Jesus: watching, nurturing, not always understanding, but always standing by, even at the cross.

WHEN DEATH COMES

Mary Elise Henehan was a mother of seven and already a widow when her son Paul called with a chilling message about her other son, Tom. "Mom, I'm afraid I have bad news. I just got a call from Tom's friend in New York. Apparently, Tom was chaperoning a dance for teens in Brooklyn. He and a friend were selling tickets at the door of the social club and three older guys tried to crash the dance. Tom refused to admit them. A little later they came back with guns and shot him. He has just died at the hospital."

Tom was a very bright young man who had recently graduated cum laude from Columbia University. His commitment to always fight for the underdog led him to stay in New York City after he graduated and work for a political party advocating workers' rights. He was idealistic and had a strong sense of social justice. That's why he was working with children in Brooklyn that fateful night. Committing oneself to make a difference in the world is not always safe.

I would like to guarantee parents that fostering a love for others in your children will bring them a happy and long life. But it doesn't always work that way. Committing to justice can be risky and painful. As heartbreaking as Tom's death was, his mother said that what helped her get through it was the tremendous support structure she had at home. Mary was already a widow, had been for many years when Tom died. Her support was her other six children and the friends in her faith community. This was also the environment in which the seeds of Tom's commitment to the poor and oppressed first began to grow. What started him on the road to his death helped his mother survive it.

As tragic as Tom's death was, it was a death with a purpose. Tom died doing what he believed in, trying to help others. What's harder is senseless death. Death by suicide or accident doesn't carry the mantle of altruism, yet it happens. To a great degree in the United States, we are shielded from death because it happens mostly to the elderly or people on TV. Until September 11, 2001, wars were distant. It's hard to make death pretty because it isn't. It's scary and painful. By talking with our children about death we can help them to recognize that people die all over the world from hunger, AIDS, and wars, and that these people have mothers and fathers who love them. This helps them understand that every life is valuable, not just those who are related to us, live close to us, or agree with us. Showing our children a graphic picture of death is not the answer. We should show our children empathy, a life well lived, and hope in the future.

The Vogt Kids Speak

I know that, when I was a junior and senior in high school, my parents were concerned about my limited social life. I only hung around with one or two guys, and mostly what we did was play late-night role-playing games like Dungeons and Dragons. What I didn't tell them at the time was that one of the reasons I didn't go to a lot of the parties with my classmates was that I knew there would be a lot of drinking going on. (My best friend often did go and he just didn't drink, but I preferred my own kind of entertainment.) These were popular kids, and my mom, especially, didn't understand why I didn't hang out with them more.

Dacian

Although I've always considered myself a strong and healthy person, diabetes has definitely made it more difficult for me to work in less-developed countries due to the strict regimen that I must follow and the need to have access to certain medical supplies. This has been frustrating as I would have certainly liked to have gone off to a remote locale with the Peace Corps, but I felt that the limitations diabetes placed on me made such a commitment difficult. Overall, however, I feel that if there is something I really want to do, I can always find a way despite such obstacles. Diabetes just makes it more difficult.

Brian

A Daughter's Response

The Birds and the Bees

As I was growing up, my parents were always giving weekend workshops for engaged couples. It was part of their job. They would stand at a podium and describe married life to twenty-somethings: everything from joint bank accounts to children to emotional boredom. When I was a young child, these weekends meant time with a baby-sitter and often pizza for dinner. As a young teenager, I made money baby-sitting for the various couples my parents had recruited to give presentations.

But once I started driving and working and living my teenage life to the fullest, these weekend events sort of dropped from my radar screen. I barely noticed that my parents were gone.

So I was taken aback when I was coming home for Christmas break from college and my brother picked me up at the airport and said, "We can't go straight home. Mom and Dad are leading a marriage preparation program, and we have to pick them up on the way home." I hadn't even realized they were still giving those talks. But we drove to the conference center and walked to the main room where my parents were giving their final talk of the day. I edged into the back of the room to wait until they were finished.

Then I started listening—and trying not to blush. I had walked into the "marriage and sexuality" talk. And this wasn't a G-rated debate on the morality of birth control pills; it was my mom discussing different types of lubrication and my dad explaining how their sexual relationship "evolved." This was walking into your parent's bedroom, times ten.

The talk ended. I waved at my parents and went up to say hello. My mom gave me a big hug, then blushed, saying "I wish you hadn't walked in at *exactly* that time." But that was it. We went on to talk about my first semester at college. It wasn't a big deal, just their sexual history. As we drove home in the car, I felt proud that these adults who were talking to me as an adult were my parents.

Heidi

Other Families' Stories

If I was invited to an overnight, my mom and dad needed to know the family. If they didn't know them, Mom would have at least one telephone conversation with the host parent. Then she would go to the house with me to drop me off so she could make sure a parent was going to be home throughout the party. I complained, but now I think it probably kept me out of a lot of trouble.

Mary Lichtenwalter, member of Holy Spirit Parish Young Adult group,
Duncanville, Texas

Our oldest daughter got pregnant while she was in high school. Although it was a wrenching experience for the whole family, I was proud that she stepped up to her responsibility and decided to make an adoption plan. I'm now very cognizant with our other children how little control I actually have over them as teenagers. I hope that they will at least see that while always loving them, I remained true to my convictions. I know they will at times be angry with me for my positions, but I'm willing to endure their anger because I care.

Marianne Bosch, mother of five, grandmother of three,
Edgewood, Kentucky

They called my great-great-grandmother, Miss Lizzie. As the story has come down to me, Miss Lizzie was a slave and was beaten to death because she refused to breed with a man who was not her husband. I don't preach about sex to our kids; I just make sure they know her story. Sometimes a story can be more powerful than "the talk."

Terri Lyke, mother of two teenagers, nurse, Chicago, Illinois

I remember driving down the tollway with our then ten-year-old son (taking a group of five soccer players to practice) when Joe (who was prone to ask questions any time and any place) asked, "Mom, why would anyone want to have an abortion?" You could never put Joe off for an answer, so as we talked briefly I suddenly realized how quiet the van had become and that I would need to call the other parents that evening to let them know of how we passed a billboard about abortion and "unwanted pregnancy" and that as Joe and I talked the other boys were listening.

Anne C. Keough, mother of four young adults, Duncanville, Texas

When I was just out of college, I spoke with over 1,000 high school students on behalf of a crisis pregnancy center about the beauty of saving sex for marriage. During my own high school years I sometimes felt pressured by dates, and it may have simply been fear that kept me from "going along with the crowd." But with every "no" I said "yes" to something else. As I grew older, I learned that waiting for sex wasn't just about saying "no" but also about saying "yes" to that total gift of self and that promise of forever that comes with marriage. In my visits to classrooms, I was amazed to discover how hungry teenagers are for this message—especially those who had been hurt. A young woman at a Cincinnati school wrote, "I would like to hear more about the fact that it is never too late to start over." I feel it has been a privilege to bear to these students the hopeful message of new beginnings and of the beautiful expression of love that sex can truly be in marriage.

Kate Bergman, 24, graduate student and residential counselor for Senate pages, Washington, D.C.

Two of my children went through treatment for drugs and alcohol while they were still in high school. I didn't have a clue that they were abusing drugs or alcohol. Each child has gone through his or her own particular set of problems, poor choices, etc. Our response was to turn to God in an active way, attend parent programs and Alcoholics Anonymous. We have learned to let go, support, listen, and call for psychiatric help when needed.

Gail McDonough, mother of four young adults, St. Louis, Missouri

In regard to drinking or drugs or anything else I thought was questionable, my parents let me know I could always use them as an excuse: "My Mom would kill me if I did that." She also gave me a good line to say if offered a drink ("Tell them you're taking a decongestant"), so I wouldn't look like a jerk in front of my friends.

Stephanie Babb, member of Holy Spirit Parish Young Adult group,
Duncanville, Texas

Our daughter, Kathleen, developed an eating disorder when she was about eleven. In hindsight, we can now see that we were an overcommitted family trying to pack too much into a day. Not every child in this environment would become anorexic, but to Kathleen it translated into feeling out of control. At first I felt guilty but eventually realized that I couldn't know about every single thing that happens in the family. It was not an easy or quick recovery, but recover she did with the help of counseling and all of us being honest about our family's lifestyle and what needed to change.

Wendy Northrup, mother of three young adults, peace educator,
Ashland, Virginia

We talked about sex openly and early, often at the supper table, but I tried to make it part of other casual conversations as well. We limited sexually explicit movies and television and reading material until we felt that the kids were ready or willing to share it with us. We tried to teach them respect for their bodies, talked about pornography and how it dehumanized, and how intimacy was no longer intimate when it had been shared too many times. We listened to their arguments and tried to respect their opinions on any number of sexual issues, while still letting them know what we believed, why we believed it, and what difference believing it had made in our lives.

Kathleen Chesto, mother of three young adults, author, teacher, Southbury, Connecticut

I don't know exactly what my parents did, but it must have been something because all three of us grew up sexually responsible in a time when that was the exception. Maybe it was the supper table conversations where we talked about sex.

Becky Roberts, 28, married, finishing social work degree, Watertown, Connecticut

When I was about twelve, I checked out some pornography on the Internet. I pretended that I was eighteen. It wasn't that hard to find. After a while I asked myself what this was doing for me and decided it wasn't that great; it wasn't real anyway, and it wasn't worth the risk of getting caught. Sometimes a kid just has to learn through trial and error. Although I never got addicted to it, I know kids at school who are really into it and often that's because their parents are interested in that kind of stuff themselves.

Anonymous, fifteen-year-old boy

When my husband, Sky, died, our seven children ranged in age from three to eighteen. The one thing I would have done differently was not to hide my mourning from the children. I took care not to cry in front of them because I wanted to be strong for them. They thought they had to hold it all in too. Eventually we got family counseling, and that was very good. Our youngest, Matthew, was able to express his sorrow that, "My father will never know that I can read."

Mary Elise Henehan, widow, social worker, and mother of seven, Kalamazoo, Michigan

Matters of Life and Death

What kind of health issues does our family most often face (common colds, chronic illness of some kind, lots of accidents from sports, anxiety and worry, a long-term disability, etc.)? Are there any lifestyle changes that would help our family be healthier?

Do I like how I look? What part of my body would I change if I had the power?

Is anybody in my family, including myself, unhappy with their weight? Is it a valid concern requiring a weight program or does it stem from the need for self-acceptance?

Does our family exercise (run, play sports, go to the gym, etc.)? Is the exercise indoors or outdoors, organized or spontaneous? Is anybody a weak link in the healthy body department? What would it take to change this?

Are there any addictions in my family of origin or my current family? (Consider alcohol, drugs, nicotine, food, sex; even work, hobbies, TV, or computer-related addictions.) How did (does) my family deal with the addiction?

Am I satisfied with the physical, intellectual, emotional, spiritual balance in my life? If something is out of kilter, what would it take to bring it back in balance?

Have I talked with my children in an age-appropriate way about their sexuality? If not, when would be a good time to do this?

If you could pick one contribution you'd still like to make to the world before you die, what would it be?

CHAPTER 7

Peacemaking
How to Get On with Getting Along

Heidi and Tanya were both four years old, next-door neighbors, and best friends. That doesn't mean they didn't fight. I had given Heidi a treasured doll from my childhood that Christmas, and the girls wanted to play with it. The problem was that they both wanted to have it at the same time. A tug-of-war ensued as they both pulled from opposite directions. The head came off. I don't know if they were more upset about breaking the doll or fearful of my reaction. I shared both these feelings myself. In a flash of parental wisdom, all I said was, "When people fight over something, everybody loses" and put the doll away—for several years.

Peace and property are inextricably linked. Whether it's in the home or between nations, fighting breaks out when you have something I want. It might be a doll, it might be land, it might be oil. It is unrealistic to expect that we can equalize the whole world in terms of material goods. Children learn from an early age that some people have more, some less, than others. We begin to teach peacemaking during those mundane tugs-of-war over toys.

Not all conflict, however, is based on need or greed. Sometimes the root of conflict is pride or quest for power. In these cases the "property" is self-esteem or reputation. Another source of conflict is simple ignorance and fear of the unknown. This is the conflict that results in racial tension, wars over religion, or clashes over conflicting values.

If a person is going to make a difference in the cause of peace, he or she has got to learn to get along with others. The most brilliant, energetic, and committed activist will be ineffective if he or she can't work well with other people—friends, enemies, and everyone in between.

My husband and I have long worked in the arena of peacemaking, from quelling racial tensions in the sixties to protesting the Vietnam War to working for a nuclear freeze in the seventies. And then we started having children. We wondered if we could still maintain as active a role in these civic issues. We couldn't. Attending meetings every night of the week did not mix well with being responsible parents. We did find, however, that some of the same principles we learned about dealing with national or international conflicts could be applied in the home. Eventually, we realized that we were learning more about the root causes of fighting and how to resolve conflicts through our little community of the family than we had ever learned as activists. It seemed to be simply a matter of transferring these principles to larger and more distant groups of people.

We were also struck with how easy it was for tempers to flare in the family, for each of us to fight for our own way, and for squabbles to be a constant companion. If this little community of people who were of the same race, religion, and economic level, who held similar values and were bonded by love and genetics could fight over who sat where in the car, was there any hope for the world?

Gradually we refined our parenting skills, which meant honing communication and problem-solving skills. It took longer for us to recognize that the source of our arguments with one another was the need that both of us had to be right. Each step we took, we found ourselves ruminating about how the family was just a microcosm of the world and that the same principles we used to settle fights at home might indeed be used with any group or nation that experienced anger and was in conflict.

BASIC PRINCIPLES OF GOOD COMMUNICATION

Just as nurturing children of compassion and commitment starts with basic good-parenting practices, teaching children to be peacemakers starts with the basic communication and problem-solving skills that have been known to family life educators and insightful parents for years. I'll summarize them here. The bibliography notes references for readers who might want to review the literature in more depth.

If a verbal and nonverbal message conflict, the nonverbal message is more powerful.

This is another way of saying that actions speak louder than words. If I tell a child that hitting is not the way to solve a problem yet I use spanking as a punishment, my words are hollow. If a nation says it wants peace but won't sign a nuclear nonproliferation treaty . . .

If a positive and negative message conflict, the negative message is more powerful.

If a teacher says to a student, "You are a good and worthy human being, but you're not very smart," the child will focus on the message that he or she is not smart. If I receive ninety-five positive evaluations and five negative evaluations of a program I've just done, I have been known to sit and stew over the five.

Listening is not the same as being quiet.

Effective listening means assuring the speaker that you understand what he or she is trying to say. Even though it can sound trite at times, the classic active listening formula of "I hear you saying that . . ." still holds magic for defusing many arguments before they escalate. Once we understand the person's (or country's) needs, *and they know we understand,* negotiation is possible.

Separate morality from feelings.

Feelings are neither right nor wrong; they simply are. Morality comes into play if I act to hurt another. "I feel angry at you for taking my toy (neutral), so I'm going to take something of yours (wrong)."

Use "I" statements rather than "You" statements.

Speaking for yourself like this helps defuse defensiveness when sharing negative feelings. "I felt upset when you didn't keep your promise." Instead of "You make me so upset when you don't keep your promises."

Affirmation and appreciation keep relationships healthy.

Some psychologists refer to emotional bank accounts, in which positive input is considered a deposit and negative input is a debit. If all that is exchanged is negative, the bank account will soon be overdrawn. A child (or friend or colleague) can handle the occasional negative feedback if it is given in the context of regular positive feedback.

Never say "never" or "always."

It's hard to eat those words later, and you will eat them, because such blanket statements aren't true anyway. Furthermore, when you say that your child "never" listens, you're not giving him or her any credit at all, and that is hurtful.

BASIC PRINCIPLES OF CONFLICT RESOLUTION

Some concepts have been proven again and again. They are worth repeating here.

You can ask a person to change but you can't make the person change.
Changing yourself is hard enough. Others may decide to change as a result of your influence, but that's their decision. "You should stop being so mean to me. I wish you'd quit it" probably won't work for long, if at all. Treating the other person with respect might not magically prompt a change, but it might eventually have an impact.

Don't get in the middle of other people's conflicts.
Whether it's between toddlers or nations, it's best to exercise healthy restraint before judging who's right or wrong. Unless one side has an unfair advantage or there is physical harm, urge them to settle it themselves.

Consider using one of the five C's of conflict resolution.

- Concede: I don't care that much, I'll give in.

- Compromise: Take turns or meet in the middle.

- Chance: Toss a coin or pick numbers.

- Create a New Solution: Brainstorm a new way that everyone likes.

- Consensus: Mix compromise and creating solutions, so dialogue leads to a mutually agreeable decision that everyone can support even if it's not their preference.

Provide a safety valve.
Sometimes anger is too intense to allow clear thinking, and a cooling-off period is needed. For families, punching a pillow or punching bag, getting away, going for a walk, listening to calming music, or writing down feelings

might help. For groups, taking a break, looking for a way to save face, or bringing in a mediator may be appropriate.

Use forums such as family meetings.

A family meeting gives each person in the family a voice and a place to take grievances. Knowing how to hear everyone out and come up with a mutually agreeable solution is a life skill transferable to all stages and places of life. We used family meetings periodically with more success than not. Anyone could put an agenda item on the list that was always on the refrigerator. When the kids were young, the length of discussion was measured in minutes. We learned it was important to write down our decisions, and thus the kids learned the power of being secretary. Our biggest problem was that as the kids got older they started to notice a pattern. It seemed that every time we'd have a family meeting they would end up with more work. We backed off having formal meetings, and if a decision needed to be made we would disguise it as dinner. This is also the source of one of our family's favorite Dad quotes: "Well, why don't we try it for a week (or a month) and then evaluate."

BASIC PRINCIPLES OF CHILD DISCIPLINE

Discipline is not solely about whether one is strict or lenient. It's not just about doling out punishments. At its essence, child discipline is primarily about being a disciplined and calm *parent* so that you can think clearly enough to know where to draw a line and how to follow through. Sometimes this means saying "no."

Try a nurturing no.

When "getting to yes" is not working, the wise parent tries a different approach. Parenting educator Sharon Froom suggests that children need two arms around them: a "yes" arm and a "no" arm.

The "yes arm" affirms the person and behaviors that are appropriate. The "no arm" stops behaviors that are inappropriate and not allowed. A formula that helps parents implement this is: ask ➜ warn ➜ consequence. Here are some examples.

For toddlers:

Mom: "Please come help me pick up your toys."

Toddler: (ten minutes later) "Can I have a drink?"

Mom: "After you help me pick up your toys." (You can't have a drink until you help me.)

For young children and preteens:

Mom: "You need to pick up your room before dinner."

Child: "I'll do it as soon as this show is over." (forgets)

Mom: "Don't forget to do your room, we're eating in half an hour." (No dinner until it's done.)

For teens:

Dad: "The trash needs to go out before you go out with your friends."

Teen: (two hours later) "My friends are here. I'm leaving."

Dad: "Not until the trash goes out." (You can't leave until it's done)

All this sounds so simple, but there are many ways parents mess this up:

- Rather than let the consequences play out, they nag, lecture, and use their anger as punishment.

- They pick consequences that are too harsh and thus evoke resentment.

- They use consequences that are too soft or irrelevant to the child.

- They forget or get distracted and don't follow through.

- They get derailed by the child's anger, and the original expectation gets lost.

In my years of doing family therapy, one of the concepts I find most difficult to get across to parents is that not spanking does not have to equal being lenient.

From a conversation with Sharon Froom, therapist and

parent educator, Kalamazoo, Michigan

Find alternatives to corporal punishment.

Although many parents were raised with corporal punishment with no apparent lifelong scars, almost all family-life professionals today have abandoned this as an effective strategy. The advantage of getting a powerful message across quickly is outweighed by its disadvantages. It sends a mixed message that hitting is an acceptable way to solve problems for the parent but not for the child. Because it takes little thinking on the parent's part, it short-circuits learning better ways to discipline. And because it usually takes place in an emotionally charged setting, otherwise reasonable parents are vulnerable to stepping over the line into child abuse. Stressed parents with minimal coping skills are even more at risk to use corporal punishment as a first and only option. When used as a last resort, it means that we're already too angry to think clearly or moderately.

To eliminate corporal punishment from our behavior, however, we need to have other disciplinary options that work. Here's a start:

- Let natural or logical consequences be the teacher.

- Use time-outs when natural consequences are not practical (rule of thumb: use one minute for each year of the child's age).

- When children are young, physically stop them, hold them, or separate them from others when necessary.

- If a lesson doesn't need to be learned, distract the child and redirect play.

- As parent, stay calm, hold your ground, and be a nonanxious presence.

- When the setting allows, talk with the child about what was wrong and discuss better ways to deal with the problem

I confess that I have spanked my kids but not often. I don't think they've been scarred for life. Looking back at those situations now, I think that if I had made a firm commitment not to spank, it would have forced me to go beyond my impulses and to think harder about other more creative and effective ways to discipline when I was at my wit's end. It takes intelligence and effort to resist the impulse to spank and to think of an alternative solution. But intelligence and the willingness to expend effort are marks of a mature adult.

A WORD ABOUT CHILDREN'S PLAY

In regard to peacemaking, much has been discussed about encouraging cooperative games and discouraging war toys. Parents sometimes say to me, "I used toy guns as a child, and I turned out OK. Besides, if you don't buy them a gun they'll just make one with their finger anyway." I'll speak to that from my own bias. Many kids will, in fact, create guns in the absence of toy guns. But war and killing are real and ugly. Real people get hurt. I don't believe that war games are child's play, especially in today's climate of gang warfare and school shootings. To glorify or trivialize war as a game puts our children out of touch with reality. It teaches them to solve a problem by using a gun or brute power rather than using their intellect or creativity. It also makes it appear that shooting someone has no real consequences. The child just gets up and continues to play. Because children are children, this line between fantasy and reality often gets fuzzy—maybe not for every child and not every time. But for children who are vulnerable or at risk, simulating violence can lead to the real thing.

In our own home, we didn't buy what we called war toys. We thought that our children had enough to stimulate their imaginations and that they didn't need this negative trigger. We bent the rule when it came to squirt guns, as long as they were pink or yellow—in other words, as long as they were clearly child's toys and not simulating a real gun. (Note: In our family it has been determined that Risk is not a war game. It has been redefined as a strategy game.)

We also became known as the gurus of cooperative games. Once the children realized what we were doing, however, this didn't go over as well because they thought the games sounded wimpy. A few of them caught their fancy but if asked now, I bet most of our kids would groan if I suggest playing a cooperative game. It just sounds too prissy, and we're a family of competitive individuals.

DEALING WITH BULLIES

One of the most perplexing dilemmas for parents who want to teach their children to be peacemakers is how to deal with bullies. A natural impulse is to protect the child through adult intervention. For example, most schools teach students to call a teacher or monitor when bullied on the playground. This is good, but adults aren't always going to be available. Another approach is to teach the child to defend him- or herself, perhaps through martial arts. There are schools that teach Aikido or Judo in a way that emphasizes self-discipline and self-defense rather than aggression. Often the greatest benefit of this approach is that children gain self-confidence, which makes them less vulnerable targets to the bully. But such training takes time and investment. Parents can also help a child understand that many bullies were bullied themselves when they were younger or that they feel insecure; they lash out to make themselves look powerful or important.

Sometimes, however, a child just needs a snappy but noninflammatory reply. In his book, *Sticks and Stones,* Scott Cooper provides some retorts. My favorites are the "Mighty Might" and the "Reverse Tease."

In the "Mighty Might" the child simply replies to a taunt with "You might (or could) be right." For example:

Parent: Let's say I'm a kid at school and I start ragging on your basketball skills by saying, "Gee, can't you make any of your shots?"

Child: You might be right.

Parent: I might be right? I am right. Just look at your shots.

Child: You might be right.

Parent: Is that all you've got to say, "You might be right"?

Child: You might be right.

The calm (and monotonous) repetition of "You might be right" is the trick to making this work. It's hard to fight with someone who's agreeing with you. Yet the victim saves face by holding the mental reservation that "Then again, you might *not* be right."

In the "Reverse Tease" the victim agrees with the bully in a funny, sarcastic way.

For example:

Parent: Hey, what's your problem, don't you know how to walk?

Child: You're just too kind.

Parent: Yeah, well, you look like a penguin when you walk.

Child: Thanks, I've always wanted to be a penguin.

Parent: Just look in the mirror, you've become one.

Child: Oh my gosh, you're right, call my parents!

The parent or teacher helps the child learn either of these techniques by practicing many typical jeers that might be used and letting the child respond with "You might be right" or by turning the tease into a joke.

GETTING ALONG WITH PEOPLE WHO ARE DIFFERENT FROM ME

So far I've talked chiefly about dealing with squabbles that occur primarily in the home or immediate neighborhood, mostly with younger children. These are important fundamentals, but we must go beyond learning to get along with people who are our friends and acquaintances and who are similar to us (same ethnic group, same socioeconomic status, same background). It can be more complex when the people we deal with have different cultural assumptions, values, and experiences from ours. Often the difference is visible, such as skin color, ethnicity, poverty, or handicap. Other times it may be interior, such as different values or sexual orientation. We wanted our children to be able to reach out with compassion beyond the home to those who were different from them and to make a difference in how the larger world works.

Letter writing and petition signing are actions that affect the larger world and can be taken without leaving the comfort of our homes. Since young children aren't capable of writing a letter to political representatives on their own, we parents would explain a current peace cause, such as wanting the government to institute a nuclear freeze, and ask the children if they would like to sign it. Seeing us occasionally write a letter to the editor planted an idea in their minds that could come into play as they got older.

Although some of our children had left home by the time the Family Pledge of Nonviolence had been written, it became a tool for the rest of us to explore what it really meant to be a person of peace. Most of our kids' resistance to taking the pledge revolved around the section that deals with

Family Pledge of Nonviolence

Making peace must start within ourselves and in our family. Each of us, members of the
_____ family, commit ourselves as best we can to become nonviolent and
peaceable people:

To Respect Self and Others
To respect myself, to affirm others and to avoid uncaring criticism,
hateful words, physical attacks and self-destructive behavior.

To Communicate Better
To share my feelings honestly, to look for safe ways to express my anger,
and to work at solving problems peacefully.

To Listen
To listen carefully to one another, especially those who disagree with me,
and to consider others' feelings and needs rather than insist on having my own way.

To Forgive
To apologize and make amends when I have hurt another,
to forgive others, and to keep from holding grudges.

To Respect Nature
To treat the environment and all living things,
including our pets, with respect and care.

To Play Creatively
To select entertainment and toys that support our family's values and to
avoid entertainment that makes violence look exciting, funny or acceptable.

To Be Courageous
To challenge violence in all its forms whenever I encounter it, whether at home,
at school, at work, or in the community, and to stand with others who are treated unfairly.

This is our pledge. These are our goals. We will check ourselves on what we have pledged
once a month on _____ for the next twelve months so that we can
help each other become more peaceable people.

Pledging family members sign below:

_____   _____

_____   _____

_____   _____

"Eliminating violence, one family at a time, starting with our own."

Families Against Violence Advocacy Network
c/o Institute for Peace & Justice, 4144 Lindell #408, St. Louis, MO 63108
314-533-4445 • E-mail: ipj@ipj-ppj.org
Web: www.ipj-ppj.org

169

avoiding entertainment that makes violence look exciting, funny, or acceptable (see chapter 5). It was a helpful vehicle, however, for coming up with an agreement on our family's values and strategies for being peacemakers beyond just "Be nice and don't fight." For preschoolers that might be enough, but for teens we wanted to delve deeper.

CONFRONTING INJUSTICE

"If you want peace, work for justice," said Pope Paul VI. When all is right with the world, governments are just and people are good. In such a climate, all that's necessary is calling people to their best selves and figuring out how to help the weak or disenfranchised meet their basic needs and get a fair deal. But of course we don't yet live in that world, and probably never will. Some laws are wrong, some governments are bad, some school policies are flawed, and some families are dysfunctional. All of us are selfish at times and imperfect most of the time. Sometimes the evil is in the system, sometimes in the other person, and sometimes in ourselves.

After an honest self-examination in which I uncover the part I might inadvertently be playing in an injustice, it might be necessary to take a stand against another person or the established power. Rosa Parks did this in 1955 when she refused to give up her seat to a white person. Ministers do it when they refuse to betray a confidence even when ordered to do so by a court of law. When human life or dignity is at risk, sometimes drastic measures are justified. When there are no other remedies, civil disobedience might even be considered if we are to be true to a higher value and power. Civil disobedience is a grave step, however, and should be taken only with a spirit of humility, courage, nonviolence, and a willingness to face the consequences of one's action. It goes without saying, but I will say it lest I be misunderstood, that civil disobedience involving violence to another human being is never justified—even for a good cause.

Most of us, however, are not likely to face decisions of civil disobedience. The injustices that permeate our communities may more often involve people who feel left out or disenfranchised. For example, there may be an in-group and an out-group in a school. Often those in the out-group become the troublemakers. They may be a minority, they may be poor, they may just wear weird clothes, but somehow they feel that they don't have as much power, prestige, or stuff as the in-group. It doesn't seem fair or just to them. It's tempting for the out-group, whose members may think of themselves as victims, to want to even things out by whatever means necessary. It's tempting, but not right. It's the job of parents and others in authority to reach out to those who are left out and help them rise above the injustice. Unrealistic? Perhaps. Impossible? No. Nelson Mandela did it. And if the bully, victim, or gang member objects, saying, "I'm no Nelson Mandela!" I say, "You could be."

Being wronged is not an excuse for anarchy or for disrespecting other people. If I speak against an individual or government, my words must carry the tone of respect for their dignity and lawful authority even though I may seriously disagree with their actions. Isn't this the same way a wise parent disciplines a child? Isn't this the way we want our children to relate to us?

The Vogt Kids Speak

As for war toys and violent games, it seems to me that children are indeed impressionable during their early years, and consequently you should limit what it is that they have access to. However, I also believe that once a kid gets to be around fourteen or fifteen, you should probably cut back with the restrictions and trust your kid to make his own decisions and to think for himself.

Dacian

I agree that limiting war toys was a valuable constraint. However, these limitations did not last forever. I don't remember the exact age, but once I was probably around twelve or thirteen, restrictions on these types of toys decreased. I appreciated the fact that my parents recognized my increasing maturity and eventually allowed me to make my own choices.

Brian

I know a lot of adults worry about their kids getting involved in gangs and all, but even though I go to a school in the inner city I've never noticed any problems or felt unsafe. We have gangs, but they're more like "fashion gangs." Kids like to dress the same way. There are cliques that like to hang out together, and some kids may feel excluded, but it's not like they have gang wars. I suppose some places do.

Aaron

A Daughter's Response

Someone to Listen

One of the best things my mother ever did for me was give me someone other than herself to talk to. Mothers and teenage daughters often have strained relationships. They swing back and forth between being soul mates and boxing opponents so often that the relationship gets whittled down to silence. My mother and I followed this pattern. Our discussions so quickly turned into arguments, and arguments into power struggles. Voices rose. Doors slammed. Once I laughed at my mother as she screamed at me in the car (not a good idea). Another time I slapped her (even worse). Most of the time I just answered her probing questions with silence. Even now, with my teen years well behind me, I cringe a little when I feel like she's trying to run my life again. She claims that I still shut her out occasionally.

But way back when I was too young to know that disagreeing with my parents was an option, my mother handed me a godmother. Mary was an old friend of my parents, someone they trusted. So I decided to trust her too. When I was young, I was comforted by the idea that she would take me in if my parents died. And I got presents from her every once in awhile. But as I entered my teen years, our relationship grew. Mary would stop by whenever she was in town and take me out for lunch or coffee. And we would talk the way I was sure adults talked, without a lot of judgments or advice, but opinions and feelings. Talking to Mary was a lot like talking to an older version of my friends.

I could be open with my godmother precisely because she *wasn't* going to change my curfew or tell me I couldn't go to a certain party. She just listened. In short, she was cool. She could even explain my parents to me in a way that made them seem less totalitarian. She said she understood how my mother felt because her daughter didn't talk to her either. Mary didn't get defensive when I didn't agree with her or get frustrated when I got fickle. Talking to Mary was also a lot like talking to a more objective version of my mother.

I never asked my godmother if she kept our conversations to herself. I assumed that she didn't run to inform my mother about my life, but I wonder if part of me didn't want her to tell my mother the things I couldn't say without yelling. I certainly heard some opinions very similar to my mother's from Mary's mouth. Yet when they came from Mary, I didn't feel obliged to disagree. In those years when my parents were too close to talk to, my godmother was a bridge that kept us in touch.

Heidi

Other Families' Stories

We blew it once by insisting that our teenage son attend a church-sponsored family gathering on New Year's Eve. He wanted to be with friends, so he didn't participate at all and made it awkward for everyone. By the time we "let him go," his friends were not to be found, so he felt that we had ruined his evening. Later, with our other children, we were more compromising and gave choices, e.g. "How about coming to the church gathering for a while and then joining your friends?"

Peter Edwards, father of four young adults, Fargo, North Dakota

My family is pacifist and never believed in war toys so my parents didn't buy me any G.I. Joe dolls. Well actually, they did get me one—a medic.

Josh Thompson, 21, college student, Baltimore, Maryland

It was hard, but I made sure my children knew that they had to live with the consequences of their choices. It's best if this can start when they're really young and the stakes are low, like when they're starting to walk. Let them fall down. Don't try to rescue them from all pain.

Pam Winston, single parent of two young adults, Covington, Kentucky

We decided not to allow toy guns even though we knew they could make them out of a stick or use a finger to simulate a gun. We did allow swords because that seemed more in the fantasy realm. When we visited Williamsburg, we decided to allow the purchase of a gun there because it was more like a historical artifact. When we discussed taking the Family Pledge of Nonviolence, the kids were concerned about whether they could see the latest *Star Wars* movie. Probably even more important than any of our decisions about war toys was the discussion that the pledge prompted about our values. Generally we tried to find a middle ground so that a forbidden fruit did not appear too appealing. Despite all our care to raise our children to be peacemakers and to treat them equally, we have noticed a difference between the girls and our boy. Jonathan seems to have a need to be the "warrior" in the sense that he puts himself in places of risk to test his courage and bravery. A lot of this happens in play, and we didn't notice it as much with the girls.

Alejandro and Mary Aguilera-Titus, parents of three young children, Alexandria, Virginia

I have spent my career trying to disprove that all police officers are power mongers who use authority to prop themselves up. After some work, I have been able to engage the entire alternative group in our small town who previously felt disenfranchised by all authority figures. I have always helped kids along with what I do for work, but after Columbine I am much more driven to help all I can. I know that I am not responsible for Columbine, but by God, I am not going to live through that again without the knowledge that I am doing everything I can for the teen community.

Neal Schwieterman, police officer, Paonia, Colorado

When one or more of the children/teens weren't getting along . . . they had to sit on the floor Indian style, with knees touching the person they were in conflict with, holding hands, looking one another in the eyes until they decided what the problem was about, figured out how to resolve it, and asked for forgiveness.

Anne C. Keough, mother of four young adults, Duncanville, Texas

When discipline needed to be served (we avoided using the word punishment) I would give the boys a list of three to choose from: 1) No Playstation or computer games for the weekend; 2) Write and number fifty sentences that read, "I will listen the first time I am asked"; or 3) Fold four loads of clothes and put them away.

Cindy Stevens, mother of two preteens, Whitefish Bay, Wisconsin

Late in my active-parenting years I gained some insight into how my reactions to my children's anger was compromising my parenting. I recognized that whenever my children responded to correction with anger I was quick to move from regarding them as wrong to regarding me as wrong. As a result, I hedged on consequences. I would often start talking at them rather than letting the consequence do its work. A couple of one-line mindsets proved particularly helpful: "They do not have to like it, but they do have to do it." and "I don't have to have the final word, but we both need for me to have final say." Continually repeating these words out loud would have been harsh, but keeping them in my mind kept me focused and gave me the courage not to abdicate my job as parent.

**Sharon Froom, mother of step- and adopted young adults,
therapist and parenting educator, Kalamazoo, Michigan**

Who Disturbs Your Peace?

An individual I have a lot of difficulty getting along with is _____
because . . .

I get annoyed at people who . . .

When I feel angry, it helps if I . . .

Is there anything you've read so far in this book that makes you mad or
that you disagree with? What are you doing as a result of that feeling?

CHAPTER 8

Spirituality
Sharing Faith That Will Last after They Leave Home

The family in the pew in front of us was disgusting. There were two young girls, perhaps four and seven, and they just sat there—quietly, not bothering anyone and looking at their books of Bible stories. Meanwhile our kids (seven, four, and two) squirmed, pestered each other, and made car sounds. I was sure that the parents in front of us must have drugged their kids ahead of time or threatened them with death by sugar withdrawal if they weren't good in church. Actually, we had already done the sugar withdrawal thing by saying we would stay for donuts after church only if they were good during the service. I yearned for the day when mine would be old enough to sit still and understand the service. I was sure that we were incompetent parents and that this had to be the hardest part of trying to nurture our children in the faith that we found so dear.

Of course, I was wrong again. The children in front of us weren't drugged to be quiet, and this was hardly the most challenging part of raising children in a religious faith—but it felt like it at the time. I have since decided that some children by nature are just quieter and more compliant. Not ours. Eventually, we saw worse behavior by other children in church, and it made us feel better about ourselves but not about how we introduce faith to our children.

In the short run, we tried a variety of stopgap measures, such as preparing the children ahead of time, bringing quiet (religiously oriented if possible) diversions such as books. Cheerios filled in the gaps. We tried sitting up front so that the children could see—although this made the escape route more cumbersome if crying got out of hand. We went through phases of taking the younger ones to the nursery or going to different worship services so that one of us could watch the kids at home. Some "crying rooms" were OK; others were merely places to trade germs and forlorn looks between parents. There are pros and cons to each of these methods, but regardless of the strategy, the bigger questions loomed: Was any of this instilling in our children a love for the sacred? Was it nurturing their spiritual nature?

Fortunately, at the time we were part of a small Christian community that had some very talented Montessori teachers who understood how to touch young children's lives with meaning and talk to them through symbols. Outside of church time we gathered with maybe five or six children ranging from ages two to five, and different parents would take turns designing a child-oriented service around a religious theme. We called it "kiddie lit" for "children's liturgy." We had solved our immediate problem, but what about all those other children outside our small group? As socially conscious adults, we knew we had to offer such opportunities to other families. Of course we didn't invent this wheel, but it's nice to see that now many churches and synagogues offer special children's programs.

We thought that if we kept up this approach—listening to our children's needs, searching out (or creating) interesting, relevant, and fun religious experiences—we'd be home free. We hoped that because we tried very hard to live our faith that this example would be enough. Our children would not spew the typical complaints about not wanting to go to church and would sidestep the later rebellion of dropping out when they left home.

Wrong again, at least in part. We did get complaints about going to church from various kids at various ages. Occasionally we would compromise and agree to have "church at home" if they would plan it. This meant we would use the Scripture readings of the day and talk about them in the living room around a lighted candle. Jim and I knew that according to the official criteria of our church, this didn't "count," but we believed that it counted a lot to our children. It showed them that faith happened in more places than just the church building, that we could access God wherever we were and in our own words, and that we weren't heartless ogres. We were willing to meet the kids partway—at least some of the time.

So what's all this got to do with nurturing a social conscience in children? Not everyone who espouses a faith in God has a social conscience. And not everyone who does good in the world is connected to an organized religion. And certainly there are lots of decent folk doing significant service in our world who may not believe in God or be part of a faith community. Having talked and corresponded with hundreds of socially conscious people in the course of writing this book, however, it seems apparent to me that faith, or at least a sense that there is more to life than the present, physical world, has been a significant influence in many people's decision to go beyond their personal needs and wants so as to be there for others. Whether we call it religion, faith, spirituality, or a search for the sacred in life, these are concepts that have led many people to be altruistic and to make this world a better place by their lives.

Sometimes it starts with religion. Most mainline religions have a social teaching that, when taken seriously, impels the believer to care for the poor and oppressed, to respect all people and the earth. Usually religions at least suggest that there are times when a person might be called to sacrifice his or her own desires or comfort for the common good, a higher good, or the final good of life after death.

Religions also talk about the redemptive nature of suffering—not that we seek suffering for its own sake, but that in the course of life, suffering happens. Belief in an afterlife, a reincarnated life, or solidarity with the sufferings of Jesus, Mohammed, Moses, or Buddha gives meaning to our own suffering and those who suffer unjustly. Faith in something bigger than ourselves and this world not only makes life's problems bearable, it also can stir our hearts to be generous beyond what seems necessary and to sacrifice self even when there's nothing in it for us. The witness of others who have turned the other cheek, been ready to sacrifice an only son, or risked their lives because of faith can prompt the receptive heart to do the same. Organized religion, when true to itself, not only motivates believers toward sacrificial love, it also can provide comrades and a structure in which to accomplish these noble ends.

But sometimes it works the other way. A person intuitively knows the fairness of caring for others in need and eventually sees that he or she can't do it alone, can't do it even with a lot of other people, that a higher power is needed to make sense of all of this and especially to make sense of life when it doesn't work out right or justly. They may attach to an established religion at this time or they may find like-minded, committed people who become a community for them, albeit secular, as they rally around a common cause.

Still others were brought up within a particular faith tradition but drift or intentionally move away from it as adults. They may not practice within an organized religion, but usually it has shaped how they look at life. As adults they may see the imperfections of religion in how it is lived by those around them, but they've still been touched by the notion that there is a God and perhaps even life after death. It's the old question of who is more faith filled—the person who acknowledges a God and claims a faith but does little as a result, or the person who claims no faith but acts according to the spirit of living for others?

All of these concepts were swirling around both in my brain and in Jim's as we tried to forge the way that we would raise our own children in faith. We saw plenty of people who were nominally religious. They went to church on Sunday or synagogue on Saturday. Now that we have been exposed to more religions, we know that this same phenomenon is also present within the Muslim, Hindu, and other traditions. It's faith by custom and habit. We wanted more for our children.

We wanted their faith to be active and to lead them to action, to be something that didn't depend on outside or cultural supports. In a romantic sense, I imagined, What if, as adults, they found themselves in a world that had changed so much that churches or communities of faith were not easily found? What if they were in a far-off land that had no religion or a different religion than what was their heritage? Would they have anything in them that could anchor them to the holy in a culture that might not be so anchored? We wanted them to have an interior appreciation for the value of prayer, for how symbols and ritual can be a window to the spiritual, and for how our journeys to the end of life are not individual journeys but communal ones intertwined with many other people of goodwill.

Of course, we raised them in our faith and hoped that they would choose that as their own. But we decided that we would be happy if they stayed true to the values of our faith even if the form didn't fit Catholicism or even Christianity.

These ideals guided us as we decided what to emphasize in the religious education of our children. Since we wanted them to believe on their own, we knew we had to go beyond mere rules and traditions to touch their hearts, even if it meant bending the rules at times. Here are a few principles we tried to follow.

Live what we believe ourselves.

Maybe that was easy for us because both Jim and I worked for the Catholic Church for many years. But it meant not only going to Mass on Sundays but also being active members of our parish and devoting a lot of energy to building the small Christian communities that nurtured our faith in a more personal way. Actually, by the time our kids were preteens, they assumed that they were doing much more "religious" stuff than their peers, and they probably thought that our work for the church was a burden. Mostly we tried to "do" and not preach, although they may have experienced this differently.

Make it relevant.

There were very few things we did with our children simply because they were rules. We always tried to connect a prayer, an action, or a service with a reason. We pray because it's a way of communicating with God and other people. It also helps us understand our inner selves. We do communal worship because it strengthens the community. We're doing a particular service project because it's the right thing to do; and besides, our faith compels us to do it. We always tried to give both a human reason and a spiritual reason for doing things. (Don't lie because lying is wrong—and because if you lie, I won't be able to trust you.) That way, we figured that if they ever were on that deserted island or in a crowd of people who were disenchanted with faith or morals, our kids would have more to go on than "because God, the Bible, or my parents said so." It's a corollary to the parental axiom, Do it because I said so. That may work with preschoolers, but it doesn't prepare a person for adult life, adult choices, and adult spirituality. Of course, this also makes for longer and sometimes tiring conversations. Some sophisticated kids can even manipulate the "Why" game to prolong a debate over an insignificant issue. Eventually we learned to recognize this ploy and would just answer, "Because I said so."

Ritualize important events.

This is especially helpful with young children because they find comfort in the repetition of a prayer or in a custom repeated every year, such as lighting Advent candles or inviting a neighbor to Thanksgiving dinner. Rote memorization has a role, but because we were aiming at spirituality that would last, we needed something more internalized, more from the heart. With older children, repetition isn't as important as creativity. We found that using classic elements of ritual such as silence, song, candles, water, unified movement, and tangible objects could symbolize something that words couldn't always do justice to. We wanted to stir their souls, not just pay a weekly debt.

Link faith with justice.

In my mind this is a natural connection because faith led me to be passionate about justice. But for some, especially teens, it often works the other way around. There came a time in our children's lives when the prayer services, creative as they might have been, just seemed too childish to them. We found that their idealism and energy attracted them to getting involved in the needs of the neighborhood, city, and country. Sometimes they did these activities with us as a family, but more and more that became unappealing. The preferred outlets for living their faith became Habitat for Humanity, soup kitchens, trips to Appalachia or Mexico for service, and so forth. Thank God for other adults, often a little younger than us, who were willing to supervise these outings. I'm not sure how much direct God-talk there was on most of these excursions. There didn't have to be.

Make it fun.

This may sound a little frivolous for important, deep things such as faith and justice, but we learned the hard way that we needed to meet the kids where they were. They learned to link church with positive experiences. Eventually, they would learn that this same church that understood their desire to be with their friends and eat pizza was also available to them in times of crisis or tragedy. In due course, we hoped they would learn as well that *they* were the church and needed to be there for others in crisis or tragedy. Thus, at religious events we allowed junk food that we might have restricted otherwise; we let them act out the Scriptures in crazy teenage ways; we encouraged their friends to come along; we took religious holy days and secular commemorative days such as Kwanza or the bombing of Hiroshima and created special events around them.

Let the community work.

Although parents are ultimately the primary religious educators of their children, other adults in our small Christian community managed to reach our children when we had become dumb or antiquated in their eyes. It was the other children in the community who sometimes made it acceptable to take part in a protest or talk about their faith. It was godparents; and now that we have older children, the elder ones who occasionally mentor their younger siblings. I smile and think, "Boy, they sound just like a parent."

When all else fails, pray.

When all else fails—and it will—pray. Pray for the child, pray for your children's friends and enemies, pray for their schools and teams, and pray for yourself that you may have the wisdom and courage needed to be a caring and effective parent. Prayer serves several purposes. It reminds us as parents that some things truly are out of our control and that after we've done our best we need to let go. Prayer can curb the urge to nag because we've turned it over to a higher power. I find that a strange thing happens in my own prayer in that I start out praying for the child (often that he or she will change), and I end up praying for something bigger and harder: that I will change or know what to do.

What if you're not a religious person and you don't believe in prayer? Prayer may not be your habit. There are many ways to look beyond an immediate crisis and get perspective. Prayer works for me, but for others it might be meditation, physical activity, reading, or conversations with mentors. The important thing is to stop stewing and complaining and make room for your heart and mind to gain perspective.

AFTER THEY LEAVE HOME

Now that I think back on those early days of toddlers squirming in the pew, I reflect wistfully that those were the easy days. I had control. I could rouse the children's imagination with simple or syrupy talk of baby Jesus and how much God loved them. They were inclined to believe everything I said and honor me as almost a god myself. They went to church because I took them—promising them doughnuts afterward was enough of a reward. All it took was effort.

Now that we have three young adults plus one who thinks he is, it's much more complicated. Our children have minds of their own, as it should be. Now I pray for wisdom to know when to speak and when to shut up. Did all the effort we put into those earlier years make any difference? I think so, but only time will tell.

Religion was probably the issue that elicited the most angst among the parents I interviewed. Invariably, parents would say that they felt their son or daughter had a solid spiritual base and that they were comfortable with that but that they were not active in an organized religion. Since faith was very important to many of my respondents, this was a concern. Some had made their peace with it, some had not, and many were still waiting. The jury's still out with our own young adults. I'm cautiously optimistic. I keep reminding myself that their path to God might look very different from the one I took.

I met my husband and God during my college years. I had been raised Catholic and was actively practicing—as was everyone around me in the Catholic college I attended—but I never challenged that belief until college. By inspecting my faith with the help of a supportive college community, my relationship with a personal God deepened, and my faith became my own. This is what I hoped, even expected, for our own children.

So far none of them has chosen to attend a Catholic college, but I consoled myself with the thought that any college worth its salt would have a religious presence on campus and that they would take advantage of this. Maybe. One started going to Mass very regularly during his junior year. (I don't know how much of this was commitment and how much was the enticement of playing in the guitar group. I tried the same technique with our daughter, but she had already given up interest in her flute.) I do know that all of them have had many soul-searching discussions with their peers about the meaning of life and spirituality. Sometimes parts of these discussions trickle home, but for the most part their religious practice, or lack of it, is in their hands. Some colleges have wonderful and attractive campus ministry programs, and if I could direct my child's life at this age, I would say, "Go." But mostly what I've done is ask them to check it out, give it a try, and stay close to God even if they're not close to a church.

The conventional wisdom used to be that many young adults would not associate with the institutional church after they had finished their schooling, but that they would return, at least briefly, at the point of marriage, and more permanently after the birth of their first child. Since the average age of marriage has increased to the late twenties and the gap between marriage and first child is growing, I'm not sure this will hold true in the future. Old patterns and guilt can hold some people for a while, but a ten- to fifteen-year stretch of nonaffiliation is a pretty long hiatus. It is of great concern to me that organized religions may be losing a generation or more of young people. But it is of even greater concern that we may be losing them because we have nothing to offer, or perhaps more accurately, we don't know how to translate the age-old truths of leading a religious life into a language that will touch their hearts.

As Kathleen Chesto says in *Exploring the New Family: Parents and Young Adults in Transition,*

> [Young adults] are the only group other than seniors who have increased their volunteering in projects to assist the poor and the oppressed. They are living the gospel, but they are not reading it. They are spiritual, but they are not religious. Over 90 percent claim they believe in God, but less than 40 percent believe religion is relevant. They have adopted a faith that has lost its sense of community. They have chosen the actions of faith and discarded the rituals that support those actions.

So how do we learn what touches their hearts? By listening to them. This is not to say that thousands of years of spiritual wisdom passed down through the ages is unimportant or not worth teaching. Rather, we need to become intimate enough with young adults to understand the questions they are asking, not the answers we think they need to hear. We have to listen with the ear of someone learning a foreign language. We need to listen not only to the words but also to the whole person if we are to understand the deepest yearnings of their hearts. We then need to respond in language and actions that make sense to them—which may not be the language we grew up with.

We need to listen to the young adults who are still connected with church, but even more we need to search out those who have left. Some of them may have left out of laziness or for selfish reasons, but certainly many have left because the rules were getting in the way of the spirit. The stodginess of a middle-aged church was not able to meet them where they lived their lives. Some have a hole in their soul that they are eager to fill; they just don't realize that the filling station is not on the Internet. Or maybe it is. If meeting them on the Internet is what we must do, then lets go there or find some people who can. Let's go wherever their passions are. Grace builds on nature.

Perhaps the absence of young people from many churches is a symptom of complacency or the settling in of organized religion, in which case the organized religion is being called to a deeper, more relevant spirituality. This is but one more challenge, God's way of pulling us, yanking us to reexamine our deepest beliefs and renew them. Such a challenge would be good for those of us in the middle years of life. Some will say that all young adults go through this developmental stage of leaving religion. That could be, but I'd rather err on the side of paying attention to them.

Although our own young adult children have various degrees of connection with their faith, they are in charge of their relationship with God now. I did make one request of each of them when they graduated from college. I asked them to keep seeking, to not give up on the institutional church if the first one they tried was not life-giving. There is no doubt in my mind that they are good, moral people who are deeply spiritual. Most even go to church. I have confidence that if they keep spirituality and a moral life before them as a value they will find what their hearts long for. Their paths may not look like my path, but they may pull us all onto a better path for the future.

Maybe we've reached that time and place in which traditional supports for faith have evaporated. Our daughter, Heidi, lives in a Muslim village in Africa and has been exposed to a different type of spirituality. How that will mix with what has been planted in her heart only God knows. I trust that.

The Vogt Kids Speak

When we were young (up to age ten or twelve), we really liked the annual Advent calendars Mom always did for us—especially the personalized ones.

Brian and Dacian

We had a lot of family traditions during the time before Christmas. I suppose the purpose was partly to reinforce religious connections as we waited for Christmas. My mom is big on waiting to actually celebrate Christmas until the "real" day, December 25. One thing we usually did was to adopt a family from the "Jesse Tree" at church. I remember wanting to get them Legos, but Mom thought they should get mittens.

I think the more you force someone to go to church as a young adult, the more resistance you will get. I go more often than not.

Dacian

Once a kid is in college, I don't think the parents really have any more influence as to whether or how they will practice a religion. I go to church when I find a good church, and right now I've found one.

Brian

I don't like any of the religious stuff we do. Never did, never will.

Aaron

A Daughter's Response

Church and Faith

I've finally got it. I've been trying for months to come up with the biggest mistake my parents made. Readers of a book on parenting written by my mother deserve to know.

I wish they hadn't made me go to church. It's not spirituality that I resent, but rather the many official practices that define a person as religious.

My parents' faith is active. My childhood memories are peppered with hymns sung at protest marches and prayer services for peace. Catholicism was the fabric that wove connections between working at the local soup kitchen, protesting injustice, repairing low-income housing, recycling, and breaking up fights on the street. As the poster hanging in our dining room proclaimed, "Whatever you did for one of the least of these, you did for me." In some distant way, all decisions were religious decisions.

But none of this is what first comes to mind when I think of religion in the Vogt family. Instead I see the six Vogts on our mandatory march through the church doors every Sunday morning at 10:00. When I was young, I never considered not going. But as I neared junior high age, I started noticing that Mass was being shoehorned into my weekends without anyone asking if I wanted it there. If I had a game on Sunday, I was expected to attend Saturday afternoon Mass. I was allowed to spend Saturday night at a friend's house only if I agreed to be back in time to go to church on Sunday morning and promised not to fall asleep in the pew once there.

My parents' faith is all-embracing. They integrated Seder meals and Kwanza and Earth Day into their Catholicism, but it was still Roman Catholic at heart. They expected their children to grow up with that same unquestioningly Catholic core—or that's how it seemed to me as I sat, bored and fuming, in church.

In one early catechism class I had a little second-grade epiphany as our amateur theologian lectured us to "honor our father and mother." Nobody, I realized, not even the wise college student talking to us, knew who wrote the Bible. I started imagining it as an ancient choose-your-own-adventure story—a good joke on all the priests and nuns. But I held in my blasphemous thoughts, unwilling to risk excommunication by the church or my parents.

My parents' faith is alive. They tried to bring religion to life for us. They encouraged us to find our own meanings in the Bible stories. They patiently explained the spirit behind the rituals. They created new rituals: family nights around candles, banners of butterflies announcing Easter, and even the occasional "church at home" in our pajamas. But at the same time they insisted that we attend religious education classes and Mass. I was told to find my spirituality in everyday living, but also, not to forget my holy days of obligation. The second message, more supported by the church culture, drowned out the first.

As a child, I felt that challenging my parents' religion would have been disciplinary suicide. If I stayed quiet and submitted to the rituals, they would assume I was growing up a good Catholic girl. It wasn't until I went seven hundred miles away to college that I finally started to feel I had the space to explore spirituality. Like so many nineteen year olds, I cut myself free of the Sunday religion hour and got lost instead in late-night discussions of the "opiate of the people," the yearning for a God, and the place of religion in our lives, often even without the addition of mind-altering substances.

During those years, you would have rarely seen me at church, seldom found me cracking open a Bible, and never seen me at a religious retreat. But through conversations and comparisons I started to search for spirituality. I stopped trying to hide from religion and started trying to understand it.

One morning of my junior year of college I found an e-mail from my mother waiting in my inbox. She had been reading some particularly powerful article about the demise of religion in America and was concerned about my "faith development." My mother worried, "maybe I've neglected your religious training."

The woman who had stuffed Catholicism down my throat every Sunday was worried she hadn't done enough? I was about to delete the message without response when my indignation got the better of me. I decided that this was it. I was going to tell my mother the truth. So I spent an hour typing her a detailed description of all the problems I had with organized religion in general and Christianity and Catholicism more specifically. In that particularly earnest college way, I touched on everything from political stances to sanctioned self-righteousness, to the ridiculous worship of Christ. It was my slightly more adult way of telling my parents that I wasn't sure their Bible held more of a moral mandate than a good fantasy story. "She asked for it," I thought as I pictured her opening my manifesto at her computer and realizing just how far from her beliefs at least one of her children had strayed. I hit the Send key with relish.

When I turned on my computer the next morning, there was another e-mail waiting from my mother. I wasn't sure I wanted to deal with either my mother's tirades or her hurt whimpers, but I opened it.

"Dear Heidi," it read. "Thank you for your e-mail. I thought you weren't thinking about faith at all. I'm glad to know you are. Love, Mom."

I stared at the screen in disbelief. I called my roommate in to read the e-mail. If I had known my mother's response could be so open, I might have been honest with her long ago. If only church hadn't gotten in the way of her message for so long.

My parents would be happy to see one of their "searching" children actually arrive at an answer—preferably one that involves some sort of organized religion. Unfortunately for them, I don't see my search as one that necessarily has to end, or should. But I'm no longer afraid to talk to Mom and Dad about it.

Heidi

Other Families' Stories

Our older children seem to be staying connected with the church. I can't point to any one cause but suspect it's more the cumulative impact of observing parents who were active, doing rituals at home and in church over and over again, and generally fostering an inclusive and spiritual environment. Of course we have friends who have done the same without the same results. I think half of our son's Confirmation class was just getting confirmed because it was expected and they knew they would get a lot of money. I wonder if these will be the ones who abandon their faith when they're on their own. Just going through the motions doesn't cut it anymore.

Al Prendergast, father of one teen and three young adults, Weston, Connecticut

I'm Jewish, and during my college years I went to Israel for a summer to live on a kibbutz. Although I am not actively connected with a synagogue now, I expect that will be important to me when I start a family.

Laura Ax, 25, works for Ashoka, an international nonprofit organization that supports social projects in developing countries, Washington, D.C.

I am not currently involved with a church, but I am looking for a faith-based community. I looked at the Jesuit Volunteer Corps, but they didn't have any placements in French-speaking Africa, so I'm going to Cameroon with the Peace Corps this fall.

Sarah Park, 23, works for AYUDA, a community-based nonprofit organization that provides legal services to immigrants

I am Quaker, and when I was fourteen or fifteen my parents said I didn't have to go to Meeting anymore. That freedom allowed me to go of my own volition, and that confirmed my faith.

Fred Letson, 21, college student, Greenfield, Massachusetts

I have no desire to be involved in any kind of organized religion, although I'd like for my kids to have a spiritual life, but hopefully a broadly tolerant spiritual belief system and one without so much hierarchy, sexism, homophobia, greed, etc.

M.B., 28, social worker, Brooklyn, New York

I think there's plenty of intellectual awareness out there about the problems of the world. The next step is emotional awareness: in essence, being "converted" to being compassionate, aware, active human beings rather than simply "knowing" of the problems out there. That's probably the greatest legacy of my Christian upbringing: that knowledge isn't enough; conversion in one's heart is also required.

Robert Honeywell, 36, lawyer, actor, playwright, New York, New York

Although I'm not sure what form of religion our children will hold as they move more into adulthood, I feel confident that each has a strong religious core. One practice that we initiated when they were young and that continues to this day when they're home is a weekly "Moment of Meaning." Each week a different family member would be the leader. We'd finish dinner, check in about the weekly calendar, and then the designated leader would bring a newspaper clipping for discussion, or lead a prayer, or suggest five minutes of silence—whatever he or she wanted. Although we missed some weeks, we did this more often than not.

Leif and Rene Kehrwald, parents of one teen and one young adult

When I looked at the church, what I saw was a club that believed it had a closer knowledge of God but in a subtle way was tragically shutting itself off from engaging the rest of the world. I don't think my faith and understanding of God has really changed, but my Sunday practice has. I go occasionally to a Unitarian-Universalist fellowship, and I hope for the day when people of similar beliefs will start a nature-based Sunday celebration where I can find some community.

John Stith, 26, Green Party organizer, Montgomery, Alabama

After Confirmation I got turned off from my faith partly because teachers made the role-playing games I enjoyed sound evil. My parents expected me to go to church with them until I started college. I experimented with other religions at that time and didn't go as often, but eventually I came around to a belief in God and Jesus that I could own for myself. If I had been forced to go as a young adult, I know I would have resented it. I don't take well to doing something just because I've been told to do it.

Joe Hargett, 25, computer scientist, Crestview Hills, Kentucky

Christ does not live at the Church building but rather inside each one of us. Christ is in the CEO of a Fortune 500 company as much as he is in the street kid who lives outside of my apartment building. And because he is also inside of me, if I am to honor that, I am to treat both the CEO and the street kid with the honor, dignity, and compassion worthy of a king. If religion is just about visiting a church once a week, and Christ's radical social, political, and economic message never gets translated into real life, then we become part of a farce—and kids pick up on inconsistencies. Perhaps they won't understand that they should be "putting feet on their faith," but they will understand that none of what they hear in church makes sense for them. They will get bored, and they will disconnect religion from the rest of their lives. If kids are to live their faith holistically, then it must be integrated into every aspect of life right down to the clothes we wear, the cars we drive, and the ways we invest our time. A sure way to get kids to forget religion as soon as they leave for college is to force upon them rigid social constructs supposedly based on religious precepts but that in reality are far from compassionate and loving. If the only thing deterring a child from doing something bad is fear of eternal punishment, he or she will either rebel or simply live a superficial religion.

Julia Marie Graff, 23, volunteer with Witness for Peace

REFLECTION

Soul Search

What is the motivating force or source of energy in my own life?
Is there anyone or any cause that I would be willing to give my life for?

To me, faith in God is (choose one):

- Foundational

- Supportive

- Something I probably have until something changes my mind

- Something I would like to have but I'm not sure about

- Fine for others but not the source of my commitment

- Irrelevant

How do I stay focused and centered on the really important values in my own life? (prayer, meditation, physical activity, reading, conversations with mentors, nature, etc.)

To me it is most important to:

- Be a faithful and active participant in an organized religion

- Be spiritual

- Live according to values such as honesty, service, compassion, respecting all life, being a peacemaker

When my child becomes an adult, will I be disappointed if he or she chooses a different faith from mine (or no faith)?

If nothing else, I hope my child(ren) grow(s) up to believe . . .

A time when our family had a meaningful experience of God's presence was . . .

(This could be a time of intentional or spontaneous prayer or simply an event that touched you all deeply and reminded you of God. Please consider something other than the birth of a child. As miraculous as this event is, I'd like you to search beyond the obvious.)

CHAPTER 9

Global Awareness
From Being the Center of the Universe to Exploring the Universe

These are the words of my son Brian, when he was seventeen:

I've never been to Myrtle Beach, I've never been to Hilton Head, and I've never been to Daytona Beach. Throughout my life I have heard friends talk of their vacations in places like these. I was always a little jealous until the summer of my sophomore year. During that summer I had what was undeniably the best experience of my life so far. My family traveled to the Soviet Union.

I wasn't quite sure what to expect, but I did have some preconceptions about what it would be like. I had always had a mental picture of the Soviet Union being colorless, drab, and boring. When our plane landed, this image intensified in my head. It was the middle of the night, and there was fog everywhere. All I could see was grayness. It looked so bleak.

When we entered the airport lobby, however, my outlook changed completely. We were met by the Soviet delegation, who embraced us enthusiastically. They showered us with flowers and gifts. It was then that I saw the true color of the Soviet Union, the color that tourists don't get to see. I'm not talking about magnificently painted buildings or beautiful gold church domes. I'm talking about something much more beautiful than that: the inner color that I felt from these people. From the very beginning they opened their lives to us. They talked willingly about the good and the bad.

My first experience of this openness was on an excursion to a "Pioneer Camp," which would be equivalent in the United States to a Boy Scout or Girl Scout camp. Upon entering this camp, our group of Soviet and American families was greeted by hundreds of young children singing songs. Feelings of hope and love overwhelmed me. I could not believe that we had actually been enemies with these people. During the next two weeks, we got to know our Soviet hosts extremely well. We spent many nights talking until 2:00 or 3:00 in the morning. We talked about everything ranging from the history of the Russian revolution to the high cost of blue jeans.

One person who I befriended was the guard of the camp, Arif. He was about twenty-one years old, and this was his summer employment. We were both avid Ping-Pong players. We also shared a common interest in the Beatles. Since it was hard to find many Beatles albums in Moscow, I let him copy a number of mine. One day Arif came to me with a depressed look on his face. His younger brother's birthday was coming up and because of the huge popularity of American clothing in the Soviet Union, his brother asked for a T-shirt that said something in English. It didn't even matter what it said; it just had to be American. Arif asked me if there was anything I could do. I could see the pain in his face. He was a very proud person, and it was very difficult for him to even ask me to help him. He even offered as a trade three books that he had had since childhood. It amazed me how something as insignificant as a T-shirt, something that I take for granted every day, could mean so much to somebody. Fortunately, I was able to find a T-shirt for Arif's brother.

I learned so many things from my trip. When I returned, my outlook on life changed significantly. I was not as concerned with material possessions. I also began to value friendship more and learned to withhold judgments of people before I met them. Finally, I appreciated more all of the opportunities and gifts that I had taken for granted before. I still haven't been to Myrtle Beach, Hilton Head, or Daytona Beach, and I may never get to these places—but who cares!

GETTING ALONG WITH THE WHOLE WORLD

Sound grandiose? Of course it is. Doable? No. Approachable? Maybe. Not everyone is going to be a friend, but no one needs to be an enemy. The more we are exposed to people who have different looks, customs, and lifestyles from our own—and the more we really get to know them, their hopes, and their fears—the harder it is to hate them. We feel more connected to others simply by understanding that, even though they don't lead a typical middle-class American lifestyle, they laugh, cook, have babies, deal with jobs, and eventually face death. Our spirits become larger when we take the time and energy to find these things out for ourselves.

When I hear the news of an earthquake in Turkey, I hold vigil with the Turkish people because I have known them from an exchange student who stayed with us. When I hear of the bombing of the U.S. embassy in Nairobi, I am concerned for both the Americans and the Kenyans there because we have met the people. My world of care has grown; it doesn't matter where I live.

One doesn't have to travel internationally to contribute to peace in the world—but it helps. From a parent's perspective, our family's international experiences were probably the most stimulating and rewarding. Perhaps it was because our children were getting older and we could process our experiences on a deeper level. It also was probably because my husband has instilled in all of us a love of travel. Mostly, I think it is because of the many quality, caring people we have met on five continents.

Our family is also proof that it doesn't take a lot of money to travel, just a lot of creativity, will, and adaptability. Here's how it all started. We were invited to be one of eight families to go to the first U.S.–Soviet Family Peace Camp near Moscow in 1989. We were honored, but we laughed and we scoffed. We would have to pay our own expenses, and we knew that there was no way we could afford airfare for five people. Thus began our introduction to fundraising. I never want to do it again, but between holding a dance, talking at churches, sending out numerous letters, and downright begging, we managed to raise ten thousand dollars. After meeting and falling in love with our counterparts in the then Soviet Union, our stereotypes of a godless land of communists who were bent on overtaking the United States melted. We found that children who did not speak one another's languages could still communicate and that parents have universal concerns no matter what the nationality. When we came back, we prayed for the transition that was going on in their country and rejoiced with them as the Berlin Wall fell.

Our children caught the bug too and were thus receptive when they heard about Children's International Summer Village, which eventually led one or the other of them to exchanges in Italy, Argentina, Norway, and Turkey. Meeting children from other countries who could speak two or more languages, while our own children knew nothing of their new friend's language, was humbling and helped us all to see the strengths and weaknesses of our own country

When our children were a little older, their school offered the French class an exchange with a school in France. They already knew how to ask local businesses for money, and they only had to cover one airfare. Besides, they were getting old enough to earn a little money themselves. Over the years we hosted eight French students in our home, and three of our children made the trip to France. Part of the fun was being with peers away from parents, but they also found out that just as they are not equally fond of all Americans, there's good and bad in any group; you've got to get to know people individually. Some of our guests were less likable than others. The important thing is that our children were learning not to judge by the color of their skin or the country of their origin but by the content of their character, to paraphrase Martin Luther King Jr.

BEYOND BEING THE CENTER OF THE UNIVERSE TO BEING CENTERED

Yes, for most people it's fun to visit foreign lands, and it certainly is a broadening and enriching experience, but the point is not merely to expand one's horizons. Just because I can talk (or brag) about getting to Timbuktu and back again doesn't make me a wise and centered person. It might help me get a better perspective on my place in the world, but if I'm still trying to grasp at happiness through making myself appear important and well versed in the ways of the world, I will be an empty vessel. Somewhere along life's journey each person needs to realize his or her infinite worth as an individual human being. What flows from that conviction is that just as I have worth, so does everybody else.

I'm sure these international experiences influenced Brian to spend a year working as a volunteer teacher in Indonesia after graduating from college and later to work for an international nonprofit organization supporting social entrepreneurs in third-world countries. Heidi's path took her to the Peace Corps. Dacian probably isn't headed for international work; his interests are more in the area of time travel, as in back to medieval times. But they know that they are not the center of the universe and that getting along with people who are different from them is like learning a new language. No one language is right or wrong, but understanding life through another person's language and worldview takes a lot of work.

Although traveling is a good way to see the world through another's eyes, some people can't or don't want to travel. The goal is to expose children to people who are different from them and to open their eyes to the needs of the larger world. For some, entering the world of a neighbor who is disabled or someone who is considered an outcast in our society might be the foreign land. The point is to push beyond my needs to see those of others. What are *your* passions or concerns that can stretch your family beyond the walls of your home?

Another way to bring the world into your home is to invite in a variety of people. As our children grew older, we got involved in an international hosting program called Servas. Several times a year people from various places in the world would stay a day or two and share their interests and travel experiences. Eventually, the children got old enough to host exchange students themselves. I suppose it's a risk to welcome a stranger into your home, but life is full of wonderful risks. (For more information contact Servas at 11 John St., Rm. 407, New York, NY 10038, (212) 267-0252, info@usservas.org, http://www.usservas.org.)

We've hosted at least twenty-five people, ranging in age from fifteen to sixty, from more than fifteen countries, for anywhere from two weeks to six months. Most of the people we didn't know before we picked them up at the airport. They brought gifts; they brought strange languages and ways. Some didn't eat pork, some cooked authentic Japanese or Indonesian meals for us. A couple of the relationships in the student exchanges were strained, but they were brief, and the vast majority of visitors taught us the beauty of humankind and how to be a gracious guest. One gave me mononucleosis, but no one presented any danger.

BEYOND ENGLISH, OR WHAT A DIFFERENCE A WORD MAKES

When I was in high school, I remember questioning the need to learn a foreign language. I'd probably never travel outside the United States. Even today, travel agents will proclaim that English is all you really need because almost everyone speaks English in major tourist destinations. That's probably true if the only people you ever want to be around are other tourists and people who cater to them. Language is important even for those who never plan to travel, not only because in our global society people of different tongues may cross our paths, but also because it's a symbol of trying to understand not just the literal words but another's life experience.

Language was the most immediate difference we noticed in hosting people from a foreign country. (Why did we never exchange with England?) Our children were studying French in school, but even when the exchange was with France, we always had to slow down our speech and listen with special attentiveness, sometimes simplifying the message to it's core—an important practice for communication in any language. Inevitably I would come away from these experiences with great admiration for the effort our guests made to communicate in our language. I knew I would not be nearly as fluent in theirs. It was a very humbling experience, considering I come from a nation used to thinking of itself as the most advanced and powerful in the world.

In an effort to even out this poverty of language and also to prepare for a month-long trip to Colombia, my husband decided to learn Spanish. His teacher advised him to put little labels on all the common household items around the house. This meant we were all exposed to *puerta* ("door"), *ventana* ("window"), and *baño* ("bathroom"). I've forgotten most of the words but remember something more important: Not everyone understands me (or agrees with me) just because I say it's so. This goes for communicating in English too. To care for the world we need to communicate with people who speak and understand differently from ourselves.

The Vogt Kids Speak

One of the things that I valued most during my childhood and adolescence was my parents' open-door policy, which meant that we frequently hosted visitors—both friends who needed a place to stay for a while and travelers from other countries. It was an educational experience for me and also served as a chance to develop friendships with people from all over the world. Even though at times there were temporary inconveniences, like having to switch bedrooms and entertain someone I could barely communicate with, the rewards were enormous. I think that's part of why I developed an interest in international studies.

Brian

When I was fourteen and fifteen, I was involved in an exchange program through Children's International Summer Village. I spent a month in Argentina the first summer, and my partner, Juan Ignacio, spent a month the next summer with my family. The time in Argentina was fun, and my delegation experienced a lot of new things. But when Juan Ignacio visited my home, I realized how immature he was. He wanted everything his way, even though when I was in his country I tried to go with the flow and do what he wanted. A couple of years later our family agreed to host a student from Brazil who was also my age, seventeen. Andre and I got along a lot better even though he had some of the same personality traits as Juan Ignacio. Perhaps it was because we were both a bit older and more mature. We took each other's needs and interests into consideration. I don't think the country made a difference. Both cultures seemed to like to party a lot.

Dacian

I attended a Children's International Summer Village for a month in Norway when I was eleven. I was one of four members of the U.S. delegation. Twelve other countries were also represented. I didn't notice many differences about the kids from the other countries; we were all just having fun together. I did learn to think like a thesaurus, though, since even though everyone spoke English (more or less), I was always needing to think of different words to explain what I wanted to say.

Aaron

A Daughter's Response

Vacation World

Remember how everything happened magically in childhood? I remember family vacations that way. My parents would tell us to pack our bags and get in the car, and I'd hop in with only a foggy idea that we were heading somewhere west. When the car stopped, I'd scramble out, amazed to suddenly find myself face to face with a bighorn sheep or Mt. Rushmore or Old Faithful.

Corny as it might sound, it was these 1950s style, pile-in-the-station-wagon-and-head-to-the-first-national-park family vacations that first taught me to value the world beyond my hometown. There was magic in the unknown. I remember watching the burping mud pots of Yellowstone jump and shiver like, well, like nothing I had ever seen before, and wondering, "How did my parents find this crazy, awesome place?" Then, "What else is out there?"

Yet, however far we went, my parents always acted as if they were at home. I was shy of the strangers who talked funny and dressed weird, but my parents treated everyone like old friends. My father asked park rangers how they liked their jobs. My mother struck up conversations with the campers one site over while I was still warily eyeing their children, trying to decide if they were friend or foe. And I started to get the idea that exciting places bred fascinating people.

I discovered on these trips that if one drives far enough, the world really will change. Later in life this excitement for the unknown translated into a thirst to understand other countries and cultures. As a seven year old, I was happy just to shout as we crossed another time zone and to see Old Faithful gush into the sky like magical clockwork. Corny? Yes, but pretty powerful all the same.

Other Families' Stories

I was watching *The Power of One,* a movie about apartheid in South Africa, and it struck me that I really wanted to go there to see if all of this injustice actually existed. When I got up from watching the movie, I saw a flyer on my roommate's desk that was advertising an immersion trip to Cameroon, sponsored by the University of Dayton's Social Concerns Office. When I told my mom, she asked me why I had to choose Africa. When I told her the other option was Colombia she quickly agreed to Cameroon.

I don't think that I had any idea what I was doing when I signed up. I was so excited at the prospect of seeing this new place and experiencing new things. However, when I stepped off the plane in Douala, Cameroon, it hit me like a ton of bricks. It was hot and humid. The airport was built in the sixties and had seen no renovations. I needed to go to the bathroom and the toilet looked like a really bad truck stop; it had no seat and no toilet paper. My baggage was lost. This was my first twenty-five minutes in Cameroon.

So what did I learn? I learned about being the minority, the person that everyone looks at because you look different. I learned that I could do anything if I put my mind to it. I learned how to be thankful for such things as running water, grocery stores, finished floors, electric fans, and ice cubes. I learned that a person should never go into a foreign country with the belief that they can fix things or solve problems. I wanted so badly to be involved in service when I went to Cameroon and found myself stamping books in a university library. They didn't have enough jobs to employ their own college graduates. If there were not even jobs for them, then why would they have work for us? I learned about poverty and discrimination, about assumptions that I had and assumptions that people that I encountered had. I learned about the disparities between the rich and the poor, about love and community and how those two things are universal. I met and befriended some of the kindest people in my life in Cameroon. I found that they take the time to sit and talk. They take the time to invite you in for a cup of tea or some food. They greet you with "Good morning" instead of "Hello" because a "Hello" would be rude—it's just something that you say in passing. I found that there are people thousands of miles away from us from a different culture, with different customs, but that they can become the dearest people to my heart. I guess I learned a lot.

Maureen Wagner, 22, teacher, Lumberton, New Mexico

There was a picture frame my mom hung in our house. Every few weeks she would change the picture to a new UNICEF photograph of a child from somewhere else on the globe. Later, when studying Latin America in high school for a Spanish class, it was nothing more to me than memorization of capital cities and main exports. However, years later after having traveled to Ecuador and Peru, meeting people from Argentina, Chile, Puerto Rico, and Cuba, the different histories and contexts of each country took shape and made sense in my mind. If possible, parents should find ways to make the world beyond their backyard a reality: meeting people from there, reading a book about it, even just finding it on the map or globe. I wish I had approached geography as an exploration instead of a chore.

Judy McGrath, 22, art teacher, Chicago, Illinois

All three of our children have had significant international experiences through Children's International Summer Village. I believe that what led them to this involvement was mostly stories—stories of my husband's travels through Asia and Africa before we were married and my own commitment to an international women's organization, The Grail. Stories about our experiences, books we were reading, and news from the daily paper were part of our dinnertime conversations. One book that I think influenced our oldest daughter was *Material World*. It's a book of photos of families from all over the world in front of their homes with all their stuff. Our house was also decorated with gifts and multicultural art from other parts of the globe. Indirectly I think that influenced our children to notice that the world is bigger than their country. One of the experiences that was a challenge was having an exchange student for a year. Max was eighteen and from Germany. Our children were seven, ten, and twelve. Nothing terrible happened, but I think the age mix didn't work well. The kids didn't have a lot in common with Max, and squabbles were common. The experience with Max, however, taught us to rethink relationships, stretched us to be hospitable, and forced us to communicate concepts large and small across cultural and language barriers. It was a good experience, but the learning wasn't always easy.

**Mindy Burger, art teacher,
parent of one young adult and two teenagers, Cincinnati, Ohio**

I started traveling internationally when I was eleven, and I took part in a Children's International Summer Village in Sweden. Our family didn't have much money for this kind of stuff, but they again made it a priority when I wanted to go to Argentina two years later for an interchange. When I think of what might have prepared me to say yes to international travel at age eleven, it was probably a mixture of my own reading, of hearing about my parents' interest in travel, and of seeing pictures of different places in our home. I can remember reading *The Little Princess* when I was a child and developing a real interest in India. Later as our family took road trips around the United States, I loved looking at the atlas and figuring out where we were. Traveling for its own sake, however, was never enough for me. It just opened the door to bigger questions. I developed a kind of "American guilt" because I'd see how much more a middle-class family like mine had than most of the people in the countries I visited. Traveling influenced my decision to be a peace and global studies major, although I have recently changed to politics since I think that might give me a better chance to impact unjust political systems. My friend just got back from Botswana, and we've been having long discussions, trying to figure out what we can do to help. I'm not fulfilled in what I do unless it has some greater meaning. It's never been a huge value in my family just to have a lot of stuff.

Erin Burger, 20, college student, Richmond, Indiana

We read newspapers in my house. My parents read and so we did too, and we talked about everything we read. And we argued. We had this great big atlas that got pulled out all the time so that we would know where the places were that we were discussing. We didn't have the opportunity to travel a lot as kids, but it didn't make any difference. We knew there was a big world, and we were going to get to see it. And we were fascinated with everything about it. I had friends who didn't own an atlas or a globe and didn't know where anything was. It was weird.

Liz Chesto, 24, medical student, New Britain, Connecticut

We always had a globe in our living room, which our kids were encouraged to play with when they were young. I wonder if its presence there had a constant, if quiet, influence on them, similar to the crucifix on the wall and the photos of grandparents on the fridge. As our children got older, we were blessed with the opportunity to host two teenage girls from Russia, and later to be part of an exchange group to visit them in Russia. I will never forget the night we picked up Anya and Tanya. Despite having traveled for more than twenty hours by train, plane, and bus, when they arrived at our home they pulled out a bag of Russian tea and insisted on serving us! At thirteen, Tanya was fluent in English and acted as our translator. I came to see our country a bit more clearly though through the eyes of an outsider. I also caught a glimpse of the consumer mentality that lives in me and diverts too much of my energy and attention away from what matters most.

Susan Stith, parent of three young adults, family-life educator, Portage, Pennsylvania

Who in the World . . . ?

If you could travel anywhere in the world where would you go first? Why?

Look at a map and find at least one country you've never heard of before. What's its capital? What language do its people speak? If you don't know, how would you find out?

How many languages do you know? (Most people in underdeveloped countries know at least two whether because there are multiple indigenous languages in the country or because a colonialist government brought a new language.) Consider learning a new language. If this sounds too formidable, pick a new language and learn one word a day for a month (yes, no, please, thank you, you're welcome, hello, goodbye, I'm sorry, one, two, three, four, five, mother, father, sister, brother, peace, Where is the bathroom? How much does this cost?).

What country is the farthest from where you live? How long would it take you to get there?

Pick a new country every day, week, or month. Learn about it and/or pray for its people.

CHAPTER 10

Diversity
What's the Difference—
Black, White, and
Everything In-between

"Our daughter, Andrea, seems to bring in strays—people, that is," said Andrew and Terri Lyke, Chicagoans and parents of two teens. "Our neighbors were an older childless couple, and several times they hosted foreign exchange students. Last year they again had a student, and he was a minority in our daughter's high school. Seeing his discomfort and rejection by some of the students, Andrea made a point to introduce him to her friends and include him in their social circle. It seems to come naturally to her; being African American herself she knows what it's like to be in a minority in many public places even though her high school is 90 percent black. She has compassion for the outcasts of our society, including German exchange students."

Being white, I used to think that to expose our children to other cultures and racial groups meant we would need to live in an interracial neighborhood. This is not a bad idea, but it's not the only way. Jim and Kathy McGinnis, founders of the Parenting for Peace and Justice Network, helped us understand that much could be done within the home no matter where we lived. We sought out pieces of art that depicted people of color and displayed them in our home. We mixed music and food from different cultures with our traditional fare. Since my husband loves maps, these also became wall decorations. We didn't preach a lesson. We just let the environment speak for itself.

We also made an effort to read stories of peacemakers and people from different cultures and lifestyles. At one point, we had talked and sung about Harriet Tubman, the woman who led many Southern blacks north along the Underground Railroad, so much that our children thought she was a saint. Indeed, if a saint is a person of heroic virtue who inspires us to live more courageously, she may qualify.

Inviting people to dinner became a major way of bringing into our house people who the children might not otherwise rub shoulders with. Once I bought chitlins on a whim but had no idea how to cook them. We invited over an African American coworker's family, with southern roots, to teach me how to prepare the dish and to eat with us. Inviting handicapped people over meant learning firsthand about the barrier that steps create, and taking care of an elderly parent opened our eyes to the physical limitations that we too may face one day.

Not all our guests were minorities or people in need. Some were young adults who were doing a year of service with the Marianist Voluntary Service Community (they also doubled as baby-sitters). Some were engaged couples coming for a home-based marriage preparation program. Some were activists in the community who were with us for a meeting or just needed some respite. Many were just our kids' friends who happened to be there around dinnertime. The common ingredient was conversation about other people's lives and what made them tick.

Sometimes racism needs to be addressed directly, but the underpinnings of raising children who can put themselves in another's shoes can be indirect and begin in the nursery—or at least with fairy tales. Joan Foley tells of how she used to read the story of Little Red Riding Hood to her children, and then retell it from the perspective of the wolf. How did the hungry wolf feel as he saw some food (in the form of Little Red Riding Hood) walking through the forest? How did the Three Bears feel when they noticed that someone had broken into their home? Getting out of our milieu and into the mindset of others so that we can see life through their eyes can be a building block to understanding people who are different from ourselves. What are the needs that are driving the other's behavior?

MAKING OUR CHILDREN AT HOME IN THE COMMUNITY

As our children got older, we looked for opportunities to patronize businesses or use professionals who came from different racial or ethnic backgrounds. We made it a point to occasionally attend worship services with a denomination or faith different from our own. This helped our children know what it feels like to be the "different" one.

Sometimes we would ride our bikes through different urban neighborhoods, many of them poor. This prompted many questions such as, "Why don't these people fix their houses up?" ("Because they don't have enough money.") "Why don't they have enough money?" ("Often because they don't have a good paying job, or they're sick.") "Why can't they get a good paying job or go to the doctor and get well?" ("Because their schools aren't very good, or their parents can't help them learn, or they don't have insurance to pay a doctor.") "Why aren't their schools good?" ("Because they don't have sufficient funding.") "Why don't their parents help them with homework?" ("Because they didn't have good schools themselves or have to work at night.") "Why don't they have insurance?" ("Because they can't get a good job.") Our children started to see the complexity of poverty and how the system needs to be healed on many different levels. This was one of the few times I appreciated the interminable "why" questions that would take us deeper into the root of the problem.

Although we could have driven through these same neighborhoods in a car, biking allowed us to go slowly enough to actually notice things but fast enough to avoid gawking. Sometimes we would stop at a local market to get something to eat.

Although we haven't always lived in integrated communities, for nine years after the birth of our first child we lived in a housing cooperative that had a two to one black-to-white ratio with a deliberate mix of low-income and middle-class families. It was an intentional community that had its own board of directors; the people who lived there wanted to be there and were committed to making the community work. Even with those advantages we experienced some racial tension. Some residents didn't trust board decisions until they talked with the one black board member. Some questioned whether whites were getting preferred housing units. I learned that generations of feeling like the underdog couldn't be erased merely with goodwill. I thought I was beyond prejudice and bias and so was surprised to hear some of my black neighbors question my intentions. They regarded me as privileged even though our incomes were comparable. It takes a heap of time to build trust.

It was easier for the kids because this was the only community they had ever known. Almost all of Heidi's preschool friends were black. One time when we were staying overnight with some friends in another state, their daughter (who was white) and ours were getting ready for bed when I heard Heidi exclaim, "Look Mom, she has white skin just like me!" Now I understand a little better what it means to be a minority in a predominant culture and why it's important to have people we can identify with in positions of power. We can empathize with an oppressed people, we can stand with them and support them, but there will always be a difference—a difference of experience.

Although we don't currently live in an integrated neighborhood (unless you consider people of Appalachian heritage mixing with people of German heritage integrated), we do live in an old city with many of the problems facing the urban United States today. The city is pretty segregated, but with only one public high school, black meets white on a daily basis. One of the reasons we chose to send our children to this school system rather than a private school was that it meant they would have daily contact with people from different backgrounds.

Schooling represents a hard decision for most parents; we all want the best possible education for our children. We were not blind to the reality that the public schools in the state of Kentucky were ranked among the lowest in the nation and that our particular system was one of the poorest in the state. Were we sacrificing our children on the altar of our ideals?

This is an honest challenge. We chose the Covington public system for many reasons, including the fact that it had just instituted an extremely rigorous advanced program for grades four through twelve. We knew that our own educational backgrounds had given us the tools to supplement the education our children got from the school, which we would monitor closely. We would also take active responsibility for their faith formation at home. Given these safeguards, we felt that the education our children would acquire in terms of living with diversity and developing relationship skills was worth the risk.

I am not suggesting that this is the socially responsible route all parents should take. At one time or another each of our children attended Catholic schools. Each child's needs are different, and one of our children went through parochial schools exclusively. He is doing equally well in his own way. It's not a question of whether private or public schools are better. Our purpose was to make an effort to expose our children to people who were different from them in the hope that familiarity would break down stereotypes and prejudices and provide them with opportunities to be bridges to a population that feels oppressed. To make peace with a person or a group, we must first understand them intimately. We must put a face on the race.

A VIEW FROM ANOTHER SIDE

Since I could speak directly only about how a white Irish-German, middle-class family tried to expand our experience of other cultures, I asked African Americans, Hispanics, and Asians what it felt like to grow up as a minority, often oppressed. What messages did their parents give them that helped them survive and thrive? What are they passing on to their own children? Andrew Lyke, an African American from Chicago, summed it up when he said, "Because we are an oppressed people, I've always felt I had a responsibility to church and society. I never acted only on my own but as a representative of my people. It can be a heavy burden, but it also kept me aiming high. White culture has some atoning to do, but blacks have forgiving to do."

Following are some strategies for what families can do about racism, adapted from *Families Caring,* which was developed by the Parenting for Peace and Justice Network:

Talk about current events.

Talk within your family about events that have racial implications. Encourage children to ask questions and draw conclusions.

Celebrate heroes, holidays, and cultural events.

Lift up for yourselves and your children the lives of people of color, past and present, who have fought and continue to fight for social justice. Enhance the learning by surrounding it with a party or some other enjoyable event. Many communities have cultural events (dance, theatre, art) that provide information as well as real insights into the culture, history, and life of different racial groups. Holidays (e.g., Kwanza, Cinco de Mayo, Hanukkah) can also be times to learn more about the values of other people.

Form interracial friendships.

The ability to fight racism is nurtured by the relationships we have across racial lines. Such relationships are more easily achieved if we live and work in integrated situations and our children go to integrated schools.

Seek out racially diverse role models and professionals.

Children's attitudes are affected by those they relate to in a variety of capacities (doctors, dentists, teachers, ministers, counselors). Make racial diversity one of the criteria for choosing such professionals for yourself and your children.

Never use or allow racially derogatory terms.

Children need to know that comments and/or jokes that belittle or insult the racial ancestry of any person or group are absolutely unacceptable. It is also important for them to see us confront other adults about their language.

Check TV programming.

Children can be brought into our discussions about TV shows. We can look at the simple question of numbers: How many TV series have African Americans? Hispanics? Asians? Native Americans? We can also discuss the content of these shows: Are people of color shown in positive or in stereotypical ways?

Look at your voting patterns.

Political candidates at all levels need to be evaluated in terms of their stance and activity against racism in all forms. Children can be a part of discussions about these candidates and about our voting decisions. In some communities, working on voter registration drives is a concrete way of putting into practice one's concern for the ability of all people to participate in the political system.

Write letters to the editor.

In every community there are racial incidents that occur as well as ever-present economic and political realities that reflect the institutional dimensions of racism (for example, high unemployment, infant mortality, difficulties in voter registration). Families can let their opinions be known in the community by writing letters that could be signed by the whole family.

Get involved in community projects.

It is important for both adults and children to be involved in projects in which the leaders are people of color.

Stand with the victims.

Even though the circumstances vary from one community to another, there are always opportunities to add our voices to those in the fight against racism, whether at school-board meetings, city council hearings, court proceedings, or vigils. At times these situations may be appropriate for the participation of children.

Take advantage of visuals.

The pictures and other visual representations in our homes should be truly multiracial. Children learn a lot from what they see in their home environment. It is also important to check for racial stereotyping in any of the visuals in our homes.

The Vogt Kids Speak

I always enjoyed experiencing the diversity that went along with having all kinds of different people always visiting our house.

Dacian

When my mom asked me how I felt about going to a racially mixed school, I said I hadn't really noticed. I suppose that says something in itself. I'm more aware of the economic mix since there are a lot of kids from very poor families that go to my school, but they're all colors.

Aaron

My parents made a concerted effort to introduce me to the less pleasant elements of society. My dad taught me to pick up hitchhikers. Now, most people would be aghast at such a thought. But I remember my dad often pulling the car over to pick up someone who was hitchhiking. Of course, there's always danger in this, but I believe the good that can come from it outweighs the relatively small risk. Contact with the downtrodden people of our world is necessary if we are to reach out to these people. If we close off our world out of fear, we only perpetuate the feelings of isolation and despair that are already too prevalent in our society and the world. I appreciate the example that my father set, and now I try, whenever possible, to lend a hand to those in need, even if it puts me in an uncomfortable situation. If we only help when it's convenient for us, what is the value in that?

When I was a senior in high school, one of my classmates got shot. Although David and I were not close friends, I liked him, and we had been in almost all the same classes since junior high. Nobody was quite sure what happened, but somehow he got in the way of a drug deal in his neighborhood, and that made all the difference. Even though we went to the same high school, attended the same classes, and didn't live that far from each other, his neighborhood was mostly black and poor; mine was mostly white and middle class. He had visited my home, but I had never visited his. David was partially paralyzed and in a wheelchair as a result of the shooting, and of course our whole class felt distraught at his misfortune. As tragic as this was, I don't remember feeling afraid for my own safety as a result of it since I knew that his neighborhood was a high-crime area, and I didn't frequent it. I don't know if it was poverty, race, the drug culture, or just being in the wrong place, but what a difference one or two miles make.

Brian

A Daughter's Response

One Family, Two Worlds: A Not-Too-Far-from-the-Truth Fable

Once upon a time, a long time ago, a young married couple made a choice. They had both come from upper-class families where people played bridge, met for tennis, and golfed at the country club. This young married couple decided that they wanted to leave a lot of this behind. They wanted to "live simply." They wanted to take jobs that would make a difference in the world, and maybe all the better if those jobs didn't pay well. They wanted to live in working-class neighborhoods. They wanted to live on only what they needed and to need very little. Their lives would be richer for it, they decided, more diverse. They wanted to live diversity.

And then they had children. And their children grew up among this diversity: racial, economic, and lifestyle diversity. And their children felt uncomfortable in country clubs, didn't know how to play tennis, had never heard of bridge. Their children's friends showed them how to spit and to cuss and to show off a good bit of thigh. And the parents didn't understand.

Why haven't we raised children that want to march in nuclear protests, they asked themselves? They don't seem to *care* about helping the less fortunate. Why does our daughter wear more makeup than our friends' daughters? And what is she doing with that hairspray? Why does our son only listen to heavy metal music? What is this talk of "preps" and "posers" and "wiggers?"

It was the usual generation gap, but somehow exacerbated. Exacerbated by living in a neighborhood in which the TV was the expected dinner companion, in which wealth was worn in fast cars, not in nice wooden coffee tables. A neighborhood in which getting in a fight was a rite of passage and microwaved mac and cheese was the meal of choice. Exacerbated by the fact that this was normal for the children and a tragedy for the parents.

That young married couple had chosen this urban world as their residence, but their children had been born into it and shaped by it, and didn't like being told suddenly that they weren't part of it.

"No dear you have to come for dinner at six."(But normal kids don't eat dinner around a table.)

"That movie is too violent for you." (But it's just a movie. No one else thinks this way.)

"I want to call Becky's parents before you go to this party." (But Becky's parents understand that we drink and we smoke, and you don't.)

"You need to come with us to volunteer at the soup kitchen on Sunday." (But my people are eating there, not volunteering. Don't take my world away from me.)

Of course, as the children got older, they drifted away from that world on their own. They found friends that had been similarly ostracized by their parents and started to form a new world. But the citizens of this world would never fit in at country clubs, would always have more of an affinity toward beef jerky than granola, and would gravitate toward the processed food aisle, even as they started recycling.

They moved away from home just as they began championing the causes of the world they grew up in. And the now slightly older married couple breathed a deep sigh of relief. Maybe they had succeeded after all. Their children had started to agree with them. Only with the children it wasn't ideological. It was personal. It was old friends. It was defending their childhood home from being the dumping ground of the rich. It wasn't someone else's injustice.

That married couple put a lot on their young children. They presented contradictions to children of eight years that thirty year olds struggle with. And those children will probably never live happily ever after because of it. Better that way, don't you think?

Heidi

Other Families' Stories

Since we are a bicultural couple (Hispanic and Anglo), we made a commitment early in our marriage to have our children experience both our cultures. We live in the United States, so that means a family trip to Mexico at least every other year. In addition to seeing family, these visits have had several beneficial side effects. Our own relatives live comfortably, but the kids can't help but see the poverty in the region, and of course they ask questions about it. It strengthens their identity in both cultures and stirs their sensitivity to the needs of their country. After one of these visits, six-year-old Renata decided to take an image of Our Lady of Guadalupe to her first-grade class for show-and-tell. As she put it, "I want my friends to know more about my people." Of course we also tried to expose them to a mix of races in the U.S. and thus chose to attend a very multicultural church that had a strong social-justice bent. Recently they challenged us on that, however, since it was a long drive and none of their neighborhood friends attended. We agreed to compromise and attend church closer to home some weeks. Ale's and my friends and ideals aren't the only ones that need to be respected.

Alejandro and Mary Aguilera-Titus, parents of three young children,
Alexandria, Virginia

We wanted to expose our daughter to people of other races to nurture her appreciation of differences. One day she came home from her integrated preschool saying, "I want braids all over my head." We're white; her hair is very straight. I guess she didn't want to be too different.

Laura and Steve Domienik, parents of a fourteen year old,
Kennedy Heights, Ohio

I was driving with several friends and my fourteen-year-old son when the police pulled me over for having a missing headlight. It was a residential neighborhood—my own, so I wasn't speeding and it was dusk, so I didn't even have to have any headlights on. When the officer checked my license, he realized that we went to the same parish and that we knew each other casually. However, he also found an irregularity about how the license was issued, which meant that technically I was driving on a suspended license—a surprise to both of us. This made the charge a misdemeanor and required me to be handcuffed and fingerprinted. My son ran home to tell my wife what had happened, but it made an indelible impression on him. The officer regretted that he had to do this, but he said he had no choice. I said that I understood the law, but what disturbed me was his initial decision to stop me for what seemed to be solely the black color of my skin. I tell our kids that even though we supposedly live in a free society we are often held to a higher standard. They have to be very careful. Of course it makes us angry, and we don't try to hide this from our children, but we try not to be bitter.

Andrew and Terri Lyke, parents of two teenagers, Chicago Illinois

The dumbest thing my mother did was to send me to a Catholic, all-boys high school for a year. (It was an accelerated program, and I'm sure she thought it would advance my education, which was of utmost importance to her.) The larger problem was that I was the only black student at the time and was socializing with people who had seldom, if ever, been exposed to a black person. I felt I was supposed to be a representative for the entire African-American population. Now, when you are a twelve-year-old high school freshman, there are so many other things weighing you down without the pressure of representing an entire race.

**Kareem Simpson, 23, graduate student,
formerly Korean linguist in the U.S. Army, Covington, Kentucky**

I tried to instill a respect for each individual person. Instead of telling our children, "Don't talk to strangers," I said, "You *must* talk to strangers." I wanted them to acknowledge people as they passed them on the street. Of course I also told them not to get into a car with a stranger and cautioned them about potential dangers, but I didn't want their basic reaction to people to be one of fear and suspicion.

Jo Ann Schwartz, mother of two young adults, oncology nurse,

Ft. Thomas, Kentucky

Where Are the Differences?

Where are the differences?

What kind of diversity is most noticeable to your family—ethnic group, language, economic class? Why do some differences stand out more than others?

Has anyone in your family ever been in a minority? If so, what do you remember most about that experience?

Think about the kinds of groups your family or individual members of the family are part of. Do these groups bring you into contact with people who are much different from you, or do you tend to participate with people who are—in most ways—similar to you?

What opportunities can you create that will expose your family to a more diverse spectrum of people?

Try to think of people who are different from you in that they are less advantaged or have less power than you. Try to think of people who are different from you in that they have advantage or power over you. Which situation is more common?

What sorts of differences among people are most frightening to you? Most exciting? Most encouraging?

CHAPTER 11

Service
Life Beyond Myself, My Family, My Neighborhood

Here's more from Brian, age seventeen:

When I was about ten I started volunteering at a soup kitchen in downtown Covington. When I worked there, I either washed dishes or handed out food in the serving line. I remember one particular instance when I saw a young family come in. It was Christmas day, and I had been thinking about the presents I had received. When I saw this family, it dawned on me that these children were not going to get any presents. The most that they could hope for was a warm place to sleep. Yet they still had smiles on their faces and said "Merry Christmas" to me. This made me realize how lucky I already was. I also realized that it was not the material goods that really mattered. In fact, when I looked back at the best times that I had in my life, I saw that in terms of money, they cost very little. What made the times so great were the friends that were with me.

Now, I see that I am actually very rich. How much of this insight is from volunteer work, or exchange experiences, or just a matter of maturing, I'm not sure. No, I still don't have a lot of the things that other people have, but I do have my friends and my family, and that's a kind of wealth that I can't buy with money.

When our children were young, we invited a recently immigrated Vietnamese family for Christmas dinner. We were living far away from all of our relatives; they were neighbors and alone. It seemed like the natural thing to do. Brian and Heidi (ages five and two respectively) were horrified. They yelled, "We didn't like the food they brought. We're not doing that next year."

Sometimes it works; sometimes it doesn't.

Service sounds so noble, it's hard to imagine anyone not being for it. Yet our lives are so busy and complicated that good intentions often give way to inertia or fatigue. How can families get a handle on incorporating service into their daily lives and—even more fundamental—why bother?

If you're reading this book you probably already have an intuitive sense that serving others is something we should do. But does it really do much good other than to make us feel good and virtuous? Of course, the answer you expect from a book like this is yes, it does make a difference. Here's why:

- Service changes us by forcing us to look beyond our own needs to the needs of others.

- One person's service may actually make a positive difference in some- one else's life.

- A whole bunch of people looking beyond their own needs to serve the common good will definitely make a difference in society.

But where (and when) do we start? You've probably heard the adage, Give a person a fish, he eats for a day. Teach him to fish, he eats for a year. Some have added "Find out who owns the river" to show the dimension of changing an unjust system. We've probably all experienced do-gooders who, though well meaning, mucked up a situation by interfering or "doing for" when they should have helped the person do it for him- or herself. Most people get a good feeling from giving food to a truly hungry person. Fewer people are willing to do the long-range thinking and advocacy that it takes to change a system that allows people to be hungry in a world that has the resources to feed everyone. Sometimes that hungry person needs a job, mental-health care, or specialized training so that he or she is employable. When we get to this level of involvement, it's much more complicated, and it can feel overwhelming. It's tempting to give up or at least to stay at the level of merely giving a fish sandwich.

Still, most people start at the level of giving the fish. That is fine and probably necessary, but there is a dimension of service that precedes giving the fish and another dimension that follows it.

BEFORE THE FISH: AWARENESS AND SOLIDARITY

Exposure to the plight of the poor and powerless often precedes a decision to go out of our way to serve. Sometimes our natural instincts are awakened by something we read or see on TV. Disasters near or far are examples of this. A neighbor gets cancer, and everyone on the block feels moved to help. An earthquake, a flood, a fire, a catastrophe of any kind inspires a desire to respond. But first we have to know about the need. If no one on the block is checking in with the ill neighbor, only the immediate family may know of the need—and they might be a hundred miles away. If no one's reading the newspaper or listening to the news, if no one has their ear to the ground for community needs, we might learn about only the most dramatic crises. Not that those don't merit attention, but lots of people will respond to the well-publicized calamity. The less spectacular crises also need our attention.

So often a forerunner to service is putting ourselves in a situation where we can notice that there are needs. Sometimes this comes naturally in the course of everyday life. A relative has a special-needs baby, or an accident happens right in front of our house. But often we don't see the need because we're not in the right place. Living among the poor provides many prompts for service, but most of us haven't chosen that environment. There are alternatives.

One popular means of becoming aware of others' situations is an immersion program in which students or adults visit social service agencies and spend time in poor neighborhoods talking with the people there. Individual families can do this simply by making a point to drive through a city rather than around it on the expressway. Choosing to shop in a struggling neighborhood that has mom-and-pop stores supports the economic viability of the neighborhood while raising awareness. More extensive programs offer opportunities to spend time in Appalachia, on a reservation with Native Americans, or in a developing country. If people in need are not knocking at your door, maybe you have to go to their doors, or at least to their neighborhoods, to get to know them face-to-face. Service will follow.

Of course not everyone in need wants our help. We might not be the right person or have the right skills to provide what they need. That doesn't mean it's not worth knowing people and experiencing their milieu. It will still change us and soften our hearts. Then there are others too far away or inaccessible to make personal contact practical—people in other countries, in prisons, or in dangerous areas. Service in these situations often takes the form of solidarity. I may not be able to speak Spanish or Vietnamese to get to know a person of another culture, but I can learn to appreciate a culture by reading about it or by trying to learn the language. I might fast for a meal or a day to join my heart with those who are hungry. I could give a donation to a charity that will assist earthquake victims in Turkey. For religious people, prayer is a natural form of solidarity. Most of these actions are indirect or preparatory and can be done by families with children. Some may later lead to direct service; some may be complete in themselves.

Once my husband went with one of our sons on a "homeless campout." The idea was that people who had homes would take a sleeping bag down to a park near downtown and sleep out under the stars for a night with homeless people and other people who cared about the plight of the homeless. Not one homeless person got to sleep in a home that evening because of us. So what's the point? My son was changed. He learned that it's not easy to go to the bathroom late at night in the middle of a city. Most restaurants are happy to let customers use their bathrooms but don't take kindly to unshaven men or little kids walking in and out without buying something. He learned that the stars don't always shine as a gentle rain fell on his damp sleeping bag. He learned that it's not romantic or easy to be homeless and that maybe this was a cause he would want to work for, or give money to, or pray for with a personal understanding. He was in solidarity with the people who have to live this way every night.

GIVING A FISH SANDWICH: DIRECT SERVICE

Making ourselves aware of poverty or other injustices in our community is the first step. The natural extension of this is to say, "What can I do to help?" Direct service is the most personally satisfying way of helping, and it's where most people start. It takes form in the classic scenario of serving meals at a soup kitchen or delivering holiday baskets. Direct service often involves meeting basic needs such as food, clothing, shelter, and health care. I would add education as a basic need since in our society it's the stepping-stone to being able to pay for the other needs.

Direct service often starts at home, but it doesn't end there. Infants are at the center of their own universe, and that is how it should be. As far as they are concerned, all life revolves around them and everyone else is just there to serve them—and we do. As a child matures in years, we hope that there is an accompanying maturity of ego. It starts with sharing and evolves to giving. It starts with helping out at home and can evolve into helping out in the community. It's a gradual process as parents keep in mind their child's developmental stage and readiness to explore beyond the home. Usually the child harbors at least a tinge of "What's in it for me?" This may seem selfish, and bribes may seem, well, unseemly. But I've come to think of bribes and other such motivations as ways of respecting the child's developmental stage.

We thought we had heeded this counsel when we invited the Vietnamese family for dinner. The gathering was in our home, it was small, it was simply a meal—an event that our children were very familiar with. We didn't expect a negative reaction. It may have been that even in their short memories, they already had a sense of ritual around the Christmas meal—what food we should have and how it should go. Who knows? Who knows if it was even a mistake, though they complained bitterly at the time? Since then, Brian has traveled periodically to Southeast Asia with a job mentoring social activists in that region. He loves Indonesian and Indian foods. Heidi has lived in Mali, West Africa, as a Peace Corps volunteer and has eaten *to,* a porridge made of millet, for the majority of her meals. She doesn't complain.

Extending oneself in the family setting, however, is not just for young children. Two of our teenagers like to play late-night role-playing games. They usually don't start until midnight. In addition to the fact that they are biologically inclined to late hours at this age, one of the reasons is that one of the teens, Doug, can never get to our house before midnight on Fridays. Not only does he have a job and a girlfriend, but he is also committed to playing Scrabble with his elderly grandmother for an hour every Friday night. He's a busy guy. His friends wait for him.

Often when social activists want to impact a cause like hunger in Sudan, poverty in China, or violence in the Middle East, the response is, "That's fine, but we've got plenty of problems right here at home. Why don't you put your efforts into eradicating poverty in our own country or city?" Unfortunately, there are enough needs in our world to go around.

Committing to work on one cause does not alleviate the need for someone else to work on the others. When the children are young, however, starting close to home will make more sense to them.

There are of course the ways that families have traditionally helped the poor at Thanksgiving and Christmas: delivering baskets of food or gifts, caroling at nursing homes, participating in a "Giving Tree" where children pick the name of a needy child and buy a gift for him or her, and so forth. These are good, but a valid criticism can be made: What about the rest of the year?

A number of service projects worked well while our children were young: cleaning up litter at a park near our home, buying and planting a dogwood tree in front of an inner-city school, and gathering our old but usable clothes or extra cans of food to take to Goodwill or a food pantry. (It took Jim a while to realize why we were frequently out of the okra and artichoke hearts he bought. The kids chose what to give away.)

Eventually we developed certain practices that put us more closely in touch with people working to heal the brokenness of our community. For almost twenty years now we've been serving meals at a local soup kitchen. Our commitment isn't much—two family members work every other month—but it keeps the needs of our neighbors before us and reminds us of the gap between the rich and the poor. Sometimes the kids joined us willingly; sometimes it took bribes such as combining it with a treat; sometimes we just said, "It's part of being a member of this family that we all do some service. Now which of the following projects do you want to do?"

Some projects fell our way because of people we knew. A priest friend was the chaplain at a prison. Certainly young children couldn't visit prisoners—or could they? Father Mark needed cookies for the Kairos program he conducted for the inmates. We could bake cookies with the awareness that each cookie was a way of sending our support to the prisoners and

Father Mark. Other friends staffed and lived at a Catholic Worker house for homeless families. We agreed to help them fix dinner periodically. Our children's part was simply to play with the other children. I'm not sure if they even recognized it as service. Probably best that they didn't. They just came along for the meal.

Your contacts are bound to be different from ours. But if we put ourselves in situations where we come in touch with people in need or those who serve them, all we have to do is open our ears and eyes and service opportunities will appear.

IS SERVICE SELF-SERVING?

As our children got older, we sometimes discussed what kind of service we would do at family meetings. OK, so it wasn't the kids who put it on the agenda. But generally, as long as it was active, had an element of fun, and they could invite a friend, there wasn't too much resistance. It was at this point that we also discovered the value of bribes, er, incentives. At first it often involved food (doughnuts or ice cream after an outing). At times we would mix a service activity with recreation afterward, such as playing miniature golf. Occasionally we resorted to outright money; we would pay a child to do a bulk mailing. It was still cheaper than paying a staff person. This may seem crass, but we were trying to work with motivations appropriate to their ages and emotional needs. Most folks eventually mature into doing good simply for the satisfaction and good feeling of having helped. Even that is an incentive, albeit an internal one.

Several projects that seemed to work well during these middle years had to do with fixing or building houses. Our small faith community was involved in fixing up several old houses in a run-down part of town to rent to low-income families. Kids by nature are good at demolishing things, so they joined us in clearing out debris and scraping wallpaper. As we were tearing apart these houses, we were building community as parents and kids worked side by side over a series of Saturdays.

Although they were too young to do many of the jobs at a nearby Habitat for Humanity house, they were very good at digging dirt, shovel by shovel. One site needed some earth moved to make a pathway to the house. I imagine a bulldozer could have handled the job in a half hour, but we didn't have a bulldozer. We did have a host of kids with shovels and several Saturdays. Machinery would have taken away all the fun and our feeling of accomplishment.

As the kids got into their teens, they tended to peel off from doing service with the family. Fortunately, we live in a time when a lot of schools and youth groups sponsor service projects. For many kids this is their first introduction to looking beyond their own wants and seeing how other people live. For some it is a life-changing experience. As commendable as these efforts are, they lose their full impact when they are "required." It may be a class requirement for a grade, a religious requirement such as for bar mitzvah or confirmation, or to get a Scout badge. Students may participate because it will look good on their college applications.

I used to look condescendingly on such compulsory projects of impure motivation, but I've lightened up. Probably all of us come to service, at least initially, with mixed motivations. It's human nature to want recognition and credit. This is just a more sophisticated form of incentive. The pure altruist serves others simply because it's the right thing to do even though it might cause frustration or cost money. But we don't start there. Even wonderfully generous people don't have absolutely pure motivations.

TIPS FOR SERVICE NOVICES

Through many projects, trials, errors, and successes, we've come up with four bits of advice for parents who want to involve their kids in meaningful service.

Find a cause that interests the child and is meaningful.

In your studied opinion, campaign-finance reform may be the issue that you think is most crucial to address; but your child loves babies. Maybe collecting baby items for a crisis pregnancy center or volunteering child care for parent meetings is the place to start. For beginners it's usually best to start with concrete actions that have visible results. Teens may want to work for the prevention of sweatshop labor, especially by young teens in other countries. Don't just study the issue; personalize it by checking the origin of the clothes in your own closets. Teens in our community learned that they could take action by getting involved with the National Labor Committee's "Holiday Season of Conscience" campaign. It involved signing postcards in support of fair working conditions and taking them to local retailers during the Christmas shopping season. (Holiday Season of Conscience is a project of the National Labor Committee/People of Faith Network, 275 Seventh Ave., 15th floor, NY, NY 10001, (212) 242-3002, www.nlcnet.org)

Make it fun.

Service doesn't have to be dull or painful. Eventually a person who is committed to a cause has to do some grunt work just to get the job done. But don't start with the grit and the grunt. If cleaning up a park is your service, make a game out of it, or at least have a party or fun event at the end. Bulk mailings have got to be one of the most boring tasks, so we let the kids play their favorite music (loudly) or watch TV while they work, even if it slows them down or isn't our style. Often choosing an event that has some drama to it or performing a task in a creative way can sow the seeds for coming back another time. Laugh a lot.

Do it with friends.

Not only do many hands make light work, but they also make it fun. Kids can do some of the most unlikely and dirty work if their good friends are doing it with them. This is especially necessary for teenagers.

Include food.

A youth minister used to tell me, "You can do almost anything with teenagers as long as it involves pizza and an overnight." Eating together is a natural way to build community and to get to know your coworkers on a more personal level. Nutritious food is desirable, but occasionally eating a candy bar for energy and fun won't kill anybody. Be sensitive, though, not to use food as the only reward lest some vulnerable teens develop eating disorders. Be aware that some children may have food allergies or be diabetic.

A FISHING LESSON: EMPOWERING OTHERS

Even though it may make us feel good, giving a fish sandwich to someone who is hungry is a short-term fix. To really make a lasting change in the person's life we need to step beyond the direct service role and teach the person how to fend for him- or herself. Education and training are the curriculum. I can clean up my children's rooms faster and more thoroughly than they can, but am I contributing to their dependence on me? Future roommates or spouses will not thank me. Habitat for Humanity requires new homeowners to provide "sweat equity" by laboring along with the volunteers to build their house. The homeowner not only is invested in the project, but he or she also learns building skills that will come in handy when repairs are needed.

Empowering the poor might involve giving them money. If it's a short-term or onetime need, that might be fine. But for chronic situations we need to get to the root of the problem. Does the person need a job? Does the person need training or education to get the job? Anyone who goes into teaching is choosing a career to empower others.

Does the person need child care, counseling, or mental-health services? Some of you have probably chosen professions geared to meet these very needs. Others do their empowering by employing. One of our local restaurants serves healthy but inexpensive meals. The management intentionally hires staff who are physically or mentally challenged. A local bagel shop is known to hire ex-convicts. The owner of this successful company served time himself and wants to give others a chance to turn their lives around. There are more ways to teach than in a classroom.

WHO OWNS THE RIVER: CHANGING THE SYSTEM

Most people go as far as empowering others (teaching them to fish) and then stop. Empowering is a hard enough task.

But at least a few folks need to go beyond empowering to advocating, to changing systems. Otherwise our society will continue to perpetuate a system in which we're always trying to fix something that never should have broken in the first place. Why are there poor people? Were they just born that way? Why are some people born into poverty? How do we catch something before it breaks and costs us more to fix it in money and human suffering? Generally these are political questions and have to do with how systems work. It takes really savvy people with sophisticated communication and organizational skills to move a system to change. Our role models in this area are people like Mahatma Gandhi, Nelson Mandela, Martin Luther King Jr., or Dorothy Day.

Of course, I've also seen change happen because of people who are pretty ordinary but who have a passion and the commitment to take on the powers that be. There's Peggy Charren, who advocated for improving children's television, or the group of California women who started Mothers Against Drunk Drivers in 1980. It doesn't even have to have national impact. Influencing a local company to stop polluting a stream so that the fish stay healthy can make a difference to a lot of fishers and families. Usually this kind of project has the beneficial side effect of being a hands-on civics lesson for the kids. They learn how the government works, how to do petitions, how to speak with equal respect to both the powers and the victims. In other words, no one has an automatic pass. How do we raise kids who might become the advocates for those who can't speak for themselves? Encourage them to go beyond meeting the most obvious and immediate needs, and to ask "Why? What needs to change to make this more fair?"

WHEN TO GIVE AND WHEN NOT TO GIVE

People who have a generous heart and want to help inevitably face the question of how to give not only their time to those in need but also their money. Do you give a couple of dollars to the beggar who approaches you on the street? What charities do you support?

Most of us experience ambivalence about giving money to the street person who asks for it to buy a cup of coffee. Will he really use it to buy coffee, or some other substance? My husband always gives, figuring that even if some people abuse the gift, some might really need it—and who is he to judge. Others rarely give money, figuring that it encourages a dependency and sometimes deceit. They'd rather donate to agencies that will make a difference in the total web of poverty. If they really make good on those donations, that's great. I've sat in on many discussions on how to respond to the street beggar or the guy with the sign at the intersection that reads "Will work for food." Someone always suggests going with the beggar to eat lunch together or hiring him to do some odd job around the house. That's fine if I've got the time or the guts. It's a hard call to know the best response. One family collects nonperishable food, puts it in lunch bags, and then stores three or four bags in their car. Whenever they come across someone who is hungry, they just give the person a bag.

As valuable as direct service is for our psyche and for getting concrete help to those around us, most of us can't personally help a hurricane victim in Florida. But we can contribute to the American Red Cross. We can't directly provide medical care to the indigent or food to a war-torn country, but we can give to the United Way or our church.

Donations of money are certainly an important corollary to donating our time to service. There's a limit to how much of a dent volunteers can make in the social needs of our day. Paying professionals to study the problems and come up with comprehensive and effective means to address society's needs is not just charity but justice, and it makes good sense. In order to do good work, charities need to pay staff and have supplies.

Ordinary citizens can give even more direction to their money by carefully choosing which organizations to support with their donations. In our own family we usually try to give to causes that we are personally involved in. This way we can vouch for the wise use of the funds. We leave the more well-known or bigger charities for people with bigger pockets. Paying attention to the beggar and giving to organizations that reduce the need to beg are both forms of service. To check out the validity of a charity before you donate, contact the Council of Better Business Bureaus, c/o

Philanthropic Advisory Service, 4200 Wilson Blvd., Suite 800, Arlington, VA 22203, (703) 276-0100, www.give.org for the Annual Charity Index.

How much to give? Probably more than we're comfortable with. Ten percent of one's income is the biblical guideline. Let the needs around you be your guide.

The Vogt Kids Speak

Although we took turns volunteering at the Parish Kitchen [a local soup kitchen], I don't think of it as necessarily a life-changing experience for me. I felt it was good to help people out who needed some food, but most of the people weren't that dramatically different from the people I saw around me in school and in the neighborhood, so I wasn't shocked. I don't think you can expect social analysis or a full understanding of poor people's problems from teenagers.

Dacian

I always felt that the Parish Kitchen was a good project to undertake, especially on holidays when, because we are celebrating, we often forget those who are less fortunate. I also remember working with Anawim Housing, cleaning up old houses. It probably made a huge difference whether or not a friend came along. That can really make the difference between a good and a bad experience. I know we probably did a lot of stuff when I was younger too, but frankly it's faded from my memory and what remains is just the general impression that Mom and Dad took the time out of their schedules to be involved with the community. This is a much stronger message than anything in particular they said.

My experiences in college were the most memorable since I did those on my own. My work with Habitat for Humanity was probably the most influential—the work was very tangible and it was done in a group setting, which was a real plus for me. I suppose the foundation for that, however, was laid earlier in life during the activities that I did with the family and during high school.

Brian

A Daughter's Response

Carzell

I was the child with the hard shell. I saw working at the soup kitchen as a chore. I never wanted to give money to starving children (wherever they were). I felt embarrassed when my father gave change to beggars on the street, more so when he talked to them. My brothers both seemed eager to help the world, but frankly, I didn't want to be bothered with it (although I tried my best to hide this from my parents).

Then there was Carzell Moore. My parents had received a letter from an inmate on death row. His name was Carzell. He was interned at a prison in Georgia for rape and first-degree murder. He had read one of my parents' articles in some publication he had gotten his hands on in prison and decided to write to them and tell his story. He said he was innocent. He had been framed. My father read this letter to us over dinner one night. He said that we didn't need to try to decide Carzell's guilt or innocence. In the letter Carzell asked for nothing more than a correspondence. Did we want to write to Carzell?

There was something fascinating about a death-row inmate that caught my attention from the beginning. Everything I knew about jail came from cops-and-robbers television shows. But Carzell Moore's situation was more real and more personal. This wasn't some do-gooder crusade of my parents. This wasn't community service. This was just one person who needed some people to believe in him. So I did.

My brothers and I took turns writing letters to Carzell Moore, with my parents' help. Over the years, we sent him Christmas cards and stamps. One year, he sent us presents that he had made in prison. I received a green and white knitted purse with a matching wallet. I couldn't believe that somebody who was living without all my daily luxuries was giving me a gift.

I still whined whenever it was my turn to go to the soup kitchen. But somehow I felt it would have been sacrilegious to whine when it was my turn to write Carzell Moore. It was just something I did for a person who needed me.

Heidi

Other Families' Stories

I have been involved in working with the poor for as long as I can remember. I guess it's in my bones. My parents never said much about this topic, but their philosophy was Do By Example. My mom was always fixing a meal for someone who was sick or taking clothes to someone who needed them. The only thing she said was, "Why don't you come along?" That is what I have tried to do with my own five children. I thought it was working pretty well as I watched how my first few children chose careers and lived their lives. Beth worked at a children's home and is working on a social work degree. Keith is a social worker in a depressed area of Little Rock. Marilyn teaches at an African American Montessori school. Although Naomi is the only one who chose a high-paying job, she always works for the underdog and goes out of her way to take care of others. And then there's Peter. He took a different route, and although I have always loved him dearly, I wasn't sure he had caught the care-for-the-poor message. I'm director of our local soup kitchen; he's the vice president of a private security company. I'm a peace activist; he decided to join the military. I'm a Democrat; he's a Republican. So I was a little uncertain what would await me when I went to visit him and his family on the opposite coast. It was Saturday morning, and they were all making a heap of peanut butter and jelly sandwiches. I said, "Oh, are we packing a picnic lunch?" "Yes." I didn't see how the five of us could possibly eat all those sandwiches. Then my son said, "We want to take you to see your guys." We proceeded to drive to a park where a lot of homeless men hung out. The children immediately started handing out sandwiches to whoever wanted one. It was all very natural, as if they had been doing this for a while. They had. The values had taken. I just needed time to see them in action.

M. N., single parent and director of a soup kitchen

We've always put a high priority on recycling in our home, so it wasn't hard for the kids to agree to take part in a project to clean up garbage along the river one weekend, especially since their friends were going to do it also. But I was a little more surprised when our fourteen-year-old daughter, Renata, decided to take part in a weeklong work project painting and cleaning in a poor neighborhood. It meant getting up at 6:00 A.M., sleeping on the ground, and sharing one bathroom—none of which she usually liked. She overcame her hesitancy, however, because her friends were going to do it too, and she had a wonderful time. She now feels a personal connection with the elderly lady whose house she painted.

Mary Aguilera-Titus, mother of three school-age children, Alexandria, Virginia

It is one thing to be a "decent" person and quite another to be a "good" person, one who sacrifices a little bit so others can have more. When I was about seven years old, I saw a Save the Children ad on television and told my parents I thought they should sponsor a kid so that she could go to school and be healthy. It was sixteen dollars a month at that time, and I remember my Dad telling me that if I saved up to pay for the first month, they would pay for every month thereafter. Sixteen dollars was a lot for a seven year old back then, but that small lesson remains with me: You can't just hope for things to be better in the world; you have to be willing to give up a little, or sometimes a lot, to make them better. You have to get out there in the world and pitch in with others. As a country we are far from understanding what "solidarity" means and how our comforts are intimately related to other people's pain, poverty, and in some cases terror.

Julia Marie Graff, 23, volunteer with Witness for Peace, Bogota, Colombia

One thing that helped our son get off drugs and find his life was staying in other parts of the world—over several extensive trips. It helped him see that there was a lot of excitement and challenge in the natural world and that others had it a lot harder than he did. It also gave him some needed time to grow up rather than go straight through traditional school.

Connie Ordower, mother of one teen and one young adult,
Front Royal, Virginia

Having a child with a disability changed all of our lives. Vince is the second of my six children and has Down's syndrome. Being widowed early in life meant that all the kids had to take an even greater responsibility for looking after each other. They didn't think of it as service; he was simply their brother and they loved him. Because of Vince, at one time or another each of them had summer jobs working in group homes with people who were disabled. All of them ended up being socially active in some way. To tell the truth, I sometimes sought out service opportunities for one or the other of them just to keep them out of trouble. When a given child was having trouble I tried to go with his or her strengths. One daughter loved theater, so I connected her with a couple in radical theater who needed a baby-sitter. She's now a labor organizer. With others I used the divide-and-conquer strategy. Each of my younger children spent at least one summer away with an older sibling who seemed to get through to them. A downside may be that all of them seem overresponsible adults because of it.

Carol Igoe, widowed mother of six adults, social worker,
Cincinnati, Ohio

My husband and I were both committed to social justice, but with two young children and an ill parent I often spent my time running to my parents' house to check on my father while dragging a child or two with me, all the while working full-time outside the home. I was trying to be there for my children in any spare moments since my husband always seemed to be out at a community meeting, serving on a board, or campaigning. That's why it was so disconcerting one day when my minister came up to me and said, "You must be so proud of all the public service your husband does. I want to thank you for him." I could have screamed. My husband's kids hardly knew him, and I was worn out trying to meet their needs and those of my parents. He got all the acclaim while his family suffered from his absence.

Anonymous "social justice widow,"
mother of two young adults

When I was in high school in Mexico, I was part of a really great youth group. One of our projects was to collect all kinds of goods from our upper-middle-class neighbors and take them down to the Lost City (a squatters' section of Mexico City). It was very satisfying to pass out household supplies and toys to the grateful residents, but when our supplies ran out before the people did, things got ugly. People started throwing rocks at us. It was scary and disheartening. The great thing about our youth group, though, was not so much collecting and delivering the supplies but the discussions our leaders guided us in after the rocks were thrown at us. They pushed us to talk about why these people were poor and helped us understand a little bit of how it felt to be poor. This background was significant in later prompting me to join the Jesuit Volunteer Corps, and that was a transforming experience for my life.

Alejandro Aguilera-Titus, parent of three young children,
Alexandria, Virginia

Take an Honest Look

Name at least one person who right now has life better than you do and explain why that is so.

> In my family . . .
> In my neighborhood . . .
> In my nation . . .
> In the world . . .

Name at least one person who right now has life harder or worse than you do and explain why that is so.

> In my family . . .
> In my neighborhood . . .
> In my nation . . .
> In the world . . .

Is there anything I could do to make that person's life a little easier, a little better?

If I don't know of anyone, what could I do to put myself in a place where I might discover someone? (Stand for a while at a bus stop in a poor neighborhood; spend some time at a Goodwill-type store, not just shopping but observing; read about a person who has had a hard life; walk slowly through a hospital.)

CHAPTER 12

Motivation
How We Learn to Care about Caring

A friend of mine, with her nineteen-year-old son, went to the mall to visit her twenty-two-year-old son, a manager in one of the stores. The younger son had a rugged look. He was a camp counselor and an outdoor type—long hair, beard, overalls, and flannel shirt. The older son looked like the manager he was—suit and tie, close shaven, and trim haircut. While mom and the brothers chatted, an employee of a neighboring store joined them. The employee looked at the two sons in a puzzled way, alternating his gaze one to the other. Finally, he said to my friend, "Different fathers?" In fact, neither of the brothers was adopted; they did have the same father. Both were in good physical shape and educated. But, understandably, the striking differences between the two had prompted the question.

Not only can two siblings, raised by the same parents, in the same home, with similar experiences, look very different, but they can take very different paths. One might be an easy child to raise who naturally follows the direction of the parent, is responsible, and becomes a community leader. The other may be rebellious or creative, testing the parent's patience and pride. Eventually, this second child also becomes a community leader—or maybe not. It doesn't really matter because the parent's worth does not depend on the accomplishments of the child. Likewise, the child's worth does not depend on success as society typically judges it.

Still, it is a conundrum to parents as we try to figure out what we can do to help our children mature and become generous, loving adults who care to at least make a dent for the better in the lives of others. Why is it that when we put the same opportunities before our children, one takes it and runs with it and another rejects it? Same parents, same environment, different people. Often birth order makes a difference. Has the firstborn already taken the role of doing well in school? Maybe the next one will choose sports as his or her outlet. The size of family can be a variable; parents with many children have less energy to supervise but more wisdom to know what to ignore. And of course, there's always the genetic difference. Even if the parents are the same, the genetic mix is different. Some kids defy all categories and are just easier to raise than others. We don't know why.

This book is not about a recipe for success but rather about increasing the odds, and, of course, it all depends on how you define success. In this book, success means caring about others and the world and acting on that. Sometimes that success may be quite visible and even acclaimed by society; the child grows up to become a political leader, a social activist, or a Peace Corps volunteer. Other times the success might be quiet, even invisible; the child grows up to be a faithful spouse or parent, a reliable volunteer in a school or community, or the caregiver for an aging parent. Even though I'm not a gambler, I'm all for putting the odds in favor of our children becoming either of these types of success. In the previous chapters I've talked about a lot of different arenas for commitment, ranging from the home to the world, from the environment to technology. In this final chapter I'd like to talk about the motivation that starts it all.

We can't *make* our kids care. We can't pour into them a social conscience. But we can put prompts and possibilities before them that will increase their odds. Our efforts won't be perfect, and they won't always work, but we will have tried, and that's all we can do. The rest is up to them.

So what can a parent do to foster a giving heart? Douglas Huneke, a Presbyterian minister and religious educator, interviewed three hundred rescuers of Jews during the Holocaust to see whether they had anything in common that encouraged compassionate, courageous behavior and could be taught or nurtured in others. He found ten common characteristics.

1. Adventurousness: they all tried things as kids

2. Identification with a morally strong parent

3. Some experience of social marginalization themselves

4. Empathetic imagination

5. Ability to present oneself and control a critical situation, often through some kind of public performance while growing up

6. Planning skills to implement altruistic desires

7. Exposed to suffering at an early age

8. Exposed to stereotyped individuals and observed injustices

9. A sense of not being in it alone, involvement in a "community of compassion"

10. A home where hospitality was highly valued

Although we may not expect our children to become heroes on the scale of rescuing Holocaust victims, the terrorism of September 11, 2001, and the resulting heroism has caused all of us to think more about character under pressure.

SIX INGREDIENTS FOR MOTIVATION

After interviewing and surveying more than two hundred young adults and parents, my own research led me in a similar direction to Huneke's but with a slightly different focus. In trying to understand what motivates a child to care for others and grow up to make a difference, I've come up with the following six ingredients that seem to turn kids on. I don't think that all altruistic children have these experiences in common; some experiences appear to be mutually exclusive. I do think, however, that the more of the six ingredients children have, the greater their chances of them going out of their way for others and making some positive impact on the problems in our society.

Example of parents

The premise of this book, and the factor that probably makes the biggest difference as to what children will internalize, is that they will catch their parents' enthusiasm and commitment to contribute to the common good. Often this happens when children see parents doing works of compassion and justice. Ideally, the parents will invite the children to join in the work.

Jim and I have a strong commitment to peacemaking and serving the poor. These personal interests drive us to become involved in projects that support these causes, and the kids came along when it was appropriate. Jim also loves maps and travel. Because of his passion in this area, the whole family has become turned on to geography and global concerns. When I was growing up, I thought a vacation was a week on Lake Erie. Now a vacation usually involves a passport and visa, or at least a very long car trip. You may not be a travel person, but the point is to find what you are passionate about and allow your kids to participate.

Maybe you think that you don't have a passion. All you have to do is look around or look a little deeper. If you put yourself out in the world, open your eyes, and listen, you will find a place that needs your care, your gifts, and your resources. Maybe your passion is your children. It's not such a big step to expand that passion to other children who don't have the advantages that yours do. Is your passion your career? Your job doesn't have to be in the social service field to lend itself to fair employment practices, ecological sensitivity, or modeling respectful conflict resolution. Bring the job home—at least in the sense that you let your children hear what you're trying to do at work to make it a more honest and respectful environment.

Sometimes even a fun passion can turn into a means of connecting with other people and being of service. If you like golf, you can organize a golf outing to raise money for a good cause. If you're into sports or the arts, you can nurture kids just by being available, as did an elderly grandmother who decided on her own to do arts and crafts with junior high kids once a week after school.

Both parents and young adults in my research echoed this theme: We cared about X and so we found a way to involve the kids. In the end, the easiest way to turn our kids on is for them to see what turns us on and catch it.

Intellectual curiosity

Exposing children to service opportunities and letting them get their hands dirty building a house or cleaning up a neighborhood is good, but it's not the whole picture. It's possible to become very busy with doing good but also very tired and not very effective. There comes a time in a person's development when it's important to ask the question, Why are we doing this, and is there a better way? It's not so much a matter of how smart one is but rather how to be creative and nurture the impulse to explore new possibilities.

This is why it's so important that we don't stunt children's play by teaching them to color only inside the lines or play with toys that can be used only one way. Even though our kids love computers and video games now, they grew up with lots of blocks, art materials, books, and raw materials around the house and yard that became their toys and fed their imaginations. This is when being a pack rat can come in handy. We had old tires that became the obstacle course for the neighborhood Olympics, old dress-up clothes for plays, puppets for all kinds of performances, and old sheets and blankets that we used to turn rooms into tents or caves. When you encourage creativity and intellectual curiosity, you will often have to give more of your own time—and you'll certainly have to put up with some mess.

As the children got older, intellectual curiosity took the form of challenging ideas and the established order. This can be pretty "messy" for parents as teens challenge moral and religious precepts. "I think the government should decriminalize recreational drugs, at least marijuana." "I think organized religion is not facing the crucial issues of our day or is irrelevant." "When does human life really begin?" Discussions on these issues take a lot of patience as we try to be open to the truth and new insight that our child is moving toward, yet help him or her sort out some of the fallacies or lazy thinking that get mixed in with the argument. Still, if they are going to be brave enough to ask the question, "Is there a better way to do this?" we need to encourage this intellectual curiosity. Otherwise they may apply a Band-Aid philosophy to life problems rather than looking deeper and opting for more complex solutions.

A life-changing experience

A number of young adults I interviewed said that there was nothing special or remarkable about their upbringing. Their family lived comfortably and their childhood was basically happy. The parents were nurturing and had good parenting skills but did not have any significant involvement with social issues—and neither did the children. When I questioned them about what gave them the itch to go further than their life experience up to that point, many of them said it was a life-changing experience in high school, college, or soon after. It might have been a trip to Appalachia or to a reservation with a youth group. Sometimes it was a spiritual retreat or an immersion experience in the inner city or a developing country. It might have been a stimulating college class or giving a year to AmeriCorps or a faith-based service organization. One way or another, these young people saw that the world was larger than their life, and what they saw called to them.

I don't think that the lives of these young adults were wasted before their life-changing experience. They were being nurtured in physical, intellectual, and emotional health so that when an appropriate trigger came, they were ready and able to respond. They saw the discrepancy between their lives of privilege and the lives of others who often did nothing to deserve their oppression or poverty. Standard good-parenting practices can prepare the way for a later epiphany.

Exposure to others

The people around us influence us. If I expose my children to doers of justice, hometown heroes, or people of moral courage, they will be more inclined to consider doing the same. There are two kinds of catalysts that I can think of and two ways of accessing them.

Heroes and models. These are the Mother Theresas and Gandhis plus a whole bunch of people who are still alive and closer to home. As important as parents are in a child's development, they also need to see other people feeding the poor, risking their lives for peace, and inspiring them to think they could and should do something themselves.

People in need. Coming face to face with a person or group in need elicits empathy from most who have not had their hearts hardened by violence or their own overwhelming needs. Given enough time to work, it also dissolves stereotypes. A number of my respondents mentioned that they had a sibling with a handicap, got to know a minority classmate, or traveled through a low-income neighborhood on their way through life.

Direct access. Offering hospitality by inviting people into our homes is a direct way to rub shoulders with heroes and victims. We've done this so much that the dog no longer barks at strangers. Once we invited a lonely but socially awkward acquaintance for Christmas dinner. When we asked about next year, the house was divided. What would the new roommate I'm bringing home from college think? Would the other relatives be comfortable? Judging when a family needs its privacy and when it's time to reach out can be difficult.

Of course, bringing people home is not always possible or appropriate. Going to meet others on their own turf (the housing project, the bus, the hospital) is always a good alternative.

Indirect access. Families and circumstances differ, but solidarity with the poor and oppressed needn't be limited by the size of our home or the number of people we can fit around the dinner table. Reading stories can put us in touch with the struggles of others or inspire us with the courage of a hero. For a while we used a reading from *Peace Be With You,* by Cornelia Lehn, once a week as our grace at dinner to learn about peacemakers. More recently I have discovered a book with stories more relevant to young children, *It's Our World Too—Stories of Young People Who Are Making a Difference* by Phillip Hoose. The beauty of this book is that children can more easily identify with kids close to their own age who took on projects: a teenager who repaired bikes for children in shelters or members of a local football team who broke down racial bigotry.

TV programs, movies, and the newspaper are other ways of bringing interesting people into our homes, even when they're dead or alive on the other side of the world.

Overcoming a personal obstacle

Not everyone is so lucky as to grow up healthy, in a middle-class, intact family with moral or religious training. Some folks had some hard breaks and that's what made them strong. Maybe it was growing up Hispanic in an Anglo culture. Maybe a parent's divorce really forced them to grow up fast and take charge, or maybe a disease or handicap made life harder than usual. It's difficult to know when an obstacle is going to crush the spirit and when it will be the impetus for heroic effort. What makes one child wilt and another thrive? Often a strong parent or mentor can make the difference. Education can unlock some doors, but there has to be the will to take advantage of it. Some people just seem to be born with an indomitable spirit to work hard, and others seem to fall into success with a lot of dumb luck. Not everyone overcomes a personal obstacle but for some it is their ticket to triumph.

Personal temperament

Some people I talked with didn't fit any of the previous categories. Their parents weren't active in causes or the community, they weren't significantly involved in service projects while growing up, they didn't have any particular obstacle to overcome, but there just seemed to be something in them that led them to a life of service. Some personalities just seem to be more attuned and attracted to altruism. It's not always something we can give our children. All we can do is not get in the way. We're not sure where it comes from, but we thank God.

THE INITIAL TURN-ON

If you can, start young, start small, and dream big.

Start young.

School teachers learn to start out strict and loosen up later in the school year. Likewise, it's a lot easier to limit TV to an hour a day when the child is a toddler and gradually allow extensions than to announce to a preteen that the family is going to cut back on TV. If the rule has always been "Everybody pitches in to clean house on Saturday," it won't meet with the resistance that some parents experience when they try to implement new policies that they picked up from a parenting class or from reading a book such as this one.

If you're too late for the start young approach, approach your family gently and include everyone in the decision-making process.

Start small.

Sometimes families get inspired to simplify Christmas and other gift-giving occasions, and celebrations turn into fiascos. Relatives' feelings get hurt, and the children are disappointed. Start small is a corollary to the start young axiom in that if gift giving has usually been modest, it's not a problem to splurge once in awhile, but to backpedal after family members are used to a certain amount of loot makes you look cheap. Much easier to start small and look generous on occasion.

Another way of looking at starting small is that if you want to make changes in family traditions or customs, better to make small, gradual changes than to upset everyone with your newfound zeal and commitment.

Dream big.

Just because you may be taking small steps doesn't mean your goal needs to be small. Our goal is to raise kids who will make a difference in the world, make it a better place, and love their neighbors—all of them. Holding a big dream can help us go farther than if we just had a small dream. We can't do it all, but we and our children can make a dent. Better a big dent than a little dent, or nothing at all.

WHAT TURNS A CHILD OFF?

When I asked this question of parents and grown kids, the statement that came back more than any other was: Preaching and lecturing are turnoffs. I worded the question differently for young adults: "What's the dumbest thing your parents ever did when you were growing up?" Here's a sampling of their responses.

- I wished my parents had not taken so much responsibility for me doing homework in high school because I had a hard time learning how to self-motivate in the beginning of college.

- They allowed us to see them fight but never really talked to us about it. Being in the dark about something affecting your family every day is very scary.

- Their insistence that we always come home for the night rather than spend it at someone else's house. This was due to us drinking and driving as teenagers. Although they had a rule that they would always come pick us up for this reason, we never took them up on it. It would have been smarter to let us spend the night out, (or find a way to force the issue of picking us up).

- My dad would make up silly rules and then forget about them.

- My father lectured me for hours when I did something wrong. I could understand much quicker than that. All I did was get more stubborn about the perception that his lectures were as much a mistake as the one I made.

■ When I was thirteen, they were not harsh enough with me when I started smoking. I am twenty-one now and am trying to quit.

■ There were nearly weekly church battles, and I lost every week—but all that high school church certainly didn't turn me into a Catholic.

■ If you asked me at thirteen, I probably would have told you a lot of dumb (and embarrassing) things my parents did (like keeping the TV hidden in the closet). At twenty-five, I can't think of a single dumb thing they did except my dad once melted a plastic bowl in the oven. I thought that was pretty stupid.

■ Let me drop out of baseball.

■ Left us home alone for extended periods of time when we were still teenagers.

■ My parents divorced when I was five. Unfortunately this meant that love was split between two families.

In hindsight, parents had some opinions about what was a waste of time or turned their kids off. In addition to the preaching mentioned by the young adults, trying to make them keep their rooms clean was right up there at the top. Other turnoffs included:

■ Hypocrisy: Our kids would see people doing awful things on the weekend and then see them go to Mass on Sunday.

■ Our being busy, and too much formal church.

■ Giving piano lessons.

- Not giving piano lessons.

- Making up a lot of rules, putting them on the refrigerator, and then forgetting about them.

- Yelling, which I do too much, and using too many words. Sometimes less is better.

- Cleaning the house as much as I did.

WHAT KEEPS US ALL TURNED ON

What is it that keeps a child (or anyone) going when the going gets tough? Meaningful change doesn't happen overnight. Anyone who hopes to make a difference in the world needs staying power. Yet burnout seems to be an occupational hazard for people who care intensely and throw themselves into demanding work. In observing people who have kept commitments over the long haul and reflecting on my own life, I offer these suggestions.

Work at balance.

Balance work, family, fun, and personal time. Not all of these dimensions will be in balance at all times. I can let work dominate for a while as long as I (and the family) know it is temporary. For most social activists, fun or personal time is the dimension that suffers first. If not attended to, everybody else suffers as a result.

Make a change.

A variety of jobs and a change of scenery or focus can renew many a tired spirit. Maybe you've stayed at the present project long enough. It doesn't necessarily mean you've given up the goal if you change strategies or causes. The goal just has to become big enough to encompass many different means. Stay faithful to the people you love. Change the venue or specifics if it helps.

Include friends.

Although I suppose it's possible to do good à la Lone Ranger, why should we? Friends and community don't merely make the work go more quickly; they feed the spirit. Friends don't have to be involved in the same causes; they just need to understand your cause and stand by you. Sometimes friends become your community; sometimes your community becomes your friendship base. Moses had his relatives; Jesus had the apostles; even the Lone Ranger had Tonto.

Nurture the spirit.

Some people get it from meditation, some from yoga, some from being close to nature; many find it in prayer. The point is that if you frequently empty yourself for others, it's important not to be full of yourself. It's easy to get so caught up with our generosity and the adulation of others for being so self-sacrificing that we forget what it's all about. If it's all about me, "it" will be gone when I die. Most people who are willing to live for others survive by realizing that there's something more to life than who they are and what they're doing, and they call on that power to keep going. I call that power God.

LEST WE TURN OTHERS OFF: SKILLS

Many people have good will, and that's necessary but not sufficient. Many good works have collapsed, or at least not met their potential, because the leaders and followers were lazy when it came to developing basic group skills. Charisma is nice but not enough. Below is a minicourse in skills for the journey.

Take initiative.

Lots of people have good ideas. Lots of people put them off. When I am having trouble getting started, sometimes I remember the adage: If not now, when? If not me, who? If not here, where? If I can legitimately find another time, person, or place then I don't consider my own hesitance mere procrastination.

Listen.

Introverts think before they talk. Extroverts talk in order to think. Both can be good listeners because listening is more than just being quiet. Listening to people talk about what their needs are is always the first step. We don't want to take action before we listen, lest we solve a problem they don't have. The problem with group dynamics is often not that a person hasn't heard and understood another but rather that the colleague or opponent is not convinced that he or she has been understood. Once there is understanding, if not agreement, collaboration and compromise are possible.

Collaborate.

As Mary Benet McKinney, O.S.B., says in *Sharing Wisdom,* "No one has all the wisdom. Everyone has some of the wisdom. Everyone has a different piece." It often takes more time to collaborate with others than to do it myself, but to do the best work and have it work—to have people own it—is worth it. It's quicker to clean up the child's toys myself, but . . .

Compromise.

Collaboration inevitably brings up the need to compromise. It's often hard for a person who believes strongly in a cause to feel right about compromising. Somehow it seems ignoble or unholy. Yet one thing that couples learn in successful marriages is that "my way" is not the only way or necessarily the right way. Love for each other and the common cause make it possible. Keeping our eyes on the prize allows us to negotiate the details.

Organize.

Some people are organized by nature; some aren't. Some have a knack for organizing people; some don't. Figure out which type you are, surround yourself with your complement, and hope that you don't drive one another crazy. Even with this strategy, however, I must add that it's a lot easier to live and work with organized people (assuming that they're not compulsive about it) than unorganized people. For this reason, the organizationally challenged should learn at least the basics of organization, such as how to keep track of appointments, commitments, and important papers. Really, this is just another way of saying, "Be responsible." Organizing people (without controlling them) is a lot harder than organizing things.

Learn how to run a good meeting.

Sooner or later anyone who is trying to help others will end up at a meeting. Whether it's an international symposium or a family meeting, some elements are foundational. Have a plan (agenda), let everyone know the plan (input is desirable), listen to everyone, don't waste people's time, and keep track of any decisions. Of course there's a lot more to it than this, but if you aren't experienced in leading a meeting, watch good leaders and learn or delegate the job to someone who can. Too many good works have lost people and momentum because of boring or ineffective meetings.

Be a person of integrity.

The work might be good. You might want to do it. Don't sabotage it by being incongruent. Whether you are a president or school board member, the head of an international not-for-profit or the head of a family, if you are dishonest or don't treat people respectfully it will catch up with you and hurt the cause you love. Worse, it will hurt your integrity as a person. I know a brilliant and energetic public official who wanted the best for his constituents, but he twisted the truth and manipulated people. No one trusts him anymore. I also know a leader of a movement who speaks eloquently for his cause, a good cause, but he treats his adversaries with such contempt that few people listen. His wife left him for the same reason. One's personal life may be private, but it reflects our deepest values—and that carries over to all the work we do.

Although ruthlessness and back stabbing may appear to work in some settings, eventually people will stop following a person who does these things. You may look successful, but will you be happy? Be a person of integrity, and what's important in life will follow.

The Vogt Kids Speak

For many years our family joined others to commemorate the bombing of Hiroshima on August 6. It usually involved music, readings, and then lighting candles that we floated on water. One year when I was seven, I was asked to do one of the readings. I'd say this kind of thing was both an impressive sight and a formative experience for me.

Brian

I don't consider myself very socially active, but I have a heart for anybody who is being treated unfairly, and my friends know that I will be a true and reliable friend.

Dacian

Other Families' Stories

I don't remember my family ever discussing the needs of the world, but in high school I decided to participate in mission trips to Appalachia and Mexico. Those experiences sparked my hunger for social justice. I became bitter that my parents had so much wealth in a world of so much need and that they had not exposed me to that need, indeed did not seem attuned to it themselves. It took a while for me to get over that. After college I worked for Bread for the World, and it all came together. My social conscience became an indelible part of my identity as it and my faith, already quite strong, became permanently intertwined.

Danielle Goldstone, 24, works for Ashoka, an international nonprofit organization that supports social projects in developing countries, Washington, D.C.

Last year our family pooled our money and bought a goat through the Heifer Project. Next year we think we can afford a water buffalo. Right now it's just animals, but our daughter (fourteen) says that in the future she wants to change the political systems that make people dependent on us.

Laura and Steve Domienik, parents of a fourteen year old, Kennedy Heights, Ohio

My upbringing was pretty traditional—isolated suburbia with no special emphasis on developing a social conscience—but my parents did instill in me a sense of the dignity of all humanity. Since I was technologically inclined, I majored in computer science and expected to be into computers forever. As a college senior, however, I visited a friend who was volunteering in El Salvador, and it was a life-changing experience. I signed up for an immersion experience in El Paso, Texas, during spring break that year. Now I had a problem. I was being drawn to service, yet computers were my life. I decided to join the Marianist Voluntary Service Community for a year after college to try and blend the two. My service placement was with Caracole, an agency that provides low-cost housing for persons disabled or displaced by HIV/AIDS. It involved developing a program called Sophia, which provides an information and referral database and technical assistance for service-oriented nonprofit organizations. After my volunteer year, I explored other job options and then was able to return to Caracole as a regular employee when they were awarded a large grant. I know I'm making this world a better place doing this work rather than working in the corporate sector

David Durkalski, 29 technical analyst with Caracole, Inc./Sophia, Cincinnati, Ohio

When I was in fourth grade, my parents took my brother and me out of public schools in rural Tennessee to homeschool us. My brother has Tourette's syndrome, and the school was unable to deal with it adequately. In addition, Mom and Dad wanted more input into shaping my brother's and my values. In the following years, I was exposed to a huge range of economic and educational levels among the people I knew, from my neighbor, a farmer who chewed tobacco and spent his days watching cars go by, to out-of-town visitors and exchange students. I was encouraged to respect them all. My parents have incredible curiosity. I remember my Dad saying, "There's a big world out there." I explored a lot of the world through reading. With few exceptions, my family had meals together, with Mom sometimes planning discussion topics based on current news. We also took family trips that exposed us to other parts of the States.

Amy Clark, 26, works for Ashoka, an international nonprofit organization that supports social projects in developing countries, Washington, D.C.

Our kids saw how we responded to panhandlers while they were growing up, so when our adult daughter saw a beggar on the street she stopped and said, "I'll take you to Frisch's and buy you a dinner." Later she said to me, "Dad, you didn't tell me I'd have to eat with him also!"

Joe and Lynn Niehaus, parents of four and grandparents of eight, Crestview Hills, Kentucky

Horace Mann said, "Be ashamed to die until you have won some victory for humanity." I believe that every small success along the way—one guy who thinks differently about women, one person who recycles the can instead of leaving it in the gutter, one straight person refusing to laugh along with the homophobes, one great-grandson of a slave owner who marches for racial equality—has an immeasurable impact on the world.

Shane Dickey, 28, teacher, Dayton, Ohio

When I was a child, my parents provided dinner for a neighbor who was a Polish immigrant and living alone. We children took turns delivering the meal. Sometimes if I had been cranky and complaining on a given day, my mother said that not only did I have to deliver Mike's meal but I had to take mine along to eat with him. At the time I saw this as a punishment. As I look back, however, I see it as a blessing. The stories I heard of life in the old country and coming to a new land were as much a gift to me as the meal was to Mike. Now the soup kitchen I direct serves one hundred sixty guests per day. I try to listen to the people's stories and not just feed their bodies.

M.N., single parent and director of soup kitchen

My father is a labor lawyer, and I remember marching with him as a child every year in the New York City Labor Day parade carrying a sign that read, "People Before Profits." I also remember my father taking a lower paying job than he might have because he believed in the cause. My mother chose to work at jobs that allowed her to be home when I got home from school. Since I grew up in an upper-middle-class family and didn't really have to work during high school, they encouraged me to do volunteer work during the summer. I could do anything I wanted but found that I gravitated toward service projects. Later, perhaps in reaction to the homogeneous community that I grew up in, I wanted to travel internationally. My parents supported these efforts.

Laura Ax, former Peace Corps Volunteer in Bolivia, currently works for Ashoka, Washington, D.C.

As to where I got my values, apart from my parents and really committed teachers in high school, I have to say that that first trip to Guatemala after my freshman year of college really was my political awakening. It was there that I more actively began to connect religion and politics on a much deeper level and with more urgency. It was the exposure to grave injustices that were somehow connected to me (via my government and lifestyle)—when I was still young enough to easily shape the course of my life—that motivated me to stop being lazy about my faith, values, and lifestyle (and of course it's an endless journey—I learn daily from friends and books).

Julia Marie Graff, volunteer with Witness for Peace, Bogota, Colombia

Too many people truly believe that they do not make one bit of difference. Unfortunately, that attitude itself makes all the difference.

Judy McGrath, 22, art teacher, Chicago, Illinois

Wrapping It Up

What's my passion?

Who are my heroes?

What do I believe in?

Who are my biggest supporters?

Are there any skills I still need (or need to teach my children) in order to work effectively?

Epilogue 1
Top That Flop

"Hello, Mr. Vogt, this is the Holmes Junior High School principal calling to inform you that your son has been involved in a fight and has been suspended from school for three days." This ranks right after "Hello, this is the police (or the hospital) calling" as one of the most dreaded phone calls a parent can receive. After gulping and ascertaining that no one was hurt, Jim got a few more details and called me. It seems that some girls had been teasing Aaron and ended up tripping him in the hall. He reacted by pulling one girl down to the floor with him. The whole thing probably took ten seconds, but it did happen right in front of a hall monitor, and the school has a policy of zero tolerance for violence.

This is a discouraging situation for any family, but for our family it was compounded by the fact that Jim had just finished writing the Family Pledge of Nonviolence and that our family is known for our commitment to peacemaking. None of us is proud of this incident, but it did result in some productive discussion about managing anger and exploring alternative responses. Regardless, the suspension was hard on all of us.

After my initial disappointment and embarrassment, I found a measure of healing by garnering the coveted Top That Flop award given for the most deserving ministry-related calamity of the year. The family life ministers of my region wisely voted the Vogt family as the recipient of this prestigious award that year. Humor helps, but usually only in hindsight.

I tell this story not because I'm proud of it or because I revel in the memory. An unexpected consequence of writing this book has been the discovery that many parents are suffering silently with the doubt that they did a good enough job raising their children. I found this out especially through inviting parents of young adults to focus groups. I invited only people I personally considered to be wise and effective parents. Yet a number said they almost didn't come because it was painful to remember things they wished had gone differently in their parenting. They loved their kids and thought they were good, decent people, but doubted if they rose to the standard of making a difference in the world. They were worried about being judged or facing their own self-judgment and finding themselves inadequate.

It's hard to look back on perhaps the biggest investment that a parent makes in his or her life—the raising of a child—and wonder if you did enough, did your best. This is not so much about how the child turned out, although that may be how society judges it; it is about parents evaluating themselves.

Whether it is making one's mark in the world, or just staying out of jail, there seemed to be two things that helped parents deal with their self-doubt: hearing others' honest stories of struggle and self-forgiveness.

STORIES OF STRUGGLE

Some might call these stories of failure, and in the short run it might feel like that, but remember that a parent's willingness to go beyond embarrassment to vulnerability is a gift to all the self-flagellating parents that inhabit our planet—many of them mothers. Some of the most healing experiences I've had in my own parenting life have been hearing the tragicomic stories of other good parents.

It was consoling to hear that other parents' kids squabbled in the middle of a presentation at a family retreat, complained about going to church or synagogue, even got in trouble with the law or got pregnant before marriage. These aren't challenges we seek, but when they happen (and all families have some variation of them), be gracious enough to let the lesson be therapeutic for others. (I have received the Top That Flop award not once, but twice in a row. They threatened to give me permanent ownership when I submitted an entry for the third year in a row.)

OPPORTUNITIES FOR SELF-FORGIVENESS

Ultimately, we must learn to live with ourselves. The effective parent pushes beyond the problem, the mistake, the regret and seeks forgiveness. We may seek another's forgiveness—or forgive another—if someone else was involved. But most important is that we forgive ourselves. It helps many parents to repeat the mantra: "I did the best I could with what I knew at the time." I remind myself that I am responsible for the process I use in parenting, not the outcome. And then, as we tell our kids, "Pick yourself up, dust yourself off, and start all over again." For some of us, that opportunity comes with the grandkids.

In *A River Runs Through It,* Norman Maclean wrote: "We don't know what part of us to give, or more often than not, the part we have to give is not wanted. And so it is those we live with and love and should know, who elude us. But we can still love them. We can love completely without complete understanding."

Epilogue 2
Dear Mom

I got the first few chapters of your book today, along with your letter. But as I was jotting down ideas, I started wondering: what makes *me* a success story? Or more specifically: how do you or I know that I'm the socially responsible, community-minded adult your readers deserve to learn from?

Ok, I'm a Peace Corps volunteer. I did community service in college. Hell, I did community service in high school. I recycle. I vote. I even get a religious yearning every once in awhile and go to church.

Check. I pass the good citizen test.

But does any of this mean I really care? I also pass bums on the street without giving them money or even acknowledging them. I have no problems with animals as test subjects. I never have patience for the elderly's stories or forgetfulness. I have hit other kids. If I were told I could save the world by sacrificing myself, I might just decide that the world wasn't worth saving.

The day before I received your letter, I was interrupted in the middle of breakfast by a village woman entering my compound and calling out "Good morning!" in the local language. I hurriedly set aside my oatmeal and stepped out to greet her, only to stop midsentence as I saw the burnt baby she was holding in her arms. The child's whole chest and left arm were burnt: white and red tender flesh rimmed with charred skin. I asked what had happened. The child had tripped over one of the small charcoal tea-heating stoves the night before. As I gave the woman benedictions for her child, I took her over to my garden where I had an aloe plant growing.

I tore off four large sections and gave them to the mother, explaining that she should spread the jellylike substance on her son's skin to ease the pain. She thanked me profusely, saying that her child hadn't been able to sleep all night for crying and that she would go home right now and spread it on his body. As she left, I told her to take him to a doctor because the aloe wasn't strong medicine. She thanked me.

I settled back down to oatmeal and the BBC.

And then I started thinking about what I knew. I knew the child had a very serious burn. I knew that it needed more than aloe. I knew that the woman wasn't going to go to the doctor, a twenty-kilometer walk and a fee away. I knew that the way the burn was left open to the air, it might get infected (as even my tiniest burns and scrapes have gotten infected in this country). Finally, I knew what to do to keep it from getting infected, and I had the supplies in my house: from hydrogen peroxide to antibiotic ointment to bandages, all in my Peace Corps medical kit.

The Peace Corps counsels against playing doctor without a license to villagers, but still, a young baby with a burn like that could die from the infection. And I gave his mother some shoots of aloe. Not only that, I felt good about myself for doing it. I felt generous.

I no longer feel good about it, but I also haven't done anything more to help her.

Please, write a book about me. Make me a success story. Because right now, I'm not. I so often don't care or don't act when I do. I'm not generous. I'm not forgiving. I don't turn the other cheek.

But I wish I did.

Then again Mom, you're not always generous or forgiving yourself, as hard as you try to be.

But maybe that's the point: what's important to you is important to me. Neither of us is a complete success story, but we've got the same ideas of success.

Because I think you'd agree that I'll know I'm a success story when I encounter that same woman, dump my medical kit out in front of her, and go to work.

Until I get there, it's nice to know you put me on the road.

Heidi Vogt
March 15, 2001

Other Families' Stories

Peers counterbalanced a lot of what I tried.

Carol Ramey, editor, parent of three young adults Dayton, Ohio

I had to be self-forgiving.

Tony Garascia, parent of two teens and a young adult,
therapist and author, South Bend, Indiana

For years I tried to change our son, Tom, into what I considered to be a responsible, goal-oriented person. Eventually, when he was about sixteen, I realized I needed to change *my* attitude somewhat dramatically. I needed to let him become the person he was and not the person I wanted him to be.

Jim McGinnis, father of three young adults and cofounder of
Parenting for Peace and Justice, St. Louis, Missouri

If I have any regrets about my parenting it's that I would have trusted my instincts more and not compared myself to others. I would have relaxed more.

Jo Ann Schwartz, mother of two young adults, recipient of the
Cincinnati Woman of the Year award, Ft. Thomas, Kentucky

Selected Bibliography

Bavolek, Stephen J. *Red, White, and Bruises: Spanking in the USA: What to Do Instead.* Park City, UT: Family Development Resources, 1994.

Brower, Michael, and Warren Leon, Union of Concerned Scientists. *The Consumer's Guide to Effective Environmental Choices: Practical Advice from the Union of Concerned Scientists.* New York: Three Rivers Press, 1999.

Burke, Ray, and Ron Herron. *Common Sense Parenting—A Proven, Step-by-Step Guide for Raising Responsible Kids and Building Happy Families.* Boys Town, NE: The Boys Town Press, 1996.

Chesto, Kathleen O'Connell. *Raising Kids Who Care about Themselves, about Their World, about Each Other.* Kansas City, MO: Sheed & Ward, 1996.

Chesto, Kathleen O'Connell. *Exploring the New Family: Parents and Their Young Adults in Transition.* Winona, MN: St. Mary's Press, 2001.

Cooper, Scott. *Sticks and Stones: Seven Ways Your Child Can Deal with Teasing, Conflict, and Other Hard Times.* New York: Times Books, 2000.

DeGrote-Sorensen, Barbara and David Allen Sorensen. *'Tis a Gift to Be Simple: Embracing the Freedom of Living with Less.* Minneapolis: Augsburg, 1992.

Dingle, Adele C. *A Parent Survival Kit.* Melbourne, Australia: Collins Dove, 1987.

Doherty, William J. *Take Back Your Kids: Confident Parenting in Turbulent Times.* Notre Dame, IN: Sorin Books, 2000.

Earth Works Group. *50 Simple Things Kids Can Do To Save The Earth.* Kansas City, MO: Andrews and McMeel, 1990.

Faber, Adele, and Elaine Mazlish. *How To Talk So Kids Will Listen and Listen So Kids Will Talk.* New York: Rawson Wade Publishers, 1980.

Finley, Mitch. *Your Family in Focus: Appreciating What You Have, Making It Even Better.* Notre Dame, IN: Ave Maria Press, 1993.

Garascia, Anthony J. *Rekindle the Passion While Raising Your Kids.* Notre Dame, IN: Sorin Books, 2001.

Grossman, Dave. "Trained to Kill" *Christianity Today* 42, no. 9 (August 10, 1998): 30–39.

Herx, Henry, ed. *The Family Guide to Movies and Videos.* Washington, D.C.: United States Catholic Conference, 1995.

Hoffman, Martin L. *Empathy and Moral Development: Implications for Caring and Justice.* New York: Cambridge University Press, 2000.

Hoose, Phillip. *It's Our World, Too!: Stories of Young People Who Are Making a Difference.* Boston: Joy Street Books, 1993.

Huneke, Douglas K. *The Moses of Rovno.* New York: Dodd, Mead, 1985.

Johnson, Jan L. *Growing Compassionate Kids.* Nashville, TN: Upper Room Books, 2001.

Lehn, Cornelia. *Peace Be With You.* Newton, KS: Faith and Life Press, 1980.

McGinnis, Jim, et al. *Families Caring: At Home, In the Community, For the Earth.* St. Louis: Institute for Peace and Justice, 1995.

McGinnis, Jim, et al. *Families Creating a Circle of Peace.* St. Louis, MO: The Institute for Peace and Justice, 1996.

McGinnis, Kathleen, and James McGinnis. *Parenting for Peace and Justice: Ten Years Later.* Maryknoll, NY: Orbis Books, 1990.

McGrath, Tom. *Raising Faith-Filled Kids: Ordinary Opportunities to Nurture Spirituality at Home.* Chicago: Loyola Press, 2000.

McKinney, Mary Benet. *Sharing Wisdom: A Process for Group Decision Making.* Valencia, CA: Tabor Publishing, 1987.

Menzel, Peter, and Charles C. Mann. *Material World: A Global Family Portrait.* San Francisco: Sierra Club Books, 1994.

Parks Daloz, Laurent A., et al. *Common Fire: Lives of Commitment in a Complex World.* Boston: Beacon Press, 1996.

True, Michael. *Ordinary People: Family Life and Global Values.* Maryknoll, NY: Orbis Books, 1991.

Ury, William. *Getting Past No: Negotiating with Difficult People.* New York: Bantam Books, 1991.

Vogt, Susan V., ed. *Just Family Nights: Sixty Activities to Keep Your Family Together in a World Falling Apart.* Elgin, IL: Brethren Press, 1994.

Acknowledgments

I am grateful to the many people who responded to surveys, participated in focus groups, and talked with me about their experiences. In addition to the people directly quoted in the text, the following people shared their wisdom and informed my conclusions:

Abele, Dave

Andrews, Mary

Andrews, Sara

Backes, Katy

Barry, Jon

Barry, Michelle

Beacham, Mr. and Mrs.

Bedell, Chris

Bedell, Julia

Beirne, Meara

Blend, Lesly

Blend, Michael

Borgert, Jean

Borgmeier, Gena

Brun, Vivian

Burchett, Veola

Burwinkel, Dan

Burwinkel, Hank

Burwinkel, Mary Ann

Busse, Faye

Cadorniga, Christine

Campbell, Dave

Cavanaugh, Elizabeth

Cavanaugh, Mike

Clark, Judy

Crowley, Rosemary

Dausman, Donna

Davies, Elizabeth

Durkee, Paige

Dutton, Nate

Edwards, Joan

Eggermont, Margaret

Finley, Kathy

Fleri, Dawne

Fowler, David

Freire, Lucia

Funkhouser, Anne

Ganim, Carole

Garascia, Beth

Garascia, Jessica

Gayle, Greg

Geoppinger, Anna

Gleason, Ed

Gleason, James

Gray, Joe

Gray, Sheila

Grethel, Sue

Groen, Annelies

Guersgerd, Lisa

Hageman, Connie

Hamilton, Mike

Hampel, Nancy

Hanisch, Ila Mae

Hansen, Theresa

Hargett, Stephanie

Hart, Patsy

Hartberg, Beverly

Hartberg, Darren

Hartberg, David

Hartberg, Kevin

Heaney-Hunter, Jo Ann

Herring, Bob

Hirt, Ann

Hirt, Bill

Hirt Haskins, Jenny

Hittle, Karen

Hobbs, Sherri

Hoffman, Ron

Holy Spirit Young Adults

Honeywell, Doug

Honeywell, Winnie

Horine, Donna

Horine, Robert

House, Richard

Kinner, Pat

Koppenheffer, Carol

Laird, Kathy

Lauer, Andrew

Loyes, Spayd

MacDonald, Barbara

McBride, Nancy

McDonough, Gail

McGinnis Wagner, Joan

Meister, Katie

Miller, Gail

Miller, Glenn

Miller, Kathleen

Miller, Les

Miller, Nathan

Moses, Butch

Moses, Linda

Navin, Molly

Noll, Anna

Noll, Jim

Noll, Joan

Northrup, Wendy

Noyes, Pennie

Nutter, Christi

Nutter, Mark

Owen, Kathy

Owens, Peg

Ozar, Bud

Powell, Jenny

Prendergast, Al

Prendergast, Katie

Przybysz, John

Przybysz, Lauri

Radtke, Elsie

Raycher, Jeanne

Remillard, Jean

Renze, Ellen

Repaske, Mary

Roberts, Laura

Schaefer, Barbara

Schaefer, Jeff

schmidt, joe

Schmilz, Michael

Schwieterman, Marilyn

Sharone, Lita

Stevens, Cindy

Stewart, Dick

Stewart, Mary Ann

Stubler, Kat

Thomas, David

Van Gundy, Michael

Wall, Darlene

Wall, Kevin

Westlund, Abby

Williams-Mitchell,
   Monica

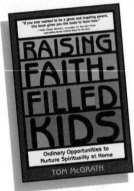